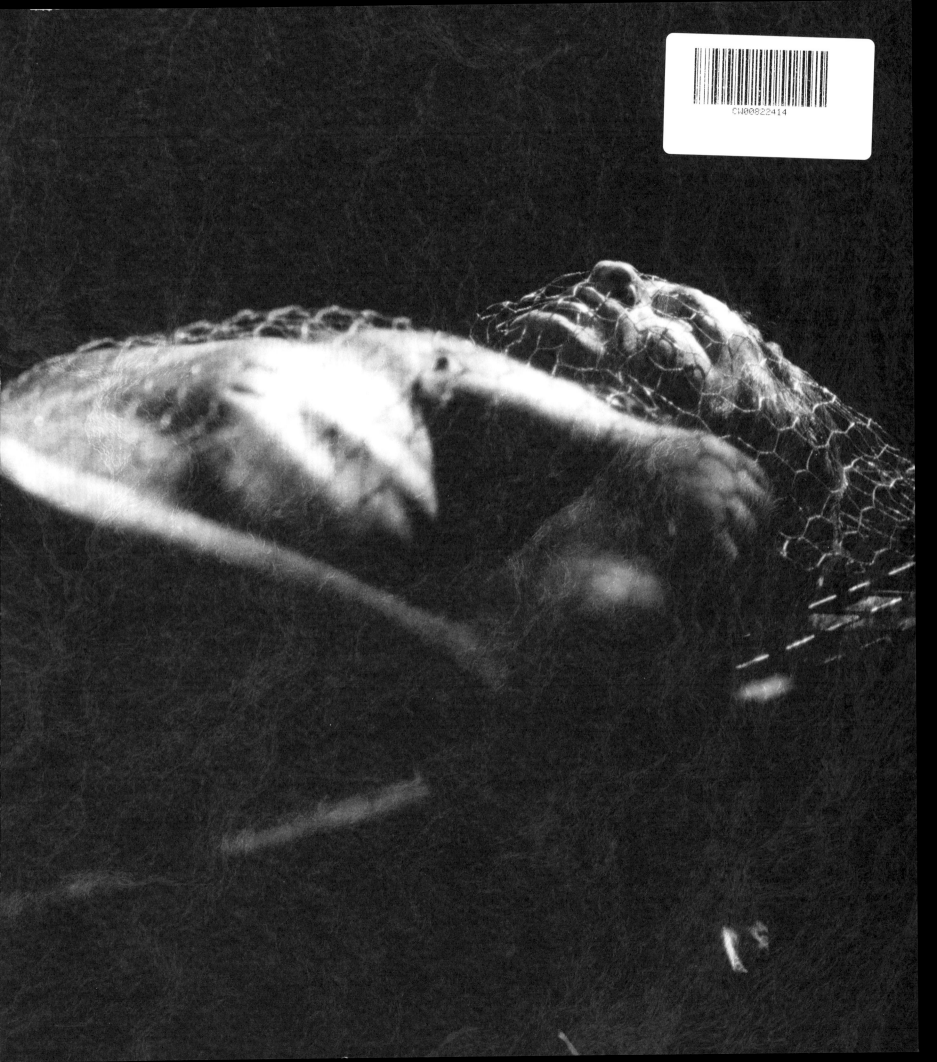

CW00822414

The Complete X-Files

BEHIND THE SERIES, THE MYTHS, AND THE MOVIES

PAGE 1: David & Gillian pose for one of their first publicity shoots in Season 1 **PAGES 2-3**: Alien spacecraft seemingly hovering on set for the first *X-Files* feature film "FIGHT THE FUTURE" **PAGE 4**: A band of Chupacabra crossing the border from Season 4, Episode 11's "EL MUNDO GIRA" **PAGE 5**: Lycanthrope from Season 1, episode 18's "SHAPES" **PAGES 6-7**: Prepping for the rebel alien attack in Season 5, Episode 14's "THE RED AND THE BLACK" **PAGES 8-9**: Chris Carter taking a moment on the set of "I WANT TO BELIEVE" **PAGE 10**: Mulder & Scully mulling over the magician's con in Season 7, Episode 8's "THE AMAZING MALEENI" **PAGE 11**: The Great Mutato poses for the camera in Season 5, Episode 6's "THE POST-MODERN PROMETHEUS" **PAGE 12**: Scully's dream monster in Season 2 Episode 13's "IRRESISTIBLE" **PAGE 13**: Doggett unwittingly takes out an alien in the early Season 8 episode "WITHOUT" **PAGE 14**: David and Gillian ready for Season 7!

INSIGHT EDITIONS

3160 Kerner Blvd. Unit 108, San Rafael, CA 94901
www.insighteditions.com
phone 415.526.1370 : fax 415.526.1394

© 2008 Twentieth Century Fox Film Corporation.
All rights reserved. Used under authorization

Library of Congress Cataloging-in-Publication
Data available.

STANDARD EDITION ISBN-13: 978-1-933784-72-4
LIMITED EDITION ISBN-13: 978-1-933784-80-9

Palace Press International, in association with Roots of Peace, will plant
two trees for each tree used in the manufacturing of this book. Roots of
Peace is an internationally renowned humanitarian organization dedicated
to eradicating land mines worldwide and converting war-torn lands into
productive farms and wildlife habitats. Together, we will plant two million
fruit and nut trees in Afghanistan and provide farmers there with the skills
and support necessary for sustainable land use.

10 9 8 7 6 5 4 3 2 1

Printed in China by Palace Press International

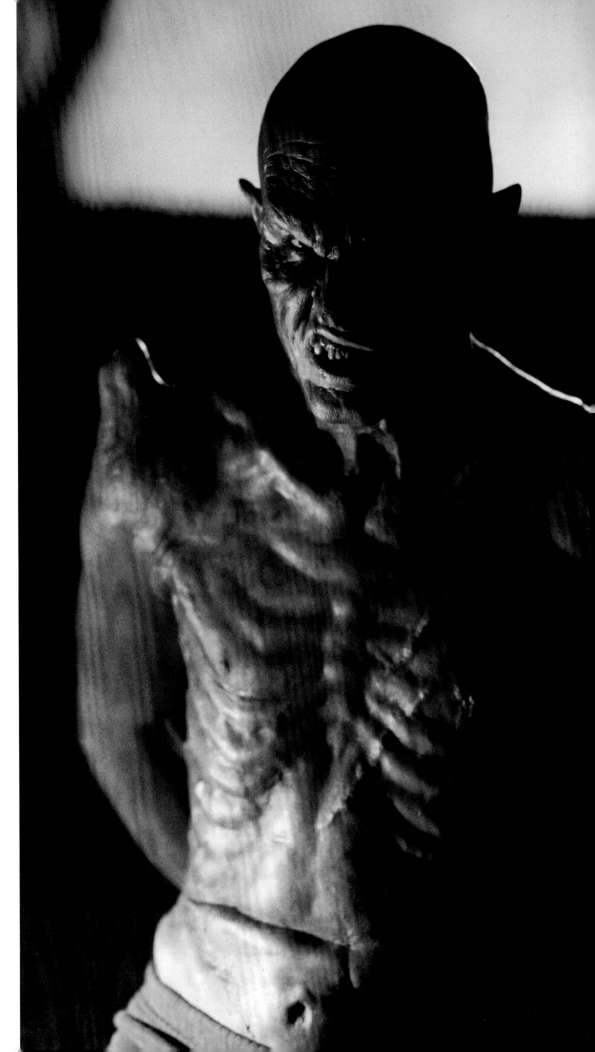

The Complete X-Files

BEHIND THE SERIES, THE MYTHS, AND THE MOVIES

by Matt Hurwitz and Chris Knowles • Preface by J.J. Abrams
Foreword by Creator Chris Carter • Introduction by Frank Spotnitz

INSIGHT EDITIONS

San Rafael, California

CONTENTS

PREFACE *BY J.J. ABRAMS*

This is a tough one. Writing about *The X-Files*. I don't know where to start. Which makes me realize that it's sort of hard to remember that time before there was an *X-Files*. Of course I have memories of 1992 and the years prior, but it's nearly impossible to believe that Scully and Mulder weren't with me throughout elementary school, high school or college. Those characters, that series, were such a force, such a creative influence, that it seems strange to imagine that they actually didn't exist at one point. Like Elenore Rigby or The Brandenburg Concertos or the Mona Lisa—these things needed to exist, and somehow there was a space in history, waiting for them to arrive; they were inevitable and perfect and, ultimately, awe-inspiring. Sublime, transportive and damn-near perfection.

Okay, yes, as I write this, I am reminded of Pre-*X-Files*. In fact, I recall what *The X-Files* meant to me, beyond its obvious and massive entertainment value.

A question I often get, and am always grateful for, is, "Where do you get your ideas?" I assume the people asking are well-meaning, curious folks who saw something I was involved in and were sufficiently entertained. They also may be intelligent, well-read people who think I'm an idiot. Either way, the answer is the same. I try, desperately, to tell stories that give me the goose-pimple feeling I got from the movies and TV series that I loved so much as a kid. Growing up, *The Twilight Zone* was the series that influenced me the most. It was terrifying, it was funny, it was moody, and rich, and heartbreaking, and poetic, and it taught me lessons I was too young to understand. But even at ten years old, I knew it was about something. It felt important, even if the ideas were a yard over my head. That series in particular sort of defined the narrative ideal. Sure, there were lesser episodes, every series has them. But by and large it was a seemingly effortless combination of truly wonderful characters and absolutely insane situations (a definition which more or less describes all of my favorite movies).

But it was old.

That is to say, it was a black-and-white artifact. Yes, the *Zone* is timeless, but it was literally from another time. It was hard to tell if that sort of genre brilliance was somehow only possible because it wasn't literally "of the now". My point is, it was impossible to separate the era of Rod Serling's series, which completed its run years before I was born, with the show itself. And it was therefore impossible to know—could another show ever do it again? Find that magic balance of humanity and terror? Could another series ever have that sort of impact? Reach that level of quality?

The X-Files was the answer to those questions; Chris Carter (whom, I've read, was a big *Twilight Zone* fan himself) managed to create a series which seemed wholly unique, absolutely inspired, a pure original and yet it delivered the same whammo punch that only *The Twilight Zone* had before it.

I remember the excitement. The relief. The sense of possibility that Carter's show provided. It wasn't just that the genre was back on network television. It was that a truly *great* genre was back on network television. *The X-Files* TV series was more than wonderfully entertaining, more than clever social commentary, more than chilling, and creepy, and thought-provoking—it was encouraging. To all aspiring writers. "There is hope," it said.

I'm not really star-struck all that often, but I was the day I met Chris Carter. It was at a local restaurant in Los Angeles. I had just created a series called *Alias*. It had yet to air, but I was in the thick of production, scrambling to figure out just what the hell the show was gonna be. Anyway, I was alone, writing notes, long-hand, over lunch. I looked up as someone entered. Taking a chair across the place was Chris Carter.

I was stunned. I mean, I had literally been sitting there, straining to structure my new series, feeling completely incapable of doing the story, cast, crew, or audience any justice, when one of the two men (Serling being the other) who most inspired me walked into the fucking restaurant.

I tried to focus a little, so as not to appear baldly sycophantic, and walked over. I introduced myself and I thanked him. What I remember (it was sort of a blur), is that Chris wished *Alias* all the success they'd had with *The X-Files*. He was a gentleman, he was supportive. He didn't just help me by creating one of the best series of all time, he helped me that day with simple, friendly encouragement.

For those who are counting, *Alias* had just about half the success of *The X-Files* (we ran for five years, Chris' show for nine). But I can assure you, *Alias* would have run for zero years—I wouldn't have been able to create it, or *Lost*, with Damon Lindelof, without the incredible impact of *The X-Files*. It is a series in whose vast shadow we all live. It is that most excellent combination of all good and weird things. It is a creation to which I am most indebted. I could not be more thankful that the truth is, indeed, out there.

FOREWORD *BY CREATOR CHRIS CARTER*

In just over two weeks, *The X-Files: I Want To Believe* opens in theaters across America, soon to premiere in countries around the world. On his online blog, Frank Spotnitz, my friend and fellow writer/producer on the movie, has been receiving emails from people across the U.S. and in places such as Peru, Russia, Germany and Slovenia, fans, excited to see Scully and Mulder for the first time since they rode off television screens and into the sunset six years ago. It is wonderful to know there are people out there who will come to see what we've been working on, but there are no guarantees we will satisfy their expectations or that they will celebrate our choices for the characters whom are most certainly the heart and soul of the show and the big reason there are fans at all. So it was sixteen years ago, when *The X-Files* made its television debut, when the jury was still out on an audience appetite for a chaste relationship between two FBI agents, one a believer in the supernatural, the other a scientist (a medical doctor) sent to spy on him and his work on a series of unsolved cases: X-files. X for the unknown. All was unknown.

Much is now known, of course, about the television show which ran for nine years on Fox and found a loyal international following in syndication and on DVD. Though it became, along with *The Simpsons*, a top-rated show on the fledgling network, its early Neilsen ratings, the genre and the vocal fans, calling themselves X-Philes, earned it a distinction as a cult show. With its first Golden Globe nomination, and then win, the cult began to grow, but the show itself remained an oddball Friday night hit. Even with an Emmy nomination for Best Drama the same year, there was never any real hope we could win (and so it was with three Emmy nods for Best Drama, though the Hollywood Foreign Press would honor us twice again.) And when it moved to Sunday night, with the biggest viewing audience of the week, all it became was an even bigger cult hit.

And then there was, again, the relationship. David Duchovny and Gillian Anderson, relative newcomers, argued, debated, sparred and bickered about cases strange and unlikely. They shared a job, an office; they shared rented cars and barbeque ribs on the road. They shared their opinions strongly but respectfully, often on their handy cell phones. They shared just about everything but a bed, and that not-so-simple choice made for an improbable romance which endured through 202 episodes and a theatrical movie.

And now, a second movie, where they share—well—more than barbeque. And, just as it was with the television show, the jury is out on the audience appetite for a Mulder and Scully whose relationship, so many years in the making, has been forged anew. But, as much hoopla is being made about their and the show's return, I would like to take this opportunity to do something I've never had a real chance to do, and may never have the chance again: thank those without whom *The X-Files* may never have been a hit at all.

Every TV series, successful or not, is a story of Survival, a weekly popularity contest in what Brandon Tartikoff (the legendary network head I worked under for several years) called "a pure selling medium." That is, a television show exists simply to sell advertising.

Every television series is a story of chemistry, not just for its cast but for those whose job it is to put forty-odd minutes (in our case) of film on the air, roughly two dozen episodes a season. Some take on the responsibility (producers, directors, editors, designers, crew) some are given it (production execs, network current programming execs, publicists). Hundreds of people scrambling eleven and a half months a year to refresh, rework and rethink a product which has to compete in a very crowded and unforgiving marketplace.

And every show is a story of opposing forces: politics, ambition, professional intrigue, counter-programming and budgeting wars. One week of bad ratings, staffing failures, a bad time slot, an over-tight studio wallet, poor promotion—all can doom a show, sink it before it gets wind in its sails. Sometimes before it leaves the harbor. Trust me, I know.

The X-Files never ran aground, however, and credit is overdue to those who worked on the pilot and the first season of the show. There were other champions in the years to come—producers Frank Spotnitz, mentioned above, Vince Gilligan, John Shiban, Paul Rabwin, Michael Watkins, Bernie Caulfield, Michelle MacLaren and Harry Bring among them. But the original framers of the first twenty five episodes deserve special notice.

Some were unlikely: Charlie Goldstein, head of production for 20th Television, fought for every penny the studio spent but saw what the show could be. In no small part because of Dan Sackheim, who produced the pilot and directed the series first episode; and because of R.W. (Bob) Goodwin, the series original producer (and eventual director of so many important mythology episodes). It was Bob who put together the Vancouver crew, including award-winners Graeme Murray and John Bartley, and led them for five years.

Bob Greenblatt and Danielle Claman bought the pitch at the Fox network—though it took two tries—and supported us in that fragile first year. Craig Erwich and Jonathan Littman ran current programming and we heard from them weekly on our stories. Key decisions were made early on by Lucy Salhany and Sandy Grushow and Dan McDermott, And Peter Chernin, whose corporate oversight of the show has spanned its entire history.

At 20th Television, Jeffrey Kramer and Dawn Tarnofsky-Ostroff were there at the inception, joined on the series by Ken Horton, future president of Ten Thirteen. Randy Stone cast the pilot and recommended Rick Millikan, our series casting director (the movie is dedicated to Randy, who passed away in 2007). Dana Walden, Nee Friedman, ran publicity and, as testament to her talent and instincts, she now runs 20th Television.

Peter Roth ran 20th Television then, though he changed hats and ran the Fox Network midway through our run. It was Peter who brought me to Fox to create TV shows and who pushed the network to hear the pitch a second time after their initial pass; who stood behind me nearly every step of the way, through the single-spaced eighteen-page outline, to the script, the filming of the pilot and through the original first season—that is, when he wasn't in front of me, hugging me, as those who know Peter will understand so well.

His influence with Rupert Murdoch prompted an encouragement to, "Go for the jugular."

Peter's insistence that I return early from a vacation with my wife to staff the show led to two timely and, in retrospect, critical hires: The writing/producing team of Howard Gordan and Alex Gansa would give the show intelligence and balance. Glen Morgan and James Wong did some of the best work on the series, ever. A very special thanks to them.

Mark Snow, of course, gave us the music. From beginning to end, on the first movie and here again on the second. We produced the bodies, it was Mark who breathed life into them. Aided ably by music editor Jeff Charbonneau, by Larold Rebhun and by Thierry Courtourier, who son's voice you hear at the end of every show, saying, "I made this!"

David Nutter joined in the first year and set a directing standard that all of us continually aspired to throughout the series. Followed by Rob Bowman, who directed *Fight The Future*. (Kim Manners didn't arrive until Season Two, but he stayed until the end, and I thank him.)

There are certainly more people than I can count, or have space to count here, who played important roles. The original editors, certainly: Steve Mark, Heather McDougall and James Coblenz. The pilot director, Robert Mandell. And J.P. Finn, our Vancouver UPM.

Actors Jerry Hardin and Doug Hutchison lived and died beautifully as Deep Throat and Tooms. Don Davis played Scully's deceased father in the great and unforgettable Beyond The Sea (We mourn his own death this year). Brad Dourif shined in that episode, and it's where Sheila Larkin, R.W. Goodwin's real life wife, started her run as Scully's mother. Mitch Pileggi and Nic Lea snuck in that first year and both stayed until the bitter end.

And there was David and Gillian, without whom it might have been just an exercise.

If I've forgotten anyone, my sincerest apologies, but my heartfelt thanks. You have changed my life and, perhaps, television history, too. May the Force be with you all.

—Chris Carter,
Malibu, CA (July 8, 2008)

INTRODUCTION *BY FRANK SPOTNITZ*

I am not big on nostalgia. Whenever I see old friends or colleagues from *The X-Files*, I am not likely to reminisce about the old days or remember the past in a haze of romantic glory.

The truth is that *The X-Files* was a lot of hard work. Whatever commercial or critical success we had always seemed distant, abstract, not to be trusted. The work, on the other hand, was very real and pressing. We were always facing deadlines—for the next story, the next script, the next edit, the next casting session, the next production meeting, the next air date. And—because of the pressure we put on ourselves to do great work—there was never enough time.

That may sound like an exaggeration, but it's not. The production cycle of *The X-Files* required that we start a new episode every eight business days. More than once, I thought of Lucy Ricardo stuffing chocolate candies down her mouth to keep the assembly line from running out of control. We couldn't let that happen to our assembly line. We wanted every nickel of every budget to go onto the screen. I'm proud (and a little amazed) to say that, in the nine years *The X-Files* was on television, we didn't shut down production once.

We set enormous ambitions for ourselves. We wanted every episode to be different and beautiful, in both its conception and execution. We wanted to create something that would not simply be viewed on a Friday (or later, Sunday) night and then be discarded. Even before the age of DVD boxed sets and video on demand, we wanted to make entertainment that people would watch again and again for years to come.

That's not to say we never stumbled. As Chris has said, "In television, when you stumble, you fall." Or, to use another metaphor, when you aim for a target as high as we did, when you miss, you really miss. So it's hardly surprising that some of our efforts did not turn out as well as we hoped. Yet I'm always amazed when I meet fans who deem what I would consider a failed episode to be one of their favorites. Who am I to argue?

Most of the time, we didn't miss. And hitting the distant target we set for ourselves gave us a satisfaction that fueled the next episode, and the next after that.

Reading this book, I am struck again by the enormous number of people whose talents went into making *The X-Files* as good as it was. Of course, no matter how good the work, none of it would've mattered had David and Gillian not been so amazing as Mulder and Scully. From the line producers and writers to the special make-up artists, second unit directors, and location managers, the excellence of *The X-Files* depended upon hundreds—indeed thousands—of people in front of and behind the camera. The beauty and power of Chris' vision reverberated powerfully through us all, demanding that we honor it by giving it our best and—in turn—reminding us why we had gotten into this business in the first place: to do good work, work of which we could be proud.

This book reminds me that—amidst all that hard work—there were, in fact, good times. Seeing all these faces, the camaraderie and feeling of family we all shared comes back to me—the sense that we were united in a common purpose: to achieve something extraordinary. And now, years after the series concluded, I can say with some confidence that we did.

The fact that people are still watching these episodes (and now, writing about them) is a dream come true. I don't need to feel nostalgic about the past. I can simply turn on the television, just about anywhere in the world, and celebrate the achievement that *The X-Files* was, and is.

PART 1
DEVELOPING THE X-FILES

THE TRUTH IS OUT THERE

In the spring of 1993, 36-year-old television producer Chris Carter was on vacation in France with his wife, Dori, when he received a phone call from production executive Peter Roth at Twentieth Century Fox Television. A series that Carter had created had just been picked up by the network; he was to return immediately to staff it and ready it for production. That show was *The X-Files*.

Chris Carter's series, which premiered the following fall on the Fox network, has endured as one of the most innovative and entertaining shows of all time. A combination of science fiction, thriller, horror, investigative procedural, drama, and—at just the right times—comedy, *The X-Files* has intrigued fans since it first aired—fans who continue to view the series' 201 episodes and two motion pictures as often as possible to try and learn more about the show and its many dark secrets.

Unlike most film industry types, Carter did not study filmmaking in college but instead earned a degree in journalism from Cal State University at Long Beach. "I put myself through college as a production potter," he recalls. "In my senior year of college, I made tens of thousands of pieces of pottery." The southern California native—a surfer at heart—nonetheless got an education for his future. "I would sit and watch TV all day long. My film school was spent at a potter's wheel."

His experience at the potter's wheel—sans the television—was also not wasted. "That's one of the things he did, and he would do it over and over and over again," notes *The X-Files* executive producer Frank Spotnitz. "It's that repetition and desire for perfection. You can see the flaws and blemishes very clearly as a potter, and he's exactly like that as a writer."

Fantasy anthologies, such as Rod Serling's *The Twilight Zone* and *Night Gallery*, *The Outer Limits*, and even '70s cop show staples such as *Mannix* and *McCloud*, fascinated Carter. But it was one show, which began as an ABC "Tuesday Movie of the Week" in 1972—*The Night Stalker*, that stuck with him.

The series featured a crusty newspaperman, Carl Kolchak, played by Darren McGavin, who followed the trails of vampires and other assorted scary villains, leaving a lasting impression. "It was scary—I thought it was just thrilling," Chris says. "*Night Stalker* was a reference and a touchstone." [McGavin would, in fact, appear twice on *The X-Files*, in the similarly crusty role of former FBI agent Arthur Dales, more than 20 years later. And the series itself would be remade for ABC in 2004 by none other than Frank Spotnitz.]

Not long after graduating, Carter landed at Walt Disney Television, originally writing features before moving on to television. He eventually found his way to NBC Productions, developing concepts for television. By the late '80s, Roth, then an executive at Stephen J. Cannell Productions, had become a fan of Carter's work and asked him to run a variety of series, including the short-lived Mario Van Peebles series, *Sonny Spoon*.

When Roth moved on to head up Fox's television division, he invited

FROM TOP LEFT: David Duchovny's Fox Mulder ponders his next move in season one's "ICE"; Is it a man, an alien, or some of both? Agents Scully and Mulder examine a recent unearthing (or maybe unEarthling) in the first of many Scully autopsy scenes, this one from the series pilot; "What is it, Mulder?" Gillian Anderson's Dana Scully would indeed be awakened by her tenacious partner countless times; Mulder and Scully try to find out what's happening to Oregon teenagers in the series pilot. CENTER: How's my closeup look? David Duchovny checks up on veteran camera operator Rod Pridy. ABOVE: This agent means business: David Duchovny as Special Agent Fox Mulder.

him for the pilot of the Chris Eliot comedy series, *Get a Life*. "I had just moved out to California about a year or two prior to that," the actor recalls. "I did a couple of films—*The Rapture* and *Kalifornia*, and I did a repeating guest spot on *Twin Peaks* as a transvestite. So I was working and wasn't really thinking of doing any television. I would audition for it, but I would never seem to get parts unless they involved wearing women's clothes."

Duchovny's manager sent him *The X-Files* pilot script at Stone's suggestion, and the actor found himself intrigued by Mulder. "I reacted to the less button-down quality of the character in the more traditional FBI sense. I got that irreverent aspect about him, and I liked his 'outsider' quality. And the searching, the questing."

Upon meeting Duchovny, Carter immediately noticed his laconic manner. "I didn't understand how smart he was," Chris recalls. "I remember telling him upon meeting him, 'I like you, and I think you're good for the part. Can you spend this week before you go in to read for this thinking like an FBI agent?' And he thought that was the stupidest thing he'd ever heard. But he went in, and he won the part."

"My film school was spent at a potter's wheel." —Chris Carter

Chris to join him and to develop a new television series. "*The X-Files* was the product of a conversation I had with Peter. It came out of the development process," Carter recalls.

His initial concept for the show came out of his love of the 1991 thriller, *The Silence of the Lambs*. "I was a big fan of that film, and I think that actually was as great an influence as anything on the show," he says. "I wanted to do a story about a skeptic and a believer. And Scully is obviously a Jodi Foster-like character. I wanted to do a show about faith and science, and to switch the traditional roles of male as skeptic and female as believer, as well as have Scully as a medical doctor, which makes her even more interesting."

Carter created an eighteen-page treatment to sell the series to Roth—which, he notes, "I do have somewhere." The treatment describes the two characters, FBI Special Agents Fox Mulder and Dana Scully, the former as "more of an MTV veejay than an FBI agent."

"I hated that, but I got it," notes actor David Duchovny, who eventually won the role.

The characters' names were, as many of the shows' characters were, drawn from Carter's life. "Mulder was my mother's maiden name, and Fox, I just thought it was a cool name—not because we were on Fox. I used to tell people that I grew up with a kid named Fox, but that was just a cover because it was such an odd name—I just liked the name Fox. Plus, David says it's better than 'NBC Mulder.'"

Scully, as one might guess, was named for the well-loved announcer for Carter's hometown baseball team, the Los Angeles Dodgers. "It's an homage to Vin Scully, the voice of God when I was growing up." Even with the passage of time, Carter, an avid baseball fan, has yet to meet his hero. "I've always been terrified to go up and introduce myself when I've been in his presence. But his daughter has told me that he knows about it."

Casting for the Lead Roles

Casting for the lead roles was handled by Carter, supervising producer Daniel Sackheim, Robert Mandel, who directed the series' pilot episode, and by the late Randy Stone, the show's casting director. It was Stone who suggested David Duchovny for the role of Mulder; Duchovny had read for

After his initial read, Duchovny went in to read for network executives, the next step in the audition process. "There were two guys—it was me and this other guy—and I think there were four girls, and we were kind of mixed and matched all day, and then they just cast us." The other unnamed party was strongly considered, though Carter was clear on his choice. "You might say I did what you'd call 'stand-up lobbying' for David—he was who I wanted," Carter recalls.

Of the four women Duchovny met that day, many of whom would themselves become big stars (*Sex and the City's* Cynthia Nixon and *Crossing Jordan's* Jill Hennessy among them), a 24-year-old redhead had already caught the producers' attention on her way through the audition process. "I told them I was 27, actually," Gillian Anderson concedes. "I came in in black jeans and messy hair. Chris likes to say I looked 'waifish,' and that I just needed a good meal and a roof over my head," she laughs.

"She was actually disheveled," Chris Carter recalls. "She was kind of like an urchin. But I knew she was Scully immediately when I saw her, even though she didn't look anything like Scully. She had a gravity about her. And those angular, beautiful good looks that couldn't be hidden. And even though she was young, she could still pull off being a medical doctor and an FBI agent. That was something I wasn't finding in any other actress."

Anderson had been living in a two-bedroom apartment in the Los Feliz section of Los Angeles, living with a boyfriend and a new dog named Ruby. "I remember the pajamas I wore and the color of the walls of the bedroom I was in when I read the pilot for the first time," she says.

The actress had been in town for about the same amount of time as Duchovny. "I'd been mostly doing films for the year that I lived there up until the time I auditioned for *The X-Files*. I had auditioned for one other TV show, *Class of '96*, and I did one episode of that. I maybe auditioned for one other thing between that series and *The X-Files*. And that was it. I did a few plays in college, and I did a couple of professional theater plays, but that was about it. I'd hardly played anything before."

Nonetheless, Carter liked her, and she, too, was invited to audition for the network—though not before getting some "notes" from Chris. "I remember heading into a restaurant and having to make a call on a public phone to talk to him about it the day before I was going in to the network."

For the network audition, Anderson instituted a complete change in appearance. "I borrowed a friend's Armani pinstriped suit that was three sizes too big for me. I went in looking a bit frumpy." The process was somewhat unnerving, though Gillian kept her cool. "I'd never been to anything like that before, where you sit outside while everybody gets called in, and then you get called back again, and you hear the applause for the previous couple that had gone in."

The four actresses took turns reading with one of the two Mulders—it was there that Anderson first met Duchovny. "I remember sitting on the stairs, and Gillian came over and said, 'Do you want to run lines?'" Duchovny recalls.

"I remember sitting there, talking to David, and he asked me where I had moved from, and I somehow gave him the impression I'd just moved from New York," she remembers. "Then he asked me more directly and got very excited, because he's from New York, but it became clear that I wasn't! There was a very clear look of disappointment from David, that I'd betrayed him," she laughs.

Even with such stiff competition, Anderson managed to find herself cast in the role of Dana Scully. "On the final audition, Randy Stone pulled me aside—and this was really naughty of him—and said around a corner, [whispering], 'You've got it.' I didn't know what to do with myself—I couldn't believe it." Making a good thing more difficult was the fact that Gillian had agreed to give one of her competitors a ride home from the audition. "The whole ride, of course, I had to keep my f*ckin' mouth shut and not tell her that I'd gotten the role. I felt awful."

The Pilot

Once cast, Carter and director Robert Mandel filmed the series pilot (Episode 1x79). Shot in Vancouver (which would remain the series' home for its first five years), the pilot introduced the characters of Mulder and Scully to each other, with the young Scully sent by FBI Section Chief Blevins, played by Charles Cioffi, to essentially spy on and debunk Mulder and his work. Mulder, known for his interest in cases involving the paranormal (thus earning him the nickname "Spooky" Mulder, heard occasionally only during the first few seasons), is kept far away from the mainstream in a basement office, featuring the now-famous "I Want to Believe" poster of a flying saucer. It is there that Scully first meets him and his "X-files"—unsolved cases typically involving unexplained phenomena (and given the "X" designation, as we learn much later—in "Travelers" (Ep. 5x15)—due to the "U" (for "Unsolved") drawer having long since become overloaded).

The two investigate a case involving the disappearance, and apparent abduction, of teenagers in rural Oregon—including a young man named Billy Miles, who, years later, would play an important part in the series.

The teens are lifted through a vortex of spiraling leaves and bright light from above in the middle of the woods—a now-iconic X-Files image. "That was a very difficult scene to create—I think the invasion of Normandy was probably a little simpler," recalled Carter. "We needed to use real leaves whipping around in a whirlwind, and we needed to use digital leaves, and we needed a special lighting effect—a lighting rig that actually took something like eight hours to construct."

Gillian Anderson remembers her induction into Vancouver's native wet—and cold—climate. "We were up on the hill in the cemetery when it was pouring down with rain. And trying to get that dialogue, over and over again, with the rain just streaming into our faces, freezing cold. I remember the impossibility of trying to spit those words out when I couldn't even feel my cheeks!"

Another character was also briefly introduced in that episode who would, by the following season, become central to the series' "mythology" storyline. In the scene in which Scully meets with Blevins, a lanky, middle-aged man is seen leaning against a file cabinet. . . . smoking a cigarette. "The leaning was my idea," says actor William B. Davis. Though in that initial episode he spoke not a single line, without a doubt, Davis's "Cigarette-Cigarette-Smoking Man" would become *The X-Files*' most complex character and one of television's most fascinating bad guys—though that would not even begin to take shape until season two.

While her stated mission is initially to spy on her colleague and explain away his unusual findings, it quickly becomes clear to Scully that Mulder is anything but the kook he has been portrayed as, and equally fast learns not to discredit his work to her superiors. "She is her own

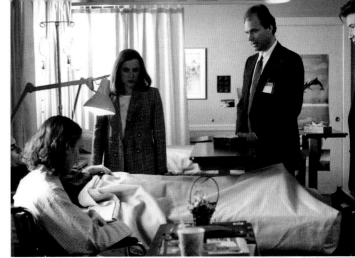

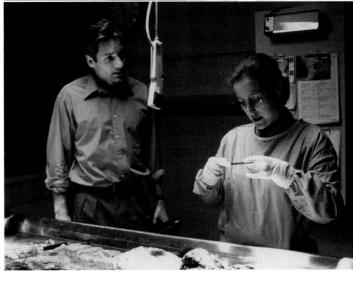

TOP LEFT: Chris Carter at work on the set of Season Five's "PATIENT X."
ABOVE: Mulder and Scully visit with abductee Billy Miles (Zachary Ansley) in the series pilot. This would not be their last encounter with Billy; A fateful encounter: Agent Scully is observed on her interview to work on *The X-Files* by an unassuming man smoking a cigarette . . . ; The results of the autopsy? Not a man, not an alien . . . an orangutan. But who put it there, and why? **FOLLOWING PAGE:** Mulder and Scully have the first of many differences of opinion: "Time can't just disappear; it's a universal invariance!" argues Scully, just before the car turns itself back on.

person, which says a lot about the character," Carter explains. "She couldn't be co-opted or used or exploited."

Assembling *The X-Files* Team

Once the pilot episode was completed in early 1993, it was then up to Peter Roth to sell the show to the Fox network, which he did shortly thereafter, prompting the aforementioned call to Carter in France to begin assembling his production team.

Among the first—and most crucial—members of the team to come aboard was co-executive producer Bob Goodwin (credited always as "R. W. Goodwin" to distinguish himself from another writer/producer named Robert Goodwin. "That happens to a lot of people," he notes). It was Goodwin, along with line producer Joseph Patrick Finn (known to most simply as J.P. Finn), who truly ran the production of *The X-Files* during its first five years.

Goodwin, born in Australia, had spent most of his life in Los Angeles, but he began producing movies for television and series work in Vancouver, eventually moving his family to nearby Bellingham, Washington. Like Carter, he was on vacation—not far away in London—when he got the call in May to return to Vancouver to begin work on a new series, *The X-Files*, which shortly was to begin shooting its initial 12 episodes.

Goodwin had known Carter since the 1980s when both were doing work for NBC Productions. "I did a series called Mancuso: FBI, and Chris had a

In what would become an iconic image from the climax of the X-Files Pilot, abductee Billy Miles is caught up in a cloud of swirling leaves as the aliens arrive for a visit with one of his classmates

"I had *The X-Files* script, and I never read it. I remember cleaning up my office thinking, 'Well, I don't need this,' and I threw it out."
—Glen Morgan

show of his own, his first series, *A Brand New Life*, so we got to know each other there," he says. Goodwin watched the pilot, met with Carter, "and the next thing I knew, I was doing the show."

"Bob was a huge factor in our success; he knew what he was doing," says Carter. "He knows how to put together a very good crew, which is what he did. And then he figured out how to get Fox to spend the money to do the show that I had envisioned."

To help with that vision, Carter began building a cadre of writers and producers, who—in those first years of the series—would set the tone for *The X-Files, a tone* that would remain for the show's entire nine-year run.

Writing/producing partners Glen Morgan and James Wong, like many of *X-Files'* key players, were staff writers for Stephen J. Cannell Productions' popular 1980s series, *21 Jump Street*—the show that essentially launched the career of Johnny Depp. "It was a great place," Morgan says, "because Cannell, being a writer himself, let writers do whatever they wanted. It was like graduate school—as story editors, you were in on casting, you were in on editing. Writers had all the power at that company."

Morgan and Wong—affectionately known simply as "the Wongs" by their *X-Files* colleagues—had gone to the same high school in El Cajon, California, and attended film school together at Loyola, becoming longtime writing partners. The two ended up eventually at Cannell, working for then-head of production, Peter Roth. "Jim and I pretty much ran *Jump Street* in its third year," Morgan says.

After Roth moved to Twentieth Century Fox, Wong and Morgan were ending their run at Cannell on *The Commish*, when Roth asked them to have a look at *The X-Files* pilot. "Peter wanted somebody to help Chris out. I wanted to go on a show at Columbia called *Moon Over Miami*, which I

figured we were going to do," says Morgan. "I had *The X-Files* script, and I never read it. I remember cleaning up my office thinking, 'Well, I don't need this,' and I threw it out."

But Roth was persistent, so the two went to their agent's office to see both the pilot for *Moon Over Miami* and Carter's show. "We watched the *X-Files* pilot, wanting to hate it. We also watched the one for *Moon Over Miami*, and it was. . . . not so good, and we went, 'Uh-oh.'" Carter's pilot appealed to them. "I liked that he had kind of merged *Close Encounters* and *Silence of the Lambs*. He had taken from all these movies that I really liked. And I loved *The Night Stalker* when I was a kid. Anyone who saw and liked that pilot understood what the show could be and knew what the show was going after. So we said, 'Let's do *The X-Files*.'"

"Jim and Glen were coming from the Cannell world, but they were lovers of just the kind of thing that *The X-Files* allowed—horror, thriller, Hitchcock—all those references that they had brought from film school," Carter notes. "I don't think they had a chance to use those muscles. But obviously they were waiting to be exercised."

"The Wongs had a fearless approach to horror," adds Duchovny. "I think in their very egalitarian way, they really expanded the tone of the show to really be scary. And they didn't care how they were gonna scare you; the point was just to scare people."

Another writing team that had a major effect on the flavor of *The X-Files* was that of Howard Gordon and Alex Gansa. The two had shot a pilot in 1992 for a new series called *Country Estates*, which came to Chris Carter's attention not long after, at the suggestion of a mutual friend. Though the series was never made, says Gordon, now executive producer for Fox's smash hit series, *24*, "I guess out of writer's curiosity, Chris read it and liked it, and he invited us to come on the show. We saw the pilot and flipped. We thought it was one of the best things we'd seen in a long time."

Gordon and Gansa immediately differentiated themselves from the other writing team, bringing their own character to the series. "Glen and Jim's contribution, as we all saw when they wrote "Squeeze" (Ep. 1x02), which was their first episode, was that this show could include a whole other genre, a wholly unique kind of monster story," Gordon notes. "But Alex and I thought of ourselves more as character-based writers. We were always looking for that character you can sink your teeth into, whether it was the frightened mother who was a little bit crazy, or the unreliable witness that Carrie Snodgrass played in "Conduit" (Ep. 1x03), or whether it was Max Fenig ("Fallen Angel," Ep. 1x08). We always built the story around a character who interested us."

"They were different kinds of writers," notes Carter. "I think Howard and Alex had come from a more thirtysomething world, and Jim and Glen were coming from a Cannell world." Adds Duchovny, "Howard had more of Chris's sensibility, more of a traditional storytelling thriller sensibility. He kind of fell in between Chris and the Wongs."

The two teams, as with all the writers, lived within an environment of healthy competition, constantly topping each other with more quality, and more outrageous, provocative writing. "We were all colleagues, and I think there was a lot of mutual respect," Gordon says. "We really all were very cooperative, but also, in some ways, I think a little bit competitive, in a very good way. We'd run ideas by each other but have the autonomy to run with our respective shows. I think that sort of culture sustained throughout the entire tenure of the show."

Carter also brought in other staff writers throughout the years, some of whom would stay and some of whom would not. Beyond the core group of Morgan and Wong and Gordon and Gansa, season one's group included Marilyn Osborne and brothers Paul and Larry Barber, the latter whose single episode contribution, "Gender Bender" introduced director Rob Bowman to The X-Files fold.

As for the remainder of the show's directors that first season, Goodwin either brought in helmers with whom he had worked before, such as Bowman or William Graham, or would poll fellow producers and production departments to take suggestions, a common practice in the TV industry. A variety of directors came and went through the first season, with only Bowman and director David Nutter (introduced in Ep. 1x07, "Ice") remaining to help define the series along with Kim Manners—yet another Cannell-ite, who would arrive the following year. "I'd get these different names and bring them in," Goodwin says. "We'd try them out, and sometimes they didn't do so good, and they didn't come back, and sometimes they were great, so we just kept bringing them back."

As for who would direct whose stories, Goodwin basically stuck to a simple production schedule, not specifically matching up writers and directors, though, as Gordon notes, for at least one year, Rob Bowman tended to end up directing his episodes.

Goodwin would often end up directing bits and pieces of season one shows himself, eventually becoming the director of record for season openers and season finales until the show moved to Los Angeles in season six. "A director needs to prep a show and then shoot it, and my job as executive producer is to prep all the other directors to make sure that they're going to shoot the kind of show we want them to shoot," he explains. "There's an awful lot of detail to stay on top of, so it would be difficult for me to be shooting an episode when I'm having to prep one that would follow me. That's why I only shot the first and last episode of each season, when there was no episode following mine."

Another important team member brought in by Goodwin was cinematographer John S. Bartley. Bartley, along with director David Nutter, was key to creating The X-Files' dark look. "I told John 'I want it dark, and I want it scary,'" says Carter . "'I want to scare people by not showing them things, keeping things in the shadows.' And John was not only excited about it; he pushed those limits."

Bartley, another Vancouverite, had gotten a call from Goodwin, who set up a meeting with him and Carter, which, Bartley says, was "kind of interesting, and then we all left. They told me what the show was about, and they told me there were 12 episodes, which I thought was perfect," though he hadn't left the meeting with much of a sense that he'd gotten the job. "Later I called up Bob Goodwin, and he called me back shortly thereafter and said, 'I tried really hard, but they still want to hire you.' That was Bob Goodwin's sense of humor!"

The look Bartley so quickly mastered, says Goodwin, was one he suggested as being reminiscent of Renaissance artist Caravaggio. "[Caravaggio] really perfected having deep, heavy shadows, and then strong sources of light," the producer says of the artist. "There would be paintings with people sitting by a window, when the room itself was pretty dark, but a shaft of light would be coming in through the window and hitting the subjects of the painting." On film, that look is produced with a combination of the cinematographer's lighting and proper set design, the latter handled by The X-Files' resourceful production designer Graeme Murray. "We wanted the show to have a very different look than most of what was found on TV at the time—more like a feature film kind of look, which John and Graeme were able to create together."

Makeup and Visual Effects

The pilot episode made use of another Vancouver artist who would play a major role in The X-Files throughout its first five seasons—special makeup effects artist Toby Lindala. "I was a 22-year-old kid, so I didn't know anything or have any credits," he remembers. "That wasn't my first concern. I just thought it was so cool to have somebody that had the venue to make the stuff for. And I loved the show—right from the pilot. It's funny, because it's really what I was into—conspiracy theories and UFOlogy, so it struck a personal chord with me."

"He was a very young guy," notes Goodwin. "But he came recommended to me, and I had him do a couple of tests, and it looked pretty good, so I just kept him on after that."

For the pilot, Lindala was called upon to create a convincing nosebleed for a young girl in the episode. "I had a little basement shop at home, and I did some testing with gelatin capsules, which I filled up with blood." Stuffed up one's nose—in this case, Toby's—the capsule was supposed to melt at a certain temperature, allowing the blood to trickle out, hopefully at just the right time. "I had it inside of about a 15-second window, but it was too unpredictable."

Ultimately, he went with a physical makeup "appliance," consisting of a carefully-hidden tube running down the actress's face. "He made that girl's nose bleed in the pilot, and I still can't believe to this day that what I saw as makeup on that girl and what I saw on camera were the same thing," Carter says. "He had to run a tube down her forehead and cover it with makeup. There was a giant cord covered with, I'm telling you, two inches of makeup over the tube that led to that appliance, and it was just angles and lighting that sold the shot. Whatever he did, it ended up working."

Once episodes were shot, it was then up to co-producer Paul Rabwin to supervise post-production duties: editing, visual effects, score production, and more. "I think he was just one of three people, including [visual effects

supervisor] Mat Beck and [production sound mixer] Michael Williamson, who worked on every single episode," Carter notes.

"They didn't have anything near the tools they have today," says Goodwin of Beck's expert visual effects work. "Today you can just go out and buy the software you need, but at that time, it didn't exist. It all had to be created. And the footage on which the visual effects were placed had to be shot differently, because those tools didn't exist. Frequently, we'd use motion control," a practice now handled by visual effects tracking software.

Musical Score

The final addition to most film and TV productions, once the film has been given its final edit (or "picture is locked," as movie folks like to say),

"It's what a good score should do, and it was never melodic. It was sounds," says Carter. "During the making of the pilot, I'd listen to Phillip Glass' *Low Symphony*. We put a lot of that in the temporary score [the music placed onto the soundtrack temporarily during editing to provide a sense of what the final music score should sound like]. Mark heard that and then tried to emulate some of it. But then, from there on out, it was Mark Snow."

Snow's music was all the more remarkable given the limitations of, for a large part of the show's run, the synthesizers of the day. With the exception of the first X-Files movie in 1998, *all* of the scores Snow created were done on synthesizers, with very little live instrument performance—and nearly all of it done on a single device. "My main instrument was the Synclavier," he explains. "It was invented by some guys at Dartmouth College in the late

> "I played the triplet figure and had accidentally left the SONY delay on, and it made that now-famous repeat." —Mark Snow

the show is given its music score by a composer, in this case, by the prolific Mark Snow, whose otherworldly music can still be heard on CBS's *Ghost Whisperer*. Snow had been recommended to Chris Carter by a producer friend. "Lucky for me, Chris didn't have any cousin or brother or composer that he had worked with before, so he was looking around," he says. "It was between me and three or four other guys though."

Carter came from his then-Pacific Palisades home to Snow's nearby Santa Monica home studio to meet his potential composer. "He was very polite," Snow recalls. "I would say very enigmatic—I couldn't quite get a read on him. He listened to some music and said, 'That's very good. I like that. Well, thank you very much; I'll get back to you.' I thought, 'God, that was interesting.'" Two weeks later, Carter returned, and the two repeated the routine, not appearing to produce something that would result in a job, but, not long after, Snow had the gig.

"Mark Snow's music is one of the stars of the show," Carter says quite plainly. Adds director David Nutter, "He had an amazing ability to tap into the emotional world of these characters. And not just in a way that is reactive to it either. It was a unique voice—it wasn't like something you'd heard before. He not only understood about 'creepy' but he understood about how to hold back. How not to give it all away and always come and hit things on the nose or Mickey Mouse the music. Every time he went at it, he just enhanced it."

"'60s and made by a company called New England Digital." While Mark had, like most composers, been scoring projects from the '70s onward with true instrumentation, by the mid-80s, he says, "It was apparent that, by God, this is going to be the future." The Synclavier would make its mark, along with Mark Snow, for nine years of *The X-Files*.

One of the first beneficiaries of Snow's music was the iconic theme for the show's main title. "Chris sent me a whole bunch of CDs of all kinds of music, from classical, Philip Glass, to rock and roll, alternative, electronic bands. It was a hodgepodge of stuff," Snow recalls. The composer made several attempts at the theme, but none seemed to fit what Carter was looking for. "Eventually, I just said, 'Listen, why don't you just let me try something—we'll start from scratch and see what happens.' He said, 'Look, whatever you do, I want it really simple. I want it not slick, not overproduced, and not the typical theme, something incredibly catchy and different.'"

Part of the accompaniment Snow worked on contained a piano, which featured a triplet line—da-ba-da-bum. "I had this Sony delay echo, either the PCM-70 or -90, one of those classic ones. I played the triplet figure and had accidentally left the Sony delay on, and it made that now-famous repeat. I thought, 'Wow, that's a whole piece right there.'"

All that was missing was a melody. "I told Mark about a Smiths song, 'How Soon Is Now?' from their *Meat is Murder* record," Carter says. "I sent it to him, and, of course, what he took from it was not the guitar at all, but the whistling, which you hear at the end of the song. That's where the whistling came from."

Says Snow, "I came up with a melody on the piano without the delay machine, but it was no good —it can't be two pianos. I tried everything— every kind of guitar, vocalizing, woodwinds, etc. But I had this one rack-mount synth, a Proteus 2, and I came upon this sound called 'Whistling Joe.' I thought, 'Whoa—this could be cool.' I played the melody, and my wife was outside and heard it and came in and said, 'That's really interesting.' I called Chris up and said, 'I think you should come over.' He was a little bit taken aback that it was so quiet, but he said, 'No, this is great. This is going to be good. This is what I want.'" Says Carter, "I liked it because it seemed to me that Boy Scouts could do it at a campout."

The next day, the two were due to play the song for a roomful of Fox executives. Upon arrival though, Snow recalls, "Chris said, 'Oh, I've got to go, I have a meeting I forgot all about. You take care of this.' So I go in and play it for all these guys in suits, who hemmed and hawed. But eventually, I think just on the strength of Chris Carter saying 'Yes,' they went along with it."

Title Treatment

The main title itself was developed with a title company, Castle/Bryant/Johnsen, with whom Carter worked very closely to create an impactful opening, featuring supernatural images, such as a terror-filled, warped face.

Carter, in fact, became very involved. "It got kind of hairy at the end—I didn't feel I had something that worked," he recalls. "In fact, the main title didn't appear on the first episode or two. I just didn't like a lot of the images. So I got in there and started saying, 'Let's find a germinating seed. Now put that split screen, and they're posing. And then let's get this guy's face, and let's warp it.' I became a man possessed. I became that warped face."

And to whom does that warped face belong seen at the beginning of every episode? "That was a guy [who] worked at the video facility where we were doing the final touches," Carter reveals.

The final touch, indeed, was the addition of a tagline, seen at the very end of the title sequence, one which would speak volumes about *The X-Files* and complete its identity. "Chris was up in Vancouver supervising what was going on up there, so I was down here in L.A. helping complete the title," Glen Morgan recalls. "And he called up and said, 'I need some space at the end for 'The Truth Is Out There.' I was, like, 'What? That's stupid.' And he said, 'No, no— 'The Truth Is Out There.' So I called the guy up and said, 'Hey, he wants to put 'The Truth Is Out There.' I think Chris was the only one [who] knew what that was going to be."

"It's really an homage to Ed Ruscha, a very well-known fine artist who did a lot of pop art," Carter explains. "I just like pithy expressions. I had come up with something else, but then that one just came all of a sudden, and it was perfect."

Indeed—The Truth Is Out There.

LEFT: Popular characters The Lone Gunmen pose with director David Nutter on the set of season three's "NISEI"; Writer/producer Glen Morgan (seen in March 2008 at the Paley Center for Media's tribute to *The X-Files*)—who, with writing partner James Wong, would concoct some of the most frightening—and outrageous—*X-Files* episodes of any of the series' writers; Producers R.W. Goodwin and Paul Rabwin, seen at the June 2008 premiere of Goodwin's '50s horror spoof, *Alien Trespass*—which co-stars Robert Patrick; Prolific *X-Files* composer Mark Snow, who created all of the music for nine seasons of the series, as well as its unforgettable main title theme. BELOW: Duchovny gets ready for the real thing in the series finale, "THE TRUTH", on April 12, 2002.

PART 2

FROM DEEP THROAT TO THE END

SEASON ONE *TRUST NO ONE*

The first episode of the regular season, "Deep Throat", drew on one of Chris Carter's primary inspirations. "The Deep Throat character in *All The President's Men* is a character that we all love," Carter notes. "So in choosing to have a character whose loyalties are mixed and/or different from those of the Cigarette-Smoking Man, I think you want to choose somebody who's got a 'similar but different' quality."

This thriller centers on a UFO conspiracy and introduces the mysterious informant who initiates Mulder into the dark underworld of America's secret government. To play "Deep Throat," Carter cast Jerry Hardin , whose role in the 1993 Sydney Pollack film *The Firm* essentially became his audition for the part. An actor's actor, Hardin seemed to have an innate understanding of the idea for this character.

"He was obviously in a position of power, hence the extraordinary amount of information he had at his fingertips," Hardin observes of Deep Throat, offering that, as an actor, "I began to create my own sense of who he was and what he did and where his information came from. David was fond of the idea that I was his father, and we thought for a while that Chris might go that direction."

Hardin was impressed by his new employer's energy and drive . "I don't think I've ever been on a television show where the writer/producer was more in touch with every aspect of how a show is put together," the actor says today.

Carter would turn again to Daniel Sackheim to help create the distinctive *X-Files* look. "It was different from most of the shows on television," Bob Goodwin observes. "It was more like a feature film look, and an even more specific kind of feature, the moody kind."

Morgan and Wong came out of the gate swinging, and indeed hit one out of the park with the next episode, **"Squeeze,"** a straight-up horror story about a liver-eating contortionist named Eugene Tooms. "We knew

we wanted to make it something other than an alien story and a government conspiracy story," Carter says.

"It was painstaking because it was the beginning of the series so the directors didn't have a clear idea of what it was that all of us aspired to," Carter recalls. "You must put the camera in certain places to scare people, and you must not put the camera in other places, because you will not scare them. There were many reshoots. There was a lot of editorial wizardry by Heather McDougall. And there was Jim and Glen, who worked on it tirelessly to make it right."

Glen Morgan notes that the actor playing Tooms was their ace in the hole: "We did so much work in editorial, and we did some reshoots, and it was all because Doug Hutchinson was so outstanding you could almost do anything. If you really look at it, it's not as good as a lot of people remember, but Doug is just really great."

"To me, those guys were honestly the home run kings," Howard Gordon would later say of Morgan and Wong. It would be his turn next at bat.

Gordon and Alex Gansa's first script, **"Conduit,"** is the emotionally-charged story of a young boy who develops a psychic link with his sister after she is abducted by aliens. The boy's mother, played by the late Carrie Snodgress, is a multiple abductee herself. "You have a character who, like Mulder, is holding the truth and is discredited," Gordon explains. "In her case, she is a single mom living in a trailer with a really plausible set of psychological circumstances which militate against her story. It's essentially like the boy who cried wolf."

The script didn't come easy, due to a bit of stage fright on the part of Gordon and Gansa. "They went off and wrote it, certain that they were going to hand me something that I wouldn't like," Carter remembers, "And of course, when they handed me something I did like, I gave Howard a

FROM TOP LEFT: Mulder enters Eugene Tooms's lair in "SQUEEZE"; Jerry Hardin as "DEEP THROAT", the first of several "informant" characters who would aid Mulder throughout his *X-Files* life; Mulder and Scully with the crime scene investigators in a deleted scene from "THE JERSEY DEVIL"; Scully ponders following the first of many of Mulder's wild hunches in "DEEP THROAT".

PILOT: In a scene from *The X-Files* pilot, Mulder and Scully examine the exhumed remains of what is supposed to be teenager Ray Soames—but there are doubts.

"Early on there are episodes where Scully's a bit cocky in the way that she delivers her lines. It's very hard for me to watch, actually."
—Gillian Anderson

noogie because he had been such a worrywart about it."

In **"The Jersey Devil"**, efforts were still being made to give Scully a life outside the FBI, in particular a romantic life: "We tried to develop a love interest for Scully only to heighten the sexual tension between her and Mulder," Carter notes. "So you see that Scully actually goes on a date in that episode."

Gillian Anderson struggled to find her rhythm with these stories. Scully was written essentially as Mulder's foil, and Anderson had not yet found her voice. "Early on there's episodes here and there where Scully's a bit cocky in the way that she delivers stuff," Anderson recalls, adding, "It's very hard for me to watch, actually."

While the show was struggling to build an audience, the producers found themselves facing a blizzard of memos from upstairs. The ghost story–slash–political thriller, **"Shadows"**, reflected the strain the writers were under.

"That one was the network demanding that Mulder and Scully should be saving people. And that's what this show should be. And they wanted a ghost story," Glen Morgan remembers, "And I just said, 'Okay we'll do that.' And I barely remember it, because I wasn't that happy with the story."

Gillian Anderson's inexperience also complicated the production of first season episodes like "Shadows": "At the beginning it was near to impossible for me. I had a really, really hard time learning the lines. There was one scene where I had to yell directions to a line of FBI agents. And here I am in my little high Scully voice; I just did not feel like I had that authority. And I think 19 or 20 takes later I kept missing my line. It was all out of

nerves," Anderson recalls, noting that, "Bob Goodwin sat me down and said, 'Look, you're in trouble. This is just the beginning, and you've got to find some way of memorizing this stuff because you're costing us money and Fox is not happy.' So there was a mixture of having a tape recorder and listening to myself going over the lines and also having this woman that they hired sit with me in the morning and go through the lines. Most of it was about just training that muscle. I simply had never had to do that before."

The energy continued to lag with the Gordon and Gansa cyber-thriller, **"Ghost in the Machine."** Carter looks back: "I don't know what happened with that episode. It was a perfectly good story, but it's hard turning a building into a villain. I don't know how cinematic that ever is. It was difficult to shoot, as well." Howard Gordon himself had a more visceral reaction to the troubled episode, saying, "Ever since that episode, I've sworn off artificial intelligence stories."

Morgan and Wong's next offering, **"Ice,"** was an homage to *The Thing From Another World* and became a milestone for the fledgling series. "In the beginning, the show used to air on Friday night, and I think for the first handful they used to set up a television monitor in the lunch area, and we could watch the episode while we were having lunch," David Duchovny recalls, adding, "I remember "Ice" being one of those moments where we all refocused and (realized) we were making a really good show. Let's keep going."

"It really showed what the series was capable of, and that's a testament to the good writing of Jim and Glen," Carter remembers, "and it was David

FROM TOP LEFT: Mulder and Dr. Diamond (Gregory Sierra) finally catch up with the corpse of the creature (Claire Stansfield) in "THE JERSEY DEVIL." Earlier in the episode, Mulder prepares to swap digs for the night with, Jack, a homeless man (Hrothgar Mathews) in hopes of catching a first-hand glimpse of the creature. The cast of the trendsetting "ICE" (including Felicity Huffman, Steve Hytner and Xander Berkeley) share a light moment on the set; Mulder and Scully's relationship is tested in the frigid episode; Future *Desperate Housewives* superstar Felicity Huffman playing Dr. Nancy DaSilva displays the source of the problem: a space worm.

ABOVE: "FALLEN ANGEL" introduced abductee Max Fenig, who would reappear three years later in season four's "TEMPUS FUGIT/MAX" two-parter. Above, Mulder and Fenig are surprised by an unknown force that has come once again for Fenig. **UPPER RIGHT:** Outside the warehouse where the two are trapped, Scully tries to stop Colonel Calvin Henderson (Marshall Bell) from blasting the building in an attempt to kill a visiting alien "FALLEN ANGEL." **LOWER RIGHT:** In a scene from "FIRE," Mulder tries to put out some fires while Amanda Pays's Phoebe Green tries to reignite an old flame in a rare romantic moment for Fox Mulder.

Bob the Caretaker (Mark Sheppard), who can start fires at will, steps in for a light in "FIRE."

"I have a terrible fear of fire that comes from my childhood...I have a friend whose house burnt down...a terrifying thing." —Chris Carter

Nutter's directorial debut. He gave it his all."

David Nutter himself was coming from a different creative sensibility altogether: "I wanted to be the next Barry Manilow and write love songs," he says today. "I'm really a very emotional, schmaltzy guy, and if I brought anything to *The X-Files*, what I tried to (do) was to enhance that part of the show. That's the thing that I'm most proud of, and what I think helped to really solidify an audience base."

Nutter is an actor's director: "He knew what we needed, and he knew not to tire us out. He knew when the actors needed to be on," Duchovny recalls, adding Nutter "was really a guy who could keep the whole film in his head, and I'd never seen that before."

Carter's astronaut thriller, **"Space,"** was shot at a time when the producers were struggling to raise funds for their increasingly-ambitious scripts.

Settings like a NASA Mission Control center had to be improvised on the cheap. "The problem with *The X-Files* is that there weren't a lot of standing sets in any of those stories," Bob Goodwin explains. "You had Mulder's office down in the basement there and you had Skinner's office, and then beyond that there wasn't a lot of stuff that you kept returning to, because every episode was somewhere different."

Carter was frustrated by the finished product, but adds, "It wasn't a great episode, although I thought it had some great stuff in it, and Ed Lauter was terrific."

Gordon and Gansa scored again with **"Fallen Angel,"** a sort of sci-fi/horror hybrid in the tradition of films like *The Terminator* and *Predator*. The episode broke ground with the multiple abductee Max Fenig, a UFO conspiracy enthusiast who prefigured the Lone Gunmen.

Carter has said that this "Fallen Angel" character "represented a kind of kook that we all believe is out there saying, 'Look up in the sky; it's up there, it's out there,'" adding, "it's a journey for Mulder and Scully to see, and for the audience to see, that these people who are crying wolf might be doing it for a reason."

David Duchovny notes that Gordon "had more of Chris's sensibility—more of a traditional storytelling thriller sensibility. And yet he also wanted to score in the horror genre. So Howard bounced back and forth, as Chris eventually did, as well."

Next up was the classic thriller, **"Eve,"** an early exploration of the super-soldier concept. "The idea came from two writers, Chris Brancato and Ken Biller," Carter recalled. In 1996, "they came in and pitched us the idea, and it was originally called The "Girls From Greenwich," and it was about genetic experiments about identical sets of twins."

The episode would be refined by Carter's go-to men: ""Eve" was an amazing episode because it was beautifully rewritten, uncredited, by Morgan and Wong," Carter recalls today, "They did a fantastic rewrite job. And those two little girls were so wonderfully understated and creepy."

"Fire" featured a telekinetic fire-starter who menaces a British family on Cape Cod. The episode introduced an old "flame" of Mulder's, Phoebe Green, played by *Max Headroom* alumni Amanda Pays.

Carter explains the impetus behind the story: "I have a terrible fear of fire that comes from my childhood. I have a friend whose house burnt down when I was a kid, and we had to spend the night in that house the night of the fire to prevent it from being looted, and spending the night in a house that just burned down is a terrifying thing. We slept on cots on floors that were still wet from the firemen's hoses. That smell leaves a horrifying impression on you. So I have this fear of fire, and I thought I'd give Mulder a fear of fire, as well." Carter also recalls an eerie synchronicity while writing the script: "I was writing that episode while the hills of Malibu were on fire." Glen Morgan would later tell *Entertainment Weekly* that Amanda Pays' appearance was no accident—the network was mulling replacing Gillian Anderson with a new actress. Little did they know …

As the producers struggled, often around the clock, to keep *The X-Files* up and running, a real-life drama would soon rock their world. Gillian Anderson had fallen in love with the show's assistant art director Clyde Klotz, and had become pregnant halfway through that crucial first season.

Glen Morgan remembers hearing the news: "I was at home, and my ex-wife comes in and says, 'Gillian's on the phone.' I go, 'Who?' She goes, 'That girl who's the actress in your show.' I knew something was up, and she finally says, 'I'm pregnant,' and started crying," Morgan remembers, adding he advised the young actress, "'Don't tell anyone. Let Jim and I figure out what to do.' But she let the cat out of the bag, and Chris was upset, and the studio was upset."

Next came time to tell Gillian's immediate supervisor Bob Goodwin. "Bob was one of the first people that I told that I was pregnant. And he was always very supportive." Anderson remembers, "The first thing he said to me was, 'I love babies,' which was really good for me to hear because of the onslaught that I then got from people who were going, 'Oh my god you're going to ruin the series!' And rightly so. It was a pretty cheeky thing at that particular time."

Afraid for her future on the show—indeed, her career—Anderson next broke the news to David Duchovny: "I think he had to sit down," she says today. "I think I kinda took the wind out of him." Chris Carter was shaken by the news and with good reason—he had put his own career on the line to cast Gillian as Scully. But the synergy of *The X-Files* had become an unstoppable force, and the writing team brainstormed on how to turn this crisis into an opportunity. "Gillian Anderson's pregnancy forced the show to create a mythology that had to account for her absence," Frank Spotnitz explains, "So, that led to the introduction of Krycek as Mulder's temporary partner, and led to "Duane Berry," "One Breath," and "Ascension." It ended up being the best thing that ever happened to the series. This mythology really ended up running through the life of the series, all because Gillian became pregnant."

A shape-shifting alien sex fiend was the focus of **"GenderBender,"** which also marked the directorial debut of yet another Cannell alumni, Rob Bowman. The director recalls that "it was the image that was in the trailers from the show which caught my eye, which was a shot of a boy in the woods with leaves circling around him. I saw that commercial and said 'That's what I want to work on.' So I called my agent and said 'Just get me a meeting.'"

Bowman soon became Carter's go-to helmsman. John Bartley notes that the director, "talked to Chris all the time. We had a cell phone there. It was on the video assist. Anyone could phone Chris Carter and get through to him," Bartley says.

Nicholas Lea made his *X-Files* debut in this episode, and became fast friends with Rob Bowman after suggesting a crucial detail in his encounter with the gender-bender in a parked car. Lea remembers, "I said, 'Wouldn't it be great if the windows are all fogged up and I have to wipe away condensation on the window in order to see what's going on?'"

Morgan and Wong's first season masterpiece, **"Beyond the Sea,"** came

from their unhappiness with Scully's character development. "People were complaining that she was uptight, that she was bitchy, and all this kinda stuff," Glen Morgan recalls, "Mulder was getting the humor, and stealing a lot of the scenes. So the intent was to produce something for Gillian to really sink her teeth into."

Gillian Anderson welcomed the challenge: "I remember getting the script and realizing that it was the first time that I really had some real material to work with. I remember sitting down with David Nutter and going through the different beats and the points and the emotional arc and wanting very much to get it right."

Chris Carter had trouble getting the episode approved. "Fox didn't want to do this episode because they said it was too close to *Silence of the Lambs*. I walked into the office of Dan McDermott—then director of current programming at Fox—and told him that Jim and Glen had their own take on it, and I think just the fact that I walked up there convinced him to let them go," Carter says today.

For Morgan, the powerful family drama of "Beyond the Sea" came from personal experience: "I had really been affected by watching my mother and how she reacted to her father dying. So there's a lot of that kind of thing in there, nearly word for word, from my mom. 'We lost your dad,' is exactly her phone call to me, how I was told my grandpa died." Portrayed by Bob Goodwin's wife Sheila Larken, Scully's mother Margaret would become a pivotal character in the series.

The producers faced some resistance when trying to raise money for the actor chosen to play the part of serial killer Luther Lee Boggs. "I remember calling Peter Roth on Thanksgiving evening, pulling him away from the Thanksgiving table, and getting him to agree to pay $15,000 to cast Brad Dourif," Chris Carter says, "I think the only reason he said yes was because it was a holiday, and he had to get back to the dinner table."

"Lazarus" further explored Scully's romantic history, pitting her against a killer whose spirit had transmigrated into the body of her former FBI agent boyfriend. "It actually was surprising to me that it was described as romantic tension. It really was a kind of adversarial relationship," "Lazarus" co-writer Howard Gordon recalls, "What was great about Mulder and Scully is that they fell in love as friends and as co-adventurers."

The drama of the episode came from Mulder's desperate yet methodical search to find Scully, who had been kidnapped by the killer. "Lazarus" was really more of a real good cop show episode in some respects," director David Nutter observes, "It was ultimately about how do we do an episode of *The X-Files* when it's a little bit more 'standard cop show' oriented?"

"Young at Heart" dealt with Mulder's backstory as a criminal profiler, pitting him against an old foe who was aging backwards thanks to a prison experiment.

ABOVE: Scully tends to a downed Mulder; Scully at her father's funeral in "BEYOND THE SEA," alongside her mother, Margaret, portrayed by Sheila Larken, wife of *X-Files* co-executive producer R.W. Goodwin. Margaret Scully would remain an important figure throughout the remainder of the series; Mulder and Scully search for clues during a visit the rural home of "The Kindred" in "GENDER BENDER." The episode marked the debut of series director Rob Bowman (pictured here on the set of season five's "Pine Bluff Variant"), who, along with Kim Manners, would set the visual standard for *The X-Files* for years to come. **BELOW:** Brad Dourif's memorable Luther Lee Boggs offers to channel the spirit of Scully's recently-deceased father in "BEYOND THE SEA," the first episode to explore Scully's emotional side. **NEXT PAGE:** Mulder and Scully arrive on the scene in "YOUNG AT HEART."

"No, no, no! Nobody talks to anybody until I get a deal! Don't underestimate my fear of dying and don't downplay my terror of going back to that chair. I know my hell's going to be to go on back to that chair over and over again but in this life, my one and only life, I don't ever want to go back again! Ever! The last time I went to death's door I looked inside. I had never talked to a minister before in my life ever until that day and he said, 'He who doth not love remains in death and he who hates his brother is a murderer and no murderer has eternal life abiding in him.' My family, who I killed after their last meal, was right there to watch me over mine...and their fear and their horror that I made them feel when I killed them was injected into me....and their collective fear alone was just one taste of hell. And then I felt myself leave my body. I thought they had already killed me...And I saw thousands of souls rushing into my body.

It is a cold, dark place, Scully. Mulder's looking in on it right now."

—Luther Lee Boggs (Brad Dourif) from *Beyond the Sea* (1x12)

Morgan and Wong tried their hand at a straight-up UFO show with "**EBE**," the episode which introduces the Lone Gunmen. "I had liked the UFO thing, but we didn't get an opportunity to write about one yet," Glen Morgan explains. "In doing research, I had been to a UFO convention at the LAX airport. And then there was a table filled with Xeroxed papers—if it was a space conspiracy the pages were blue. If it was a drug conspiracy they were yellow. The three guys behind the table were exactly like the Lone Gunmen. One was in a suit. One was kind of a rock 'n' roll thing. One was kind of a little guy. And they had space shuttle conspiracies and the whole deal. And so I put them almost verbatim into the story."

"The Three Paranoids," as they were called in the script, became immediate favorites of the core *X-Files* audience. The actor portraying Langly was plugged into the geek underground: "I went to a party with my computer science friends who showed me simple UNIX codes to find out all the places I mentioned in the newsgroup about Langly and the Lone Gunmen," Dean Haglund recalls. "And that's when I went, 'Holy crap! People are, all of a sudden, watching this show.'"

"**Miracle Man**" was one of the many episodes that would draw on religious themes. The story centers around a young faith healer who is inadvertently killing his congregants. Howard Gordon remembers it being

"The first episode where my line was, 'She's hot,' destined me to be considered a lech for the rest of my career." —Tom Braidwood

First assistant director Tom Braidwood was picked as Gunman Melvin Frohike simply because he happened to be walking past the office where the producers were trying to cast the show. Frohike came to be seen as the dirty old man of the trio. "That all resulted from the first episode where my line was, 'She's hot,'" Braidwood recalls, "which destined me to being a lech for the rest of my career." The hot woman in question was Scully, who didn't think as highly of the Gunmen: "I remember it was written that Scully thought these guys were complete lunatics," Gillian Anderson says.

The Gunmen would play an important role in the series: "That was yet another method for making Mulder seem credible, somebody you could love, because the writers were so far out and ridiculous with his theories," Frank Spotnitz explains.

significant for personal reasons: "That was the first show I actually wrote with Chris. Alex had gone off to have a baby and Chris and I wound up doing "Miracle Man" together. We had a lot of fun."

"**Shapes**" was a moody exploration of Native American werewolf myths. Nutter strove for authenticity for the rituals performed in the story: "I remember going downtown and finding this group of Indians who were playing with the drums and so forth, and I got these guys involved in this whole burning ceremony that we had," Nutter says. "We made it as real as possible, because you can't make this stuff up."

The next episode deals with environmental issues. "When I came up with the idea for "**Darkness Falls,**" Chris Carter remembered in 1996, "it was really a result of a college experience I had, where we had studied dendrochronology, which is the reading of the rings in tree trunks, and I always wondered, 'If a tree is thousands of years old, why couldn't it be a time capsule for something that had existed that far back?'"

Carter leavened the chiller with a subplot dealing with clear-cutting and eco-terrorism. David Duchovny notes that "Chris was more of a thriller guy, more of a *Three Days of the Condor* kind of a guy, and Morgan and Wong were more *Halloween Part 2* guys," the actor says, adding, "They really expanded the tone of the show to be really scary. And they didn't care how they were gonna scare you; their point was to scare people. Whereas Chris always wanted to scare you AND make you think."

OPPOSITE PAGE CLOCKWISE FROM TOP LEFT: Scully faces off with bank robber Warren Dupre (Jason Schombing) in "LAZARUS;" In the same episode, Dupre has returned in the body of her former instructor, Jack Willis (Christopher Allport), who holds Scully captive.; Duchovny and Hardin chat between takes on the set at North Shore Studios; "E.B.E." introduced the Lone Gunmen, nerds d'force who offered Mulder information otherwise unavailable. A shaken Mulder emerges with his informational benefactor, Deep Throat (Jerry Hardin) after learning that extraterrestrials do indeed exist, in "E.B.E."
THIS PAGE LEFT: Gunman Frohike was portrayed by Canadian Second Unit Director crewman Tom Braidwood; Here, a skeptical Scully gets her first dose of the Gunmen's sometimes loopy ideas.

"Morgan and Wong really expanded the tone of the show to be really scary; their point was to scare people. Whereas Chris always wanted to scare you AND make you think." —David Duchovny

"**Tooms**" grew out of Morgan and Wong's frustration with the difficult "Squeeze" shoot. "Because Doug was so great, we felt that he could do an even better job with Nutter," Glen Morgan explains, "Just wind Doug up and let him go."

"The tough part about that was how to make it—how do I bring this character back, (who) is so very special," Nutter recalls, adding that Doug Hutchinson, "came in and just enveloped who this character was. The thing I was so proud of was that you basically give him some sense of stage direction and then just let him go, let him dance."

"Tooms" also features the introduction of Assistant Director Walter Skinner, played by veteran character actor Mitch Pileggi. "I went in a couple of other times to read for Chris, just for some regular FBI guys. But at the time that I went, in my head was shaved, and they thought it was too extreme for the show," Pileggi laughs, adding, "I grew my hair back, and then I got called in for Skinner. So I went into the audition with a little bit of an attitude, because I had been in and hadn't been cast. And that's exactly what they wanted for the character."

The X-Files team was always interested in using Pileggi but hadn't yet found the perfect role for him. Rick Millikan explains: "I had brought Mitch in a couple of times for other parts. There are times where there are certain people who are right for the show, and I'll bring them in over and over until we find the right part."

Skinner is a much different character in "Tooms" than he would later become. "Initially, he was there to be pretty much a roadblock to what they were doing," Pileggi explains. "And eventually because of who he was and his nature, he understood what was happening; that these two were being dumped on and railroaded."

Pileggi was well-prepared for the role. His own father was a Defense Department contractor who was very much a real-life Skinner. "My mom was still alive at the time," Pileggi recalls, "and she and my brothers and sisters said, 'You're really doing Dad there.'"

Alex Gansa would return from paternity leave and co-write "**Born Again,**" a story dealing with the reincarnation of a murdered cop in the form of a cold-eyed young girl with lethal telekinetic powers. Co-writer Howard Gordon points out that episodes like "Born Again" show that "the brilliance and the longevity of the show is that Chris created the mythology of the show and that involved Mulder and Scully and a broader conspiracy. But the show also had the latitude to do these stand-alone episodes. So (we) had a pretty wide tent and a lot of different voices that could exist under it."

Speaking of different voices, "**Roland**" is a thriller in which a cryogenically-preserved scientist psychically controls a mentally-handicapped janitor. The title character's portrayal by actor Zeljko Ivanek would garner high praise from *The X-Files'* stars and staff.

Carter wanted to finish off the season with an unforgettable tour-de-force, and "**The Erlenmeyer Flask**" blew the entire *X-Files* concept wide open. The rough contours of the mythology were put in place: genetic

ABOVE: David Duchovny listens intently as "MIRACLE MAN" guest star Dennis Lipscomb tells a story; Mulder and Scully with Sheriff Daniels (R.D. Call). **RIGHT** (left to right): Duchovny poses with Director of Photography John S. Bartley (left) and Camera Operator Rod Pridy (right) on the set of Morgan and Wong's "TOOMS," as Gillian Anderson looks on; The return of Doug Hutchison as the liver-craving Eugene Tooms; Mulder finds a clue to Tooms's whereabouts: bile; A naked Doug Hutchison seeks his prey; Mulder and Scully locate Tooms's lair; Scully enlists the help of retired Detective Frank Briggs (Henry Beckman), who had investigated an earlier appearance of Tooms decades before; The body of an Indian victim of a werewolf in "SHAPES" is burned in a funeral pyre; Scully escorts Lyle Parker (Ty Miller) for help, not realizing he is the subject lycanthrope; Mulder and Scully recover from being cocooned by ancient mites brought back to life by loggers in "DARKNESS FALLS."

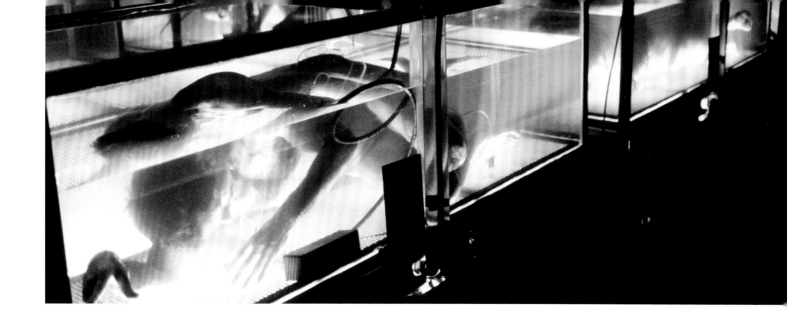

"Of course the guys were all these naked men, so we had a lot of female visitors during that shoot." —Chris Carter

experiments, toxic alien blood, government conspirators, extraterrestrial embryos, and ruthless assassins.

A highlight of this episode came when Mulder stumbled upon a storage facility filled with tanks containing human-alien hybrids. Bob Goodwin recalls, "That was a hell of a set. We built that on stage. I went and got a bunch of divers, because I needed people who could actually stay underwater," adding, "Of course the guys were all these naked men, so we had a lot of female visitors during that shoot."

The episode ends with a shocker—the death of Deep Throat. His dying words became a catchphrase for *The X-Files*—and Hardin himself. The actor remembers that, "A sci-fi shop in Glasgow called and said, would you come and sign autographs for us? Well, I went over there and there was a line for blocks around the place. I signed a bunch of young chicks' backs and arms and necks with 'Trust no one, Jerry Hardin.'"

The episode was a milestone for *The X-Files* creator. "For me it was the result of a year-long learning experience," Chris Carter recalled. He notes, "It may have been, really, the signature mythology episode; not only a sign to the audience of what we were capable of, but certainly a realization for me, of where we could take this show if we explored these different avenues." Carter concluded, "It became about mankind and about science and its misuse."

FROM TOP LEFT CLOCKWISE: A former colleague of Dr. Grable, Dr. Ronald Surnow (Matthew Walker), is sucked into a turbine at his lab in "ROLAND;" Mitch Pileggi as Assistant Director Walter Skinner; Scully has a look for herself at the cryogenically frozen alien fetus in "THE ERLENMEYER FLASK;" Mulder finds alien/human hybrids developing in tanks in an obscure warehouse. Clones would also play a large part in *The X-Files* mythology. Mulder and Scully discuss the case. **ABOVE:** Developing clones.

SEASON TWO *LITTLE GREEN MEN, FLUKEMAN AND THE ENIGMA*

"Little Green Men" picks up where "The Erlenmeyer Flask" left off. Deep Throat is dead, Mulder and Scully are split up, and *The X*-Files are shut down. Acting on a tip given by his patron in the Senate, Mulder travels to Puerto Rico to investigate alien signals picked up by a SETI listening post.

"I had written a script a long time ago on my own called **"Little Green Men"** that was about a guy who had gone down to a telescope in Chile," Glen Morgan recounts. "It was never made, but there were many elements in it that I liked, and I cannibalized it for this story."

The episode offered the first good look *The X-Files* viewers got of the aliens. "We weren't making aliens into this fanciful, new invention," Toby Lindala (Special Makeup Effects Artist) says proudly. "We were pulling real, live references from abductee reports and from other conspiracy theorists out there into the vision for them."

Following Morgan and Wong's excursion into the mythology, **"The Host"** sees Chris Carter trying his hand at straight-up horror. David Duchovny notes, "The Wongs really pushed Chris into wanting to make that a creepy, scary episode," which had formed the team's trademark in season one.

This shocking episode was inspired by a mundane observation: "My dog had worms, and I was studying these worms probably too closely," Chris

"We wanted to believe. We wanted to listen, but the tools had been taken away. **The X-Files** had been shut down." -Fox Mulder.

CLOCKWISE FROM TOP LEFT: In a flashback to his sister's abduction, a young Samantha Mulder (Vanessa Morley) is taken by aliens in "LITTLE GREEN MEN"; Mulder gets a first-hand look at an alien visit while at a SETI outpost in Puerto Rico; A young Fox Mulder (Marcus Turner) watches his sister being taken, an indelible image that would affect Mulder for the rest of his life; Future *X-Files* writer Darin Morgan makes his debut as The Flukeman in "THE HOST." **ABOVE:** Darin Morgan in March 2008 at the Paley Center Festival in Los Angeles. Though he penned but a handful of episodes, Morgan's contribution to the series was enormous, particularly in the show's ability to laugh at itself.

Carter recalls. "I had been reading a story about Chernobyl and about the extinction of species and somehow synthesized all that information and put it together, coming up with one of the, I believe, ever-popular episodes on the show."

The "Monster of the Week" in "The Host" was a human-flukeworm hybrid. The role went to Darin Morgan, who found himself bound in a stifling bodysuit for the episode's filming. "We cast Darin, and I still had just

> "David likes to do his own stunts, but he is adamant about the fact that we should see him and know it is him if he is going to risk life and limb to get up on top of a tram or a train, wherever he goes." —Chris Carter

my little basement shop," Toby Lindala recalls. "I had the four guys working with me on that episode; that was quick."

Darin Morgan recalls sitting next to Duchovny on a plane while flying to Vancouver to prep for **"Humbug."** "I leaned over and I said, 'Hey you're that guy on that show, aren't you?' He just nodded. And I said, 'Would you sign my book for me?' He says, 'Sure.' And then I ask him sign it 'To my Arch Nemesis,' and he goes, 'Why do you want me to write that?' I say, 'I'll explain later.' Then he signed it, and I said, 'I'm the Flukeman.'"

"Blood" had Morgan and Wong tackling the paranoid thriller genre head-on, dealing with a conspiracy using LED displays for mind control. The story came from Glen Morgan's own hematophobia, with brother Darin helping develop the story, earning him a writing credit. The climax of the episode was inspired by the 1966 University of Texas massacre, in which Charles Whitman killed 14 people with a sniper's rifle from atop a clock tower.

The episode featured the return of the Lone Gunmen, as well as a guest appearance by porn actress Ashlyn Gere. "*NYPD Blue* had used Ginger Lynn, an adult film actress who was retired, and got an enormous amount of press," Glen Morgan recalls. "And we said, 'When we do it, we're going to use an adult film actress who's still working. That's how cutting edge we are.'"

Howard Gordon's **"Sleepless"** came about as a marriage between two concepts. "The idea occurred to me: What if a guy couldn't sleep? What if there was a guy who hadn't slept in 25 years?" Gordon says, "Chris had the idea for a super soldier. I married the idea of the super soldier to a sleepless soldier."

The episode also marked the debut of Alex Krycek, played by Nicholas Lea. "I created him largely because Gillian was pregnant and we had to write around her pregnancy," Gordon says, describing Krycek as a "Jimmy Olsen type guy who is eager to please. The last thing in the world you would think is that he is a mole."

"They were casting this part, and it was supposed to be three episodes to begin with," Lea remembers. "And it ended up being seven years." Lea can't help but admire his signature character: "There was something heroic in his stick-to-itiveness. It's just that his point of view was a little skewed."

"Sleepless" also gave viewers their first real look at Mulder's new source, who came to be known as X (or "Mr. X"). The role went to another Cannell veteran, Steven Williams. "It was originally going to be a woman, so when I went in to read for it it was an odd read," Williams recounts. "I'm asking these guys, 'Who is this guy? What do you want me to do with this guy?'"

"Of all the sources, Steven Williams was my favorite, because he was not only a source, he had attitude," Spotnitz says today, "He was angry, he was dangerous, he was not trustworthy, and he was a character of action."

Steven Williams explains the source of X's rage: "He was giving Mulder all the information he needed; Mulder just wasn't processing it properly. I think that's one of the things that drove his anger."

The episode ends with Krycek reporting to the Cigarette-Smoking Man. Director Rob Bowman recounts, "It was a very fun, scary scene for me because he seemed to be so confident there, none of which he showed in the episode."

With Gillian Anderson's maternity looming, Carter and company developed a storyline to account for her absence. The first shot across the bow was Carter's masterpiece, **"Duane Barry,"** which dealt with a former FBI agent (and multiple abductee) who escapes from a mental institution and takes hostages at a travel agency.

"I wrote the episode of "Duane Barry" for Steve Railsback," Carter recalls. "I've resisted casting the marquee names only because it takes you out of the show; it makes the show less believable. But there are certain actors who just call out for the part."

Carter decided to helm "Duane Barry" himself. "I had to learn how to do this because I'd never done it before *The X-Files*," Carter recalls.

TOP LEFT: Mulder surveys a crime scene in "BLOOD;" The Lone Gunmen make their second appearance in the same episode; "SLEEPLESS's" Augustus Cole ("The Preacher") played by actor Tony Todd is ... just tired; "SLEEPLESS" introduced a new informant character for Mulder, Steven Williams's angry Mr. X; Chris Carter (seen here a few years later on the set of season nine's "IMPROBABLE") took his first hand at directing for Duane Barry; Kinda hot: Dr. Grissom (Claude de Martino) puts out what he thinks is a real fire in "SLEEPLESS"—an imaginary blaze that's powerful enough to kill him; Seems harmless enough: the introduction of Alex Krycek (Nicholas Lea) in "SLEEPLESS;" Mulder interrogates Scully's abductor Duane Barry (Steve Railsback), David Duchovny took "ASCENSION" literally—the actor performed his own harrowing stunts aboard the top of a mountainside tram; Duchovny discusses the scene setup with crew.
ABOVE: Producers took advantage of Gillian Anderson's pregnancy in "ASCENSION," making her enlarged belly appear to be the result of alien experiments; "3" featured David Duchovny's then-girlfriend, Perry Reeves, as a would-be vampire.

"**One Breath**" would bring the Scully abduction drama to an emotional conclusion. Carter tapped Morgan and Wong for the script, and the pair gave William B. Davis his first major speaking role as the Cigarette-Smoking Man. "In *The Godfather*, there's people in the room who are, intentionally, never identified, and I believe that that's just what Chris was doing," Glen Morgan explains, "So we said, 'Well, we're going to have to do something with him, to explain what he's doing there.'"

The former professor took a philosophical approach to the character, saying the Cigarette-Smoking Man "had made so many sacrifices in order to do what he had to do that it was as though his emotional insides were empty or destroyed. He used the smoking to keep it all at bay."

"One Breath" has Scully mysteriously appear in a hospital emergency room, clinging to life by a thread. As Mulder desperately seeks a cure for her condition—and confronts the Cigarette-Smoking Man at gunpoint—an angelic nurse ushers Scully back from the brink of death. "It was one of the only shows on television that could talk about the afterlife and what happens when you die," Morgan notes.

In response to their growing popularity online, the Lone Gunmen appear once again in "One Breath." Tom Braidwood notes, "The producers were paying attention to what the fans were talking about. Apparently they really liked us in the chat room a lot." Bruce Harwood adds, "We represented the AOL people who would chat about the show while it was on or after it had finished on Friday nights." Indeed, Internet chatter would become grist for the writers' mills. "We'd get lines directly from the newsgroup like 'nitpick the scientific inaccuracies of *Earth 2*,' Dean Haglund says. "That then made the newsgroup explode saying, 'Aha! They are really reading this shit.'"

"We'd get lines directly from the internet newsgroup ... that made us explode saying, 'Ha! They are really reading this shit.'" —Dean Haglund

"(Chris) had a really good idea of what he wanted, but for the first few that he directed, it was a bit of a struggle because he just hadn't had the experience," Tom Braidwood observes. "So as he did it, his knowledge grew, and he got better and better at it." Aided by his top-shelf production staff, Carter acquitted himself nicely. "Chris came in meticulously prepared, which is his nature," David Duchovny says. "I think his first episode was great."

The story continued with "**Ascension,**" which picks up where "Duane Barry" left off; Scully is abducted by Barry and is to be offered up in his place to the aliens. Mulder and Krycek pursue Barry to Skyland Mountain, where Krycek sabotages Mulder's efforts to recover Scully. "Ascension" climaxes with Duchovny risking his neck for a nail-biting sequence on a tram. "David likes to do his own stunts," Carter noted in 1996, "but he is adamant about the fact that we should see him and know it is him if he is going to risk life and limb to get up on top of a tram or a train, wherever he goes."

The stopgap thriller "**3**" boasts a Morgan and Wong script, based on a story by Chris Ruppenthal. The episode has Mulder investigating a "holy trinity" of vampires during Scully's absence. "3" also features Mulder's tryst with a wannabe vampire, played by Duchovny's then-girlfriend, Perry Reeves.

The Internet would also play a role in the extensive research required for the show's dense story lines. Vince Gillian notes that *X-Files* researcher Katrina Cabrera "was one of the first people I ever knew who was active on the Internet. She kept saying 'Let me look it up on the Internet,'" The writer laughs, "I would say, 'What?' I didn't know what she was talking about for years."

Gillian Anderson was back in action for "**Firewalker,**" which revisited themes explored in "Ice" and "Darkness Falls," this time in a dormant volcano. The script for the David Nutter-helmed stand-alone posed a challenge to the new mother: "It was still just a week after a C-section, and I had a fight scene, which I just kinda laughed at and said, 'Guys, this isn't gonna happen,'" Anderson remembers. "Better get some pretty good stunt doubles in here. I can't lift my leg that high.'"

Chris Carter's brutal "**Red Museum**" was originally conceived as a crossover between *The X-Files* and David Kelley's CBS series *Picket Fences*. When those plans fell through, the episode was rewritten as a mythology episode dealing with schoolchildren and cattle being injected with alien DNA. The dense narrative deals with the alien conspiracy and religious cults and introduces the spiritual concept of possession by walk-ins, which later plays a crucial role in the Samantha abduction. The episode climaxed with the death of Deep Throat's assassin, the Crewcut Man.

LEFT: In an unconscious state in "ONE BREATH" following her abduction, Scully has a vision of her deceased father, who tells her, "We'll be together again, but not now. Soon." **ABOVE (left to right):** A mysterious nurse leads the unconscious Scully back to the world of the living—but is the nurse herself alive? The Cigarette-Smoking Man; The unconscious Scully; Mulder visits his recovered partner; Mulder and Scully examine the evidence in "RED MUSEUM;" The pair visit the flock in the Church of the Red Museum; A strange spore bursts from the neck of a volcanic scientist (Shawnee Smith) in "FIREWALKER;" Scientist Adam Pierce (Tuck Milligan) leads Mulder and Scully to the volcano; Terry O'Quinn (now of *Lost* fame) as Lt. Tillman in "AUBREY;" A monster in Scully's (not pictured) dreams in "IRRESISTIBLE."

"You can't do the combination of sex and death on network television."
—Chris Carter

"Excelsius Dei" explored the fountain of youth concept, in this case an herbal potion concocted by a nursing home orderly. The episode gave the staff headaches—both during the shoot and the editing process—but is memorable for a nail-biting scene in which Mulder is trapped in a flooded bathroom.

The serial killer drama **"Aubrey"** marked the first appearance of future *Lost* star Terry O'Quinn, who came to be known as "Mr. Ten Thirteen" for his prominent roles in *The X-Files*, *Millennium*, and *Harsh Realm*. Coincidentally, O'Quinn's appearance would precede the episode that would ultimately inspire Chris Carter to create *Millennium* the next year.

"Irresistible" introduced Donnie Pfaster, a funeral home employee whose taste for dead flesh drives him to murder, a theme that was shot down by Standards and Practices. "When I handed the script in, it was really for a necrophiliac episode," Carter recalled, "and that just didn't fly. You cannot do the combination of sex and death on network television," adding that he called Pfaster a "death fetishist, and all of the sexual content was implied."

In the episode, Pfaster's crimes have a powerful effect on Scully, who was eventually kidnapped by the killer. Carter would borrow a disturbing motif for their encounter from the annals of true crime: "There are reports of people who had been under the spell of Jeffrey Dahmer, who actually claimed that he shape-shifted during those hours when they were held hostage; that his image actually changed."

Gillian Anderson would take on the emotional demands of episodes like these in stride. "It was all extremely technical, so I think I learned early on to leave my work at the door and not take it home with me," she says today.

"Die Hand Die Verletzt", a dark parody of the satanic ritual abuse scare, marked *The X-Files* premiere of director Kim Manners. This was the culmination of a longstanding ambition of several key members of *The X-Files*

staff. "Jim, Glen, and I had all worked at Stephen Cannell together," John Bartley remembers. "We all looked at each other and said, 'We've got to get Kim Manners on this show.'"

Manners would quickly distinguish himself on the show, earning praise from stars and staff alike. "The thing about Kim is that he's so emotional about his work," Bob Goodwin recalls. "You watch him at the monitor while he is doing a scene, and you can't imagine how anybody can live on that kind of level. He just throws himself into it, body and soul. It would just drain me." "Die Hand" co-writer Glen Morgan notes that, "Kim was a very passionate guy. I'd drop in on him in Vancouver when he was shooting something emotional, and he'd be in tears."

But another shake-up was soon to come: "Die Hand Die Verletzt" would be Morgan and Wong's last episode before leaving to produce their own series , *Space: Above and Beyond*

Next up was Howard Gordon's **"Fresh Bones,"** a bleak horror tale seasoned with social commentary. Daniel Benzali guest stars as the commander of a Haitian refugee internment camp, who keeps his subjects under control with the use of voodoo.

Carter recovered from the loss of Morgan and Wong by recruiting an old friend. A graduate of the American Film Institute, Frank Spotnitz would eventually become Carter's right-hand man and remains so to this day. The writer/producer/director had originally met Carter in a reading club they both belonged to.

After Carter hit the jackpot with *The X-Files*, a screenwriter friend of Spotnitz's asked him to arrange a meeting with Carter. The call was made, but Carter demurred. As Spotnitz recalls, Carter, however, said to him "'If you have anything, I'd love to hear your ideas.' So I thought of three ideas. I guess I thought it was going to be my buddy Chris and me, and it wasn't

like that at all. I pitched these three ideas, which I thought were good and he shot them all down, one by one."

Soon after, however, Carter gave Spotnitz a second chance when Morgan and Wong gave notice. Spotnitz remembers, "That was a Thursday, and I started on Monday. I have to say, from day one, it was very difficult. It was sink or swim. There was no allowance for the fact that I'd never worked in Hollywood before and this was my first job."

Spotnitz hit the ground running with the MythArc two-parter, "**Colony**" and "**End Game.**" "One of my first pitches was, 'It's been so long since Mulder has seen his sister, what if she came back?'" Spotnitz recalls. "What if a girl came back, or a young woman, and said, 'I'm your sister?' How would he know it's not her?"

The story begins with Scully and Mulder investigating the murders of several physically identical abortion doctors, which leads them to uncover an illegal cloning program. The story featured the first appearance of the Alien Bounty Hunter, a Terminator-like figure suggested by David Duchovny and played by Brian Thompson (who himself had a bit part in the first *Terminator* film).

The story ratchets up the suspense with the appearance of an alien clone of Samantha Mulder. It also introduces Mulder's parents, played by Peter Donat and Rebecca Toolan. The two-parter features a brutal fight scene between Skinner and X, and ends with Mulder clinging to life after chasing the Bounty Hunter to a Russian sub docked in the Arctic Circle. Of the fan-favorite fight scene, Steven Williams says, "It was so much fun to do. And for ages folks asked me who won that fight"

"Frank wrote with a velvet hammer," Rob Bowman observes. "There's a lot of intrigue in the way he writes and gets under your skin." About the introduction of the Alien Bounty Hunter, Spotnitz remarks, "Those two episodes

OPPOSITE PAGE, TOP LEFT: Mulder and Scully examine a voodoo marking left behind at the scene of a mysterious death in "FRESH BONES;" American military officer Colonel Wharton (Daniel Benzahi) has added Haitian voodoo to his arsenal.
FROM UPPER LEFT: Special effects makeup expert Toby Lindala applies some final touches to Kevin Conway, whose Private Jack McAlpin sees himself differently in his rearview mirror. The two agents track down Wharton practicing his craft in a cemetery; Gillian Anderson poses with seasons one thru three director of photography John Bartley (front right), Marty Sound (front left) and other crew; Frank Spotnitz with Chris Carter (seen during the filming of "I WANT TO BELIEVE"—Spotnitz, who joined *The X-Files* team in season two, would make a permanent and indelible addition to the series; Likewise, director Kim Manners (seen shooting season nine's "Audrey Pauley") would join in season two, and, with Rob Bowman, would turn *The X-Files* upside down; "The Fresh Bones" death mark.

were really a turning point for the series. Until that point, the alien mythology was fairly oblique. When this happened, I also recall that the other staff writers were very unsure about whether this was a good idea."

The energy level would recede for "**Fearful Symmetry,**" a strange stand-alone dealing with the abduction of zoo animals by aliens. It was seen as a disappointment to the staff, filming was difficult, and numerous rewrites and reshoots were done to salvage it. However, writer William Gibson would tell Frank Spotnitz later that it was one of his favorite *X-Files* episodes.

Gordon and Gansa's "**Død Kalm**" guest-stars John Savage and deals with a ship's crew infected with a mysterious aging disease. The makeup work required was an added burden to Duchovny and Anderson, and producers worried that aging makeup was never convincing enough on television. "The twist we came up with is that they looked like they were getting older, but they weren't really getting older," Frank Spotnitz explains. "It was the water that was affecting their tissue and making them look this way."

Darin Morgan would unwittingly turn *The X-Files* formula upside down with his first script, "**Humbug.**" "Glen had a tape of Jim Rose performing his sideshow act," Morgan recalls. "And they just said, 'Use this guy and do something with circus freaks,' which looking back was awfully weird because we didn't have a commitment or anything to Jim at all." Darin would work in seclusion on "Humbug" for the better part of the season and emerge with a script that astounded everyone. Not everyone, however, was sure it was right for the series.

"I remember hearing that Fox was very nervous at the time that this was not a good thing to do with this show, which at that point was turning into a real hit for them, and it was too soon to make fun of it," recalls writer Vince Gilligan, who joined the *X-Files* team around this time. "And to Chris's and everybody's credit, they went ahead and did the episode."

Kim Manners was picked to helm but was hesitant. "Kim was really, really terrified of doing the episode," Morgan says. "If it had come later, he would have loved directing it, but I just think everyone was just really scared." Today Manners sees "Humbug" as a turning point for the series: "That was the dawning of the realization that it needed to poke a little fun at itself because if it didn't, it was in danger of becoming a concept that was going to be pretty

hard for the audience to buy into every week," he says.

Breaking the comedy line took its toll on Morgan. "I've always harbored a little bitterness to all the comedies that followed because I really took a beating from a lot of people for being the first one," he says, laughing. Carter notes that humor had been part of the series all along: "Everybody was funny," he notes, "But we didn't know how funny the show could be until Darin Morgan came along."

Fan reaction was unanimous. "At that time, we were still doing fan conventions, so the feedback we received was immediate and overwhelming," notes Spotnitz. "As soon as you mentioned 'Humbug' or Darin, people screamed."

Like so many other season two episodes, **"The Calusari"** was a pitch-black horror story, this time about a child possessed by the evil spirit of his stillborn twin brother. The writer here had a unique insight on the topic. "Sara Charno had been a doctor of Eastern medicine who had become a television writer, and so she had a lot of esoteric knowledge that none of the rest of us had about all kinds of things," Frank Spotnitz recalls.

Though the script was strong and the shoot went well, Spotnitz remembers that the first cut of the episode didn't pass muster. "Chris spent a lot of time in the editing room trying to figure out how to make this more terrifying," Spotnitz says, "That was an important experience because I saw how much better something could become if you didn't give up."

Carter and Gordon teamed up for **"F Emasculata,"**—a politically-charged thriller in which a prisoners were used in the experimentation of a viral plague, leaving Mulder and Scully trapped when the prison was quarantined. Toby Lindala's crew outdid themselves on the effects: "When we saw the pustule bursting on film, we just laughed because it was just so over-the-top grotesque," Frank Spotnitz recalls, adding that this episode "was atypical in that the Cigarette-Smoking Man made an appearance in a stand-alone episode. Chris didn't like mixing mythology with stand-alones."

Another pivotal figure in the *The X-Files* would make his bones in season two. Vince Gilligan was as an aspiring screenwriter who fell in with *The X-Files* almost by chance. "It was probably spring or summer of 1994 when I happened to be out on a business trip and got to meet Chris, and Howard Gordon and Sarah Charno were in the meeting," Gilligan explains. "That's the

OPPOSITE PAGE, FROM TOP LEFT: : A Samantha clone (Megan Leitch) visits with Mulder's mother (Rebecca Toolan); Mulder with "Samantha"; "You'll only win the war if you pick the right battles, Agent Mulder. This is a battle you can't win," X tells Mulder in "END GAME," the first episode written by Frank Spotnitz; The set of the giant frozen submarine conning tower set from "END GAME." **RIGHT**: A lone survivor aboard the sub at the North Pole, or is it the Alien Bounty Hunter? Mulder soon finds out; An aged Mulder and Scully from Howard Gordon's "DØD KAIM." "I think that episode alone will keep me forever turning down anything that has to do with full prosthetic makeup. That was painful," Anderson notes. Mulder comforts Willa Ambrose (Jayne Atkinson), whose zoo animals have been the targets of the latest alien experimentation in "FEARFUL SYMMETRY". **FOLLOWING PAGE**: What a bunch of freaks: Members of Dr. Blockhead's sideshow—with Mulder and Scully—notice something amiss at the funeral of Jerald Glazebrooks in Darin Morgan's "HUMBUG," one of many an X-File fan's favorite episodes.

"When we saw the pustule bursting
on film, we just laughed because it
was just so over-the-top grotesque."
—Frank Spotnitz

way Chris was. Whoever was in the room he'd invite along for the meeting. Chris is very good in the sense that in working with him you get to be your own producer even if you don't technically have that job title."

Gilligan's *X-Files* premiere, **"Soft Light,"** features Tony Shalhoub as a physicist whose shadow has become a kind of lethal black hole. Gilligan remembers that his script was reworked by Chris Carter and Howard Gordon: "They rewrote that episode to make it shootable by getting rid of the shadow element and its ability to move independently of the actor," the writer says. "This saved an enormous amount of money in animation costs."

Spotnitz's first stand-alone **"Our Town"** tells the story of workers at a chicken factory infected with Mad Cow disease. Mulder and Scully investigate only to discover a cannibalistic cult led by the factory owner. Spotnitz recalls that Howard Gordon pitched in with crucial story point for the teaser: "Howard was always interested in finding the interesting personal conflict that was split wide open by the supernatural. Like my second episode, "Our Town," it was Howard's idea to begin it with an illicit love affair. That becomes the event that busts open the terrible secret that the community is hiding about the cannibalism."

Rob Bowman was picked to helm the story and found himself challenged by the climatic human sacrifice scene, in which the cult leader dons a ceremonial mask. "The mask scared the hell out of me only because I thought, 'Boy, if I don't shoot this right it's going to be silly,'" the director recalls.

Season closer **"Anasazi"** was inspired by Chris Carter's vacation to Sedona, Arizona, and his fascination with the vanished native tribe that gives the episode its name. The story begins with a radical anarchist being hunted by death squads after hacking into secret government files on UFOs, and ends

OPPOSITE PAGE, *TOP LEFT:* The Bearded Lady in appropriate funeral attire from "HUMBUG;" Dr. Blockhead (Jim Rose, whose troupe actually appeared in the episode) feeds Humbug's The Conundrum what he wants—anything; Is it Charlie or is it Michael? Young Joel Palmer as a brother possessed by the spirit of his dead twin in "THE CALUSARI;" A bursting pustule in "F. EMASCULATA" is about to work its magic on an escaped convict (John Pyper-Ferguson); Scully searches for the bug behind the pus. Writer Vince Gilligan (seen here in 2008) joined the fold in season two, with his first episode, "SOFT LIGHT;" The result of a dangerous shadow in "SOFT LIGHT."

ABOVE: Mulder beside a rescue helicopter in soft light; Walter Chaco (John Milford) preps a silenced Scully for her own slaughter in Frank Spotnitz's "OUR TOWN;" Whatcha readin'? Rob Bowman looks over Gillian Anderson's shoulder while the actress reads the latest edition of *Time* on the set of "OUR TOWN" as Script Supervisor Helga Ungarait makes some notes; Anderson and Duchovny on location of "OUR TOWN" after the previous night's bonfire; The Executioner's mask; Toby Lindala tends tends to the boss's on the ol' Chaco Chicken assembly line in between shots.

"David, to this day, will still leave me phone messages saying 'You killed my father.'" —Nicholas Lea

with a railroad car filled with alien corpses—and Mulder being firebombed by the Cigarette-Smoking Man's goons. "Anasazi" would also introduce the Navajo code-talker Albert Hosteen (played by Floyd Red Crow-Westerman) who would later become an important player in the unfolding mythology.

The Southwestern setting of the episode presented a special challenge to the production team: "Vancouver had an awful lot of locations, but the one thing they didn't have was desert," Bob Goodwin remembers. "So we found an old abandoned quarry east of Vancouver someplace. I got a bunch of photographs of the different rock formations in Sedona, because it has all those beautiful reds and oranges in the rocks and all that. We sent the art department out there, and we painted this whole half a mile of cliff red."

Co-written with David Duchovny, "Anasazi" ramped up the personal stakes for Mulder—the Syndicate was poisoning his building's water supply and Alex Krycek reappears to assassinate Mulder's father. Nicholas Lea jokes, "David, to this day, will still leave me phone messages saying 'You killed my father.'"

The episode also features a brutal fistfight between Mulder and Krycek. "The stunt coordinator was stuck in traffic, and he couldn't make it, so David and I choreographed that fight," Lea proudly recalls. "I had to snap my neck over and over again, looking like I was taking the punch. So, Bob Goodwin ordered a massage therapist to my room the next morning. That's the kind of guy Bob Goodwin is."

In 2005, Carter recalled that the end of "Anasazi" episode "brought a lot of interest to the show ('How can you do this? How can you kill the lead character?')" He finally concluded that "Anasazi's" fadeout "heightened interest in the show, and David was instrumental in coming up with that idea." The continuation of the storyline in the next season would plant the

SEASON FINALE, "ANASAZI" **TOP LEFT:** Scully is asked to account for Mulder's erratic behavior to a panel of FBI bureaucrats; Gillian Anderson has fun with one of them—her boss, Chris Carter, sitting in for a cameo; Scully tends to Mulder after the murder of his father. **RIGHT:** Floyd "Red Crow" Westerman as Navajo—and alien—interpreter Albert Hosteen; The Cigarette-Smoking Man, as always, at the center of things; Scully, can you hear me now? Mulder inside a tanker car stacked floor to ceiling with "merchandise"— corpses of alien/human hybrid experiments; Toby Lindala tends to one of his creations, in this case the shriveled remains of an alien; The alien corpse.

SPECIAL AGENT FOX MULDER

Fox Mulder is a driven man. As a teenager, he watched as his young sister, Samantha, was abducted by aliens, and since that time has made a life of finding ... the truth. The truth about what happened to his sister, the truth behind conspiracy, the truth behind the unexplained.

"He is fearless," explains Chris Carter. "Mulder is fearless about his convictions. He's ascetic, in that he is single-minded. He is convinced, but not beyond a shadow of a doubt. He's relentlessly pursuing, philosophically and religiously and scientifically, the meaning of life."

To Carter, Mulder's quest is, essentially, a search for God. "I kind of realized that through my own journey. It became clear that that really is what it is. That's what everything is in life. It may be supplemented into something else, but everything is a search for meaning."

Mulder's search is one which he no doubt would have continued, even had he never met Scully, particularly due to his drive to find the truth. "His lack of interest in what others think of him is very strong," says David Duchovny. "That was a very strong characterization point for me to hone in on, just because it's such a rare quality in somebody, and, for me, a sign of strength."

Even when facing the most horrific of monsters—be they human, subhuman or otherworldly—Mulder always exhibits not only a sense of fearlessness, but also empathy. "That was a beautiful quality of Mulder, which he used quite a lot and had a very effective response from people," says Gillian Anderson.

"That was written into the character," says Carter, "but I think that David understood it completely and actually helped to distinguish the character with those traits. It actually comes from him—he has a tremendously big heart for the freaks and mutants and disenfranchised and misunderstood."

The writers took full advantage of that quality, often allowing him to get information from individuals no one else wanted anything to do with. "Mulder finds these people who have been shut up, who have been marginalized, people who no one else would listen to," says Howard Gordon. "That's the client interest. And that allowed us to do a procedural that stands on its own. But with Mulder, in asking that question and helping that person, he's also pursuing his own quest and getting himself that much further. It made every show become, in some way, very personal."

"It's a useful quality because it's rare," Carter notes. "It is an opposing force in that it is otherwise against everyone's instincts. It is a show of compassion that I think is moving inherently. My feeling is kindness is a virtue and cruelty is a weakness, and that it shows Mulder's virtues."

His sense of being a loner and an outsider quickly brought out something both in Mulder and in Duchovny. "As the show developed, it really turned into a decent sense of humor, a sense of the absurd," the actor remarks. "The guy had to have a sense of the absurd, because most of the cases that he was investigating became absurd."

That sense of humor was something Duchovny was able to zero in on and make his own. "There was some humor in the pilot, but I think we really honed it as the years went on into something that I felt was a really strong part of the show." While the writers quickly got a grasp of that quality in Mulder, it was Duchovny's delivery that sold it. "The humor was written, but I would say that was just the foundation," says Carter. "David built the house on top of it. He's just a funny person. And he knows I tried to modulate and/or keep the tone appropriate. Because the show could become very silly very quickly if it were all to be funny all the time. But he's good at walking the fine line of tipping it back toward serious when it needs to be."

But it wasn't all on the page. "David added a lot of that stuff," recalls Anderson. A lot of it was in the script, but every once in awhile, David would come up with a real winner or really improve something." Says Duchovny, "The humor of the writers was very much a part of their scripts. I would not normally ad lib in humor that some of them wove in. I respected that and was thankful for it. It was more in the straight ahead investigative shows, the creepier, scarier shows, that I would try to make sure that we kept this kind of humanity alive through the humor of it." With the passage of time, David's memory has faded, regarding particular ad libs. "I can't remember which things were mine though. Let's just say anything you find funny, I made up. And anything that is attempting to be funny but is not, that's Howard Gordon."

"I have been on the bridge that spans two worlds; the link we all cross to our own true nature. You were here today looking for a truth that was taken from you. A truth which was never to be spoken but which now binds us together in dangerous purpose. I have returned from the dead to continue with you, but I fear that this danger is now close at hand, and I may be too late."

—Mulder to Scully from **The Blessing Way** (3x01)

SEASON THREE *THE MYTHOLOGY TAKES ROOT*

"The Blessing Way" kicks off Chris Carter's favorite season with a bang: Mulder clings to life in a Native American healing ceremony, and the Syndicate—the secretive group of government officials to whom the Cigarette-Smoking Man belongs—sends out a hit squad to ice Scully as she tries to recover the digital tape with the UFO documents.

The staging of the **"Blessing Way"** ceremony was drawn from personal experience. Chris Carter explained that "Mulder's journey into his own past through the Native American ritual was something I actually attempted to do as well, by going and partaking in just this kind of event."

The episode also introduces John Neville as the Well-Manicured Man, who warns Scully of the Syndicate's designs against her. "We had this rival who was sort of the white knight to the Cigarette-Smoking Man's black knight in this chess game that we were playing," Frank Spotnitz says.

The Syndicate sends Krycek and Luis Cardinale to kill Scully, but they

prophecies were then added to the mix. "The white buffalo that appears at the beginning of the episode was something I had read about, an actual white buffalo calf had been born, and the Indians—the Native Americans—felt that was an omen of something about to happen," Carter said in a 1997 interview.

The two-parter offered the first insider view of the Syndicate. Rob Bowman had a unique insight on the group and shots them accordingly. "They represent betrayal from the Watergate days," the director says. "They wield power without conscience. That was always scary to me. That's why I liked it."

"We met on *The Commish*," Lea boasts about Melinda McGraw (Melissa Scully), "I got to kill her."

mistakenly kill her sister. Although it was never made clear in the episode who had actually killed Melissa Scully (Melinda McGraw), Nicholas Lea takes credit for the hit, noting that he was dating McGraw at the time. "We met on *The Commish*," Lea boasts, "I got to kill her."

"Paper Clip" keeps the tension at white-hot intensity. The episode begins with a voiceover drawn from Navajo prophecy and mythology, using stories Navajo medicine men shared with Carter. Other Native American

"Paper Clip" has Mulder and Scully discovering a massive secret database in an abandoned mine and encountering furtive aliens in a dark tunnel. Mulder also gets an eyeful of a massive UFO while Scully is still inside. Gillian Anderson laments, "She was missing seeing everything. The mothership flying through the air, the alien, whatever it was. I always missed everything."

Kim Manners explains the importance of keeping the aliens in the

---

FROM TOP LEFT: Navajo Healer Albert Hosteen from "THE BLESSING WAY;" Rob Bowman with his first A.D./character actor Tom Braidwood (The Lone Gunmen's Frohike); Mulder watches as the alien ship takes off in "PAPER CLIP"—it's a shame Scully didn't see this; Mulder being healed by the Navajos in "THE BLESSING WAY;" Duchovny and Anderson between takes, as Scully dashes to her sister's aid; David and Gillian enjoy a light moment with two-thirds of the Lone Gunmen—Byers (Bruce Harwood) and Langly (Dean Haglund)—from the set of "PAPER CLIP."

shadows. "Chris knew not to let the audience in on anything that Scully and Mulder hadn't discovered, so the discovery was through their eyes," he says.

Meanwhile, the Cigarette-Smoking Man tries to do away with Krycek with a car bomb and nearly succeeds. Rob Bowman notes, "It's a rude awakening for Krycek. He's cocky because he's playing both sides. He hasn't had anything really bad happen to him yet."

The scene was hampered by problems with the pyrotechnics. "We rehearsed it and rehearsed it, and it didn't work. It doesn't exactly fill you with confidence," Lea explains. "But we did get it right, and I got maybe 30 or 40 feet away from it, and the concussive pressure of the explosion almost pushed me to the ground. You really feel alive when you're doing those things."

Skinner plays a crucial role in the episode, blackmailing the Cigarette-Smoking Man into calling off the hit put out on Mulder and Scully. "He's also not a company man," Carter says of Skinner. "He walks that fine line between believing in Mulder and Scully and protecting them." The confrontation with the Cigarette-Smoking Man provides one of the X-Phile nation's favorite lines as Skinner says to his adversary, "This is where you pucker up and kiss my ass." Mitch Pileggi enjoyed the opportunity to stick it to the Cigarette-Smoking Man: "It was always fun playing with him because of the nature of the characters' animosity toward each other," he recalls.

Howard Gordon describes the premise for "**D.P.O.**" as "kind of *Beavis and Butthead* and weather," noting he was exploring "this idea of a basically impotent kid, a kid who was a loser, with this power. Imagine a kid with a gun."

The episode was also notable for the two young actors who guested; Giovanni Ribisi and Jack Black. Rick Millikan remembers the casting process: "When Giovanni came in and read, I remember Chris wasn't sure about it. I didn't think he had the vulnerability Chris was looking for," Millikan says. "We brought him back, and I had a conversation with him outside, just to say, 'You know, bring a little more humanity to it. Don't make it such a caricature.' He went in, he did it, and that was it."

Black's powerful personality didn't go unnoticed on the set. "Jack was a sweet kid," Anderson remembers. "But that loud kind of brassy voice that he has, that was there way from the beginning."

Howard Gordon has a memorable experience on the guest stars' off-day. "I wound up spending the day with Jack Black and Giovanni Ribisi playing video games," The producer fondly recalls.

With "**Clyde Bruckman's Final Repose,**" Darin Morgan returned to the fold with a landmark episode that would earn both the writer—and guest star Peter Boyle—Emmy Awards. The episode didn't begin as the dark comic romp it became. "Up until that point, my favorite episode was "Beyond the Sea." So I went back, and I watched that one several times; I wanted to write an episode that was dark in that kind of vein," Morgan explains. "My original intention was to be very dark and depressing. I ended up putting jokes in it just because I simply couldn't help myself."

The episode grew out of Morgan's typically skewed take on psychics and clairvoyance. "My brother had a research book that included intensely graphic

"My original intention was to be very dark and depressing. I ended up putting jokes in it just because I couldn't help myself."
—Darin Morgan

"You can't imagine anyone other than Peter Boyle in the role now for what resulted in an Emmy Award-winning performance and a highlight not just for *The X-Files* but for primetime television."   —Chris Carter

OPPOSITE PAGE, TOP: Jack Black's guest appearance at the ill-fated video arcade in ""D.P.O."; Mulder and Scully look skyward after lightning indeed strikes more than twice in "D.P.O."; Giovanni Ribisi's Darin Peter Oswald, the title character in "D.P.O.," taunts the heavens. THIS PAGE, TOP LEFT: Peter Boyle wishes he didn't see what he sees in Darin Morgan's "CLYDE BRUCKMAN'S FINAL REPOSE;" Clyde and Mulder; Bruckman leads Mulder and Scully to the body of a murder victim; Mulder taking it all in.

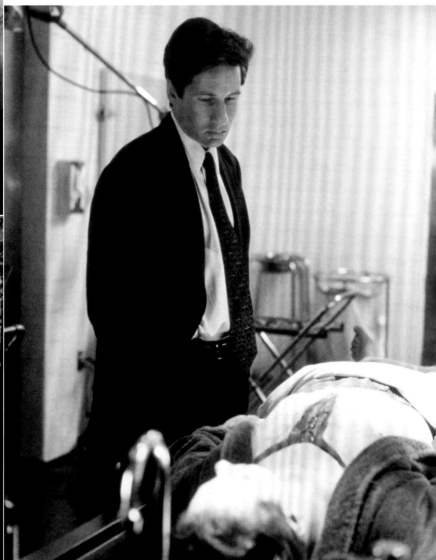

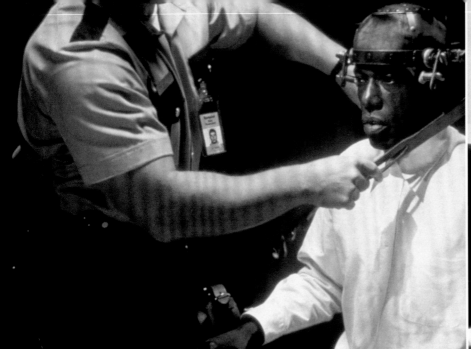

"On Death Row...we are left, emotionally, with the fallout and the vestiges of these people's lives." —Chris Carter

crime-scene photos," he explains. "The idea was that if you can foresee the events of someone's life, you should be able to foresee their death; and if you could foresee their death, you would be seeing pictures like this all the time."

Rick Millikan recalls suggesting Peter Boyle for the role. "I had said to Chris, 'I think Peter would be perfect in this.' His initial reaction was he thought Peter might come across as a little too crazy, to which I said, 'And? Isn't that what we want?'"

"I don't think Peter Boyle knew quite what to make of this whole thing in the beginning," Anderson recalls, "But we had some really sweet scenes together, and I think by the time we got to those he warmed up a bit. He was a lovely man to work with."

"Peter had real issues with death, because of his own past close calls with health issues and so forth," director David Nutter explains. "So, in the dream sequence in which he is lying in a field of flowers in his underwear, he didn't like shooting that. He wasn't into that at all."

Toby Lindala recalls Boyle's discomfort with the scene: "What he said to me was 'This is the worst day of my life.' And then I went about my job, 'Okay, sorry. I'm just going to try to make this quick and painless for you then.'"

"The List" is a prison drama spiked with a gruesome reincarnation. Written and directed by Chris Carter, the episode guest stars J. T. Walsh as a corrupt warden. *The X-Files* art department went to bat on the episode, building a convincing death row set out of thin air. Carter also gives Scully some Mulder-like quips such as, "Woman gets lonely. Sometimes she can't wait around for her man to be reincarnated."

"2SHY" is a monster-of-the-week written by Jeffrey Vlaming about a fat-sucking mutant who combs Internet dating sites for his lonely female victims. The combination of horror and romance was tailor-made for David Nutter, who explains, "So much of the reasoning that I thought was powerful in the material that was written for the show was the fact that the bad guys or the creatures in the show—the reasons they did things were not because they were just there to do evil, but to survive."

"The Walk" features the first script by new writer John Shiban, who would later become one of the primary executive producers on the show. Writing for *The X-Files* posed distinct challenges for the new recruit. "Ask any writer on the show; I guarantee you, and they'll say the hardest scene in the story is Mulder and Scully's first scene in Act One because that's where they have to come together on a case, yet they have to be at odds," John Shiban explained in a 2001 interview.

In "The Walk," Shiban told the story of a quadruple amputee Gulf War vet who used astral projection to get revenge on the officers he served under. An astounding effort by the effects team would handle the amputations, so Rob Bowman looked for an actor who could convey the rage and

FROM LEFT: Neech Manley (Badja Djola) prepares to meet his maker—and take revenge—in "THE LIST." The episode was written by new staff writer, John Shiban (below), who joined the troupe in season three; Mulder and Scully examine the remains of a victim in "2SHY;" Not much left: the killer's digestive juices stay on the job; Home away from home: Lucy Householder (Tracey Ellis) returns to the scene of her teenage captivity, where her captor has held yet another prisoner in "OUBLIETTE;" Lucy helps Mulder find the missing girl, as she experiences the girl's current trauma herself. Director Kim Manners was so impressed by Ellis's dark performance that he cast her six years later in season nine's "AUDREY PAULEY."

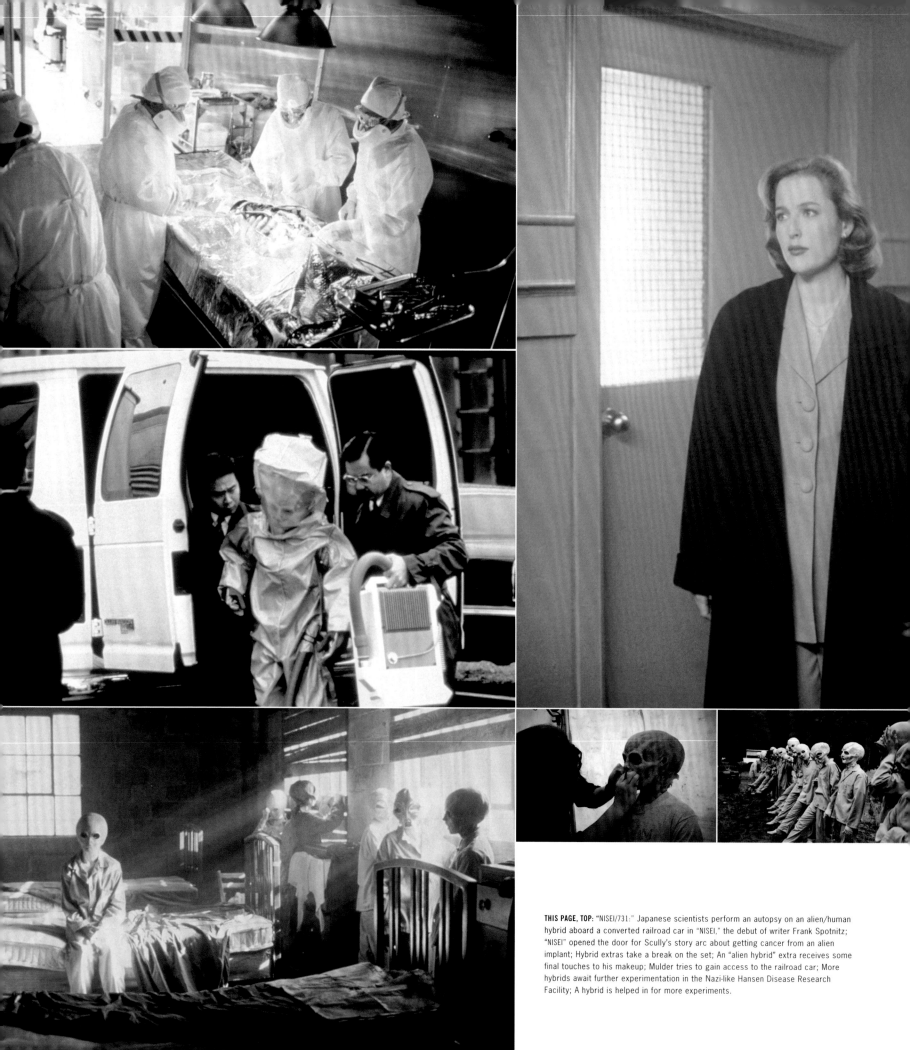

THIS PAGE, TOP: "NISEI/731:" Japanese scientists perform an autopsy on an alien/human hybrid aboard a converted railroad car in "NISEI," the debut of writer Frank Spotnitz; "NISEI" opened the door for Scully's story arc about getting cancer from an alien implant; Hybrid extras take a break on the set; An "alien hybrid" extra receives some final touches to his makeup; Mulder tries to gain access to the railroad car; More hybrids await further experimentation in the Nazi-like Hansen Disease Research Facility; A hybrid is helped in for more experiments.

intensity the role called for. "I needed an actor who could push back with equal and opposite force and not be intimidated by David," Bowman explains. "Ian Tracey is a very sturdy physical guy and an incredibly strong actor, and when he read Mulder the riot act there in the bed, that's what it had to be."

"Oubliette" is a heart-wrenching drama about a kidnapped girl forming a psychic link with her abductor's prior victim, Lucy Householder (played by Tracey Ellis). Mulder races to rescue the girl and absolve Lucy, whose intimate knowledge of the case has caused her to be accused as an accomplice. Director Kim Manners was especially impressed with Ellis' skills and noted, "We worked very, very hard—all of the directors on *The X-Files* anyhow—to find the nuances to make the performances real."

"Nisei" begins a two-parter that ties Scully's abduction to medical experiments by a group of Japanese war criminals. "I had this idea about Japanese medical experiments," Spotnitz explains. "People know about the Nazi medical experiments, but people don't realize that the Japanese committed atrocities, as well."

There was a snag in the production, however. "Bob Goodwin called Chris and said, 'This is unproducable. You can't do this,'" Spotnitz recalls. "'It's way too big. We don't have the time or the money to do it, and you've got to throw out the script, basically.' I was devastated, and Chris was scratching his head, and they came up with a solution which was, 'Let's make it a two-parter.'"

The episode ends with Mulder jumping from a bridge onto a moving train. Part of the stunt was performed by the actor himself. "I'm not a guy that says I have to do all my own stunts; I'm just the guy that says 'Is it going look better if you see my face?'" Duchovny says. "If it doesn't matter, then I'll let some other guy hurt himself, for sure."

The shocking teaser for **"731"** drew upon the horrors of the Holocaust; a group of human alien hybrids is rounded up by soldiers, gunned down, and buried in a mass grave. The shadow of Nazi atrocities hangs over the two-parter, with all of the imagery of trains and camps.

The script called for a train car to be blown up, and the effect was performed without using miniatures. "Nisei" helmsman Nutter recalls, "That was something that Chris would always repeat, 'You can't just settle for anything. You always have to try to reach higher and do that.' So that's what we always did."

Of Mulder's last-minute rescue by X from the exploding train, Chris Carter cheekily says, "It's clear that sometimes there are characters that need to bear the burden of exposition as the *deus ex machina*."

"Revelations," a Scully-centric fable about a possible Christ child, turned out to be the last episode directed by David Nutter. The longtime *X-Files*

THIS PAGE, **TOP**: Why waste a good bad guy? Scully watches as Simon Gates is ground to pulp at a paper recycling plant as she rescues the miraculous Kevin Zegers in "REVELATIONS;" Mulder and Scully talk with Kevin Kryder's principal about the mysterious wounds which have shown up on his hands—stigmata. **FOLLOWING PAGE**: More hybrids await further experimentation in "731" in the Nazi-like Hansen Disease Research Facility.

director said his decision to leave was in part motivated by the tremendous enthusiasm and drive he saw in Manners and Bowman. "When you're working on a show in the early stages, you have this parental feel for it, and you want it to do well," Nutter explains. "When they came on as producer/directors, I felt that I wanted to go out and try to do different things and that *The X-Files* was in excellent hands."

"War of the Coprophages" was Darin Morgan's cockroach-centric updating of the panic created by Orson Welles' *War of the Worlds* broadcast. The episode had some hilarious scenes, but Morgan wasn't happy with the final result. "The other day my girlfriend was saying, 'I never understood that episode,' and I guess I don't either." Morgan sighs, "It was an episode that had a lot of what I thought were really good ideas and never quite got it to work. I was really disappointed with that episode. Some people love it."

The episode's highlights included a beautiful entomologist named Bambi, and a clever gag effect in which a cockroach appeared to be walking across the television screen. "I was hoping to fool some people into thinking that the cockroach was real, the same way some people were fooled thinking that the *War of the Worlds* was actually going on in reality," Morgan explains, adding ruefully, "But we did not get any reports of people throwing their shoe at their TV."

In "Syzygy," Carter used sexual tension and gallows humor to leaven a very dark and brutal tale of two high school cheerleaders who fall under adverse astrological influences and embark on a gleeful murder spree. "Syzygy" offers memorable scenes of Scully smoking cigarettes in a fit of jealousy over Mulder's interest in a sexy detective and Mulder trying to spoon orange juice concentrate into a bottle of vodka, as the stellar alignment causes the agents to lose their own inhibitions.

"There's *The X-Files* of the stand-alone, and then there's *The X-Files* of the mythology," Duchovny observes. "And then there are the comedic *X-Files* as

"I had been wanting to do this since the beginning of the show. I wanted to see a WWII pilot at the bottom of the ocean, in his fighter, pounding on the glass of his cockpit." —Chris Carter

well, in which the characters are really not quite the characters that we know."

Howard Gordon's "**Grotesque**," a dark exploration of obsession and

demonic possession, delves into Mulder's history as a criminal profiler. The episode also features Kurtwood Smith as Mulder's former mentor from the Behavioral Sciences unit.

The next two-parter would begin with "**Piper Maru**," which introduces the Black Oil, an alien virus that passes from host to host. The shocking image in the teaser had come from a nightmare Carter had several years before. "There was something I had wanted to do since the beginning of the show," said Carter. "I wanted to see a WWII pilot at the bottom of the ocean, in his fighter, pounding on the glass of his cockpit."

The Black Oil motif signaled an effort to focus the mythology. "In the early days, I thought we were going to have more freedom to have all kinds of aliens," Spotnitz remembers, "And by season three, I realized, 'You know, this

THIS PAGE, ABOVE: Mulder meets Dr. Ivanov (Ken Kramer) and his robotic cockroaches in "WAR OF THE COPROPHAGES;" Beauty is only skin-deep: Mulder and Scully discover an artistic but possessed murderer's horrific secret—there are people under those gargoyles. . . . **RIGHT PAGE:** Whose side are you on? Mulder finds Alex Krycek in Hong Kong selling secrets abroad in "PIPER MARU;" Skinner is gunned down by an assassin (Lenno Britos) in a Washington coffeehouse after being warned not to reopen the case of Scully's sister's death; "Destroy the bodies," orders the Cigarette-Smoking Man in "APOCRYPHA"—even though the men are not yet dead. "Isn't that the prognosis?; Something's the matter with Alex. . . Krycek emerges from an airport rest room in "PIPER MARU" after being infected with the Black Oil, an alien infection mechanism that would carry throughout *The X-Files* mythology; In "APOCRYPHA," the Black Oil oozes from a World War II submarine captain, the start of the "BLACK OIL" saga; A crewman exposed to radiation in "APOCRYPHA" who won't last long.

is all going to have to tie together in one central narrative and all make sense.'"

The two-parter also featured a subplot in which Scully searches for her sister's killer, and Anderson handled the emotional demands of the story with aplomb. "You look at season one and look at season three and that girl exploded as an actress in terms of talent and capability," Manners says, admiringly.

"Piper Maru" took its name from Gillian Anderson's daughter (who is also Chris Carter's goddaughter) "I thought it was a really sweet gesture on Chris's part," Anderson says.

The storyline continued with "**Apocrypha**," drawing in most of the players in the mythology, including Krycek, the Lone Gunmen, and the Cigarette-Smoking Man. The actors themselves were never quite sure where all of this was going. "It's all relatively mysterious and murky because there was no Bible," Davis observes. "I found myself feeling that I had to watch all the episodes, especially in the early years." It wasn't just the actors who were challenged by the material.

"Apocrypha" was a challenge for me because Rob Bowman had been the master of the mythology shows," Kim Manners states. "I had studied his mythology shows because they were completely different animals than stand-alone shows."

"Apocrypha's" gruesome denouement features Krycek expelling the Black Oil into a receptacle on an alien spacecraft. Nicholas Lea recalls the grueling preparations for the scene: "It's a mask that went over my face with all these tubes that went through my hair and out my back and down my back down behind me, and they were pumping all this 'oil' out of my face. It took them over an hour to put it all on. I couldn't see, and I had to breathe through a

THIS PAGE, TOP: "PUSHER's" Robert Modell gets Mulder to point aim for his partner, rather than his adversary; Modell (Robert Wisden) in the almost-banned Russian Roulette sequence; Duchovny on the set of the hospital sequence of the episode; Mulder and Scully try to save a S.W.A.T. team member whom Modell has gotten to light himself aflame.
OPPOSITE PAGE: Scully questions archaeologist Dr. Alonso Bilac (Vic Trevino) after the disappearance of a graduate student in "TESO DOS BICHOS;" Lucy Liu's guest apperance as the very ill daughter in "HELL MONEY."

straw. And then, just as they finished, everyone broke for lunch. I was so pissed."

With the shocking thriller **"Pusher,"** Vince Gilligan became a major creative force on *The X-Files*. The episode presents the character of Robert Modell, a psychic assassin who can gently talk his victims into killing themselves. "I remember turning in the draft, and I was very proud of it. And I remember saying to Chris, 'This is the best work I'm ever gonna do for you,'" Gilligan remembers. "And he was annoyed when he heard it. He said, 'Don't say that. Don't think that way. You've always got to better yourself.'"

Gilligan recounts that casting was difficult—at one point he suggested Harvey Fierstein for the role—but at the last minute Robert Wisden "came in and read for the part of Modell and just blew us away. He was the perfect choice for that role, and that was quite a bit of good luck on our part." Gilligan continues. "At one point, Chris even considered Lance Henriksen (pre-*Millenium*)."

Director Bowman was equally impressed by Wisden: "What was interesting to me about it was Modell's performance; his ability to almost reassure his victims." Bowman would save the day with some creative blocking when Standards and Practices cried foul over the graphic Russian Roulette scene between Modell and Mulder.

Mitch Pileggi didn't enjoy the scene in which his secretary, Holly, attacks him under Modell's command. "David was ridiculing me about that," Pileggi recounts. "He would say, 'Remember your little secretary that beat the hell out of you?'"

John Shiban's supernatural thriller **"Teso Dos Bichos"** was undermined at the last minute when the producers discovered that household cats are very hard to train. A terrifying sequence in the script called for hordes of housecats to attack Mulder and Scully, but it fell apart when the cats did what cats usually do—which is pretty much nothing. Things went from bad to worse, Shiban would later recall, when it was revealed that Gillian Anderson was severely allergic to cats.

Kim Manners thought it was the end of his *X-Files* career: "The best three acts of television I ever directed. The fourth act was an absolute disaster. I begged Chris, 'Please, let's revisit the leopard in the teaser because I'm never going to make these cats scary.'"

"Hell Money" is unusual in that the story doesn't revolve around an actual X-File but, rather, on an organ-harvesting scam run by the Chinese mafia. A pre-stardom Lucy Liu guest stars.

"José Chung's from Outer Space" is an *X-Files* masterpiece from Darin Morgan. "The teaser was the only idea I had before joining the staff, Morgan explains. "Two kids out on a date, they're abducted by aliens, and a third alien comes and abducts all of them."

The story came together from a strange experience during a casting session. "We had a guy come in to audition who was very short, maybe he didn't look like Truman Capote, but he sounded like him," Morgan recounts. "After that I remember saying, 'Oh, maybe that's the way to do the story, you have a Truman Capote-type writer writing the *In Cold Blood*

"I begged Chris, 'Please, let's revisit the leopard in the teaser because I'm never going to make these cats scary.'" —Kim Manners

"It was one of the hardest episodes to shoot because Charles Nelson Reilly was so funny, he would have people laughing between takes and during takes." —Tom Braidwood

version of an alien abduction, and then the rest was a piece of cake."

Since Capote himself was unavailable, Morgan offered up a very strange alternative. "I wanted Rip Taylor to play it," Morgan says. Taylor was unavailable, so "Charles Nelson Reilly came in to audition and Frank and I both turned to each other and said, 'Wow, he was really good.'" Rick Millikan remembers Reilly's audition, saying, "At first we were a little unsure, and then after the fact, there was no question."

The script called for two "men in black," mysterious figures Morgan plucked from UFO literature. Jesse "The Body" Ventura was cast for one, but Morgan was stuck for the other. "And then for the other man in black, my brother suggested Johnny Cash," Morgan says, "which was perfect because he was the original man in black." Cash was unavailable, so *Jeopardy* host Alex Trebek was offered up instead: "Alex wanted to do it, and Chris said,

'Let's just put him in here,'" Rick Millikan says.

Stuntman Tony Morelli volunteered for the thankless role of Lord Kinbote. "They did this neat thing where they made him look like he was a stop-motion character," Toby Lindala recounts. "He had a mechanical Cyclops head and a full suit; he was set up on stilts and, oh, it was torture."

Rob Bowman was ambivalent when he was assigned the script. "I loved the show; I didn't want to make a show that made fun of my series," the director says. "I did feel I had to shepherd that concern through the making of it. Darin is a very good writer, but I didn't want to make fun of my show."

"They think I'm just making fun of *The X-Files*," Morgan protests, "but there's an awful lot of actual—well, I guess you can't call it scientific—but anecdotal evidence of what alien abduction was supposed to be like."

The shoot was thrown into chaos by their live-wire guest star. "Charles Nelson Reilly never stopped talking during or after his scene," Tom Braidwood recalls, "It was one of the hardest episodes to shoot because he was so funny; he would have people laughing between takes, and during takes."

For Gillian Anderson, episodes like "José Chung" were like dessert. "That's what kept it fun and that's what kept it worth doing all the time," the actress states.

Sadly, Morgan would not write for *The X-Files* again, having decided he was not cut out for the frantic pace of the show. "It's pathetic being burned out after just four episodes in two seasons," Morgan laments. "It's quite sad, but I guess I was not suited to be a television staff writer."

"I talked to Darin recently about trying to get him to write something," Duchovny explains. "And he was saying 'I tend to get hired by shows, and then I write episodes that make fun of the show that I'm working on.'"

"Avatar" was a collaboration between David Duchovny and Howard Gordon. "David had the premise for an idea," Gordon explains. "We worked together on it. The idea was that the job that people like he and Skinner do

THIS PAGE, FROM LEFT: Agent Scully listens with tepid interest to Charles Nelson Reilly's idea for a book about aliens in José Chung's "From Outer Space"; "Now, do you believe him, Mom?"; 1½ year old Piper Anderson and her mother greet an alien on the set of "JOSÉ CHUNG;" Charles Nelson Reilly keeps 'em smiling on the "JOSÉ CHUNG" set; Reilly has a similar effect on Gillian Anderson. **RIGHT PAGE:** Mulder finds the fake-dinosaur-foot boot of missing bait shop owner Ted Bertram in "QUAGMIRE," but no sign of Bertram—or his supposed killer, the mysterious serpent, Big Blue; Mitch Pileggi prepares to shoot the episode's "final report" scene with Duchovny and Anderson.

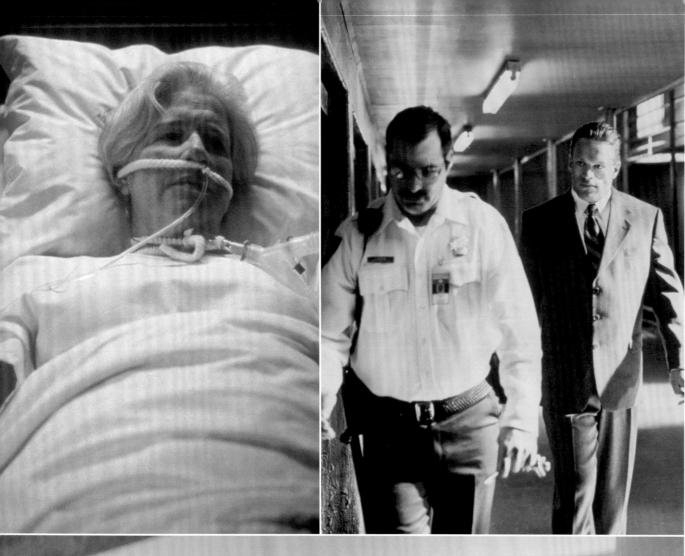

TOP LEFT: Mulder visits his mother in the hospital, after she has suffered a stroke following a visit from The Cigarette-Smoking Man; The unstoppable Alien Bounty Hunter (Brian Thompson), ventures into the prison where Jeremiah Smith is held; A tense scene between Mulder and Cigarette-Cigarette-Smoking Man from "TALITHA CUMI" at the hospital where Mulder's mother lays bedridden. **RIGHT:** Healer Jeremiah Smith (Roy Thinnes)—or at least a Jeremiah Smith—is questioned by Skinner and Scully; The Alien Bounty Hunter.

"David Duchovny happened to be flying on a plane with Roy Thinnes right about the time I was writing the episode, and suggested that (he) play the healing man, Jeremiah Smith, and I thought it was a great idea."
—Chris Carter

comes with a tremendous price. You lose your marriage. There was a part of me that was actually losing myself to the show at that point, so I related to it personally."

The story features a ghostly apparition protecting Skinner from a Syndicate plot against him; it begins with the assistant director being framed for a woman's murder. "The girl that he picks up in the bar and takes upstairs who ends up dead in the morning was Amanda Tapping. I worked with her on *Stargate Atlantis*," Pileggi says. "We get a lot of laughs about that."

Vince Gilligan notes that Pileggi essentially made his own future on the show. "Skinner was meant to be a bad guy, and yet Mitch is such a good actor that they thought to themselves 'Let's not take this character in the direction we thought we were gonna take him in.'"

"Quagmire," an episode about a Loch Ness-type monster featured some humorous pinch-hitting by Darin Morgan who was called in to look over a script written by Kim Newton. However, Gillian Anderson remembers the episode for a different reason, noting a particular day on set. Ironically, this day "was actually the only time that we ever had a weather day on the show," Anderson recounts. The rains were so heavy that "when we sat down next to the log for the shot, the water was up to our waists."

"Wetwired" was based on a script by effects supervisor Mat Beck about murders caused by hallucinations, which were caused by subliminal signals transmitted over cable television. The signals affect Scully, sending her into a paranoid fit. The episode, once again, featured a rare appearance by Cigarette-Smoking Man in a story that was not specifically tied to the mythology.

Steven Williams recalls that one of his favorite scenes on the show came at the end of "Wetwired" with the Cigarette-Smoking Man: "We're sitting in the car, and he asks, 'Who is Mulder's informant?' And I turn to him and go, 'That

person is still not known.' These two guys; you don't know where they stand with each other either. Who is the subordinate in that duo?"

Season closer **"Talitha Cumi"** featured yet another story contribution by David Duchovny, this time drawing upon the story of The Grand Inquisitor from Dostoevsky's novel, *The Brothers Karamasov*. The story introduces the shape-shifting alien Jeremiah Smith who revives the victims of a massacre at a fast-food joint.

The role of Smith would go to the star of the '60s UFO series, *The Invaders*. "David Duchovny happened to be flying on a plane with Roy Thinnes right about the time I was writing the episode and suggested that (he) play the healing man, Jeremiah Smith, and I thought it was a great idea," Carter recalls.

In addition to the scene in which the Cigarette-Smoking Man plays the Grand Inquisitor to Smith's Christ, Talitha Cumi begins to reveals that the villain was more important to Mulder than anyone could have previously imagined, revealed in a scene where Cigarette-Smoking Man taunts Teena Mulder about her dead ex-husband.

Davis affectionately recalls his favorite line: "'He was a good water skier—not as good as I was. But then that could be said about so many things, couldn't it?'" He laughs, "Implying that I was also a lot better in bed."

SEASON FOUR CANCER, BLACK OIL, AND SMALL POTATOES

"Herrenvolk" follows Mulder and Jeremiah Smith as they flee the Alien Bounty Hunter to a farm in Canada. There they find a colony of human drones—many of whom are clones of Samantha—who are raising bees for the alien conspiracy. Back in Washington, Scully contacts X in hopes of getting to the bottom of a mysterious inoculation database that surfaces while Skinner is investigating Smith. X warns Scully that a plot is afoot against Mulder's mother, and he is killed in retaliation. Finally, Mulder's new informant Marita Covarrubias (played by Laurie Holden) is introduced.

LEFT TO RIGHT: Vanessa Morley—no relation to the Cigarette-Smoking Man's brand of smokes—as Mulder's younger sister, Samantha, in "HERRENVOLK," looks like Samantha, sounds like Samantha. . . there's just a few too many of 'em: Mulder meets one of several clones of his long ago-abducted sister, as Jeremiah Smith looks on; Director R.W. Goodwin works with the young actors on the set; Mulder and Smith on the run from the Alien Bounty Hunter; A new informant character, Marita Covarrubias (Laurie Holden) is introduced; Mulder and Marita meet; Scully signals X for help by placing a taped "X" on Mulder's window. Unfortunately for X, it will be their last such meeting. . .

The scenes with the bees presented a new challenge to the crew. "As with most things on *The X-Files*, we wrote it first and then tried to figure out how to do it later on," Carter reflected. The bees were allegedly harmless drones, but people on set were stung nonetheless, including Vanessa Morley, who played the Samantha clones.

Steven Williams found out he was off the show in typical *X-Files* fashion. "Chris Carter called me up personally," Williams recounts. "'Got good news; got bad news. The good news is we're gonna bring you up for another episode next week. The bad news is you're gonna take a bullet.'"

Following the cancellation of *Space: Above and Beyond*, Chris Carter asked Morgan and Wong to return to *The X-Files*. Still smarting from their show's premature end, Glen Morgan had a specific agenda in mind. "I said, 'Look, I'll do four *X-Files*, but I'm telling you right now, I'm writing them specifically for my *Space* cast so that the world can finally see them,'" Morgan recalls today.

"As was always the case with Glen and Jim, they had very specific ideas about what they wanted to do," Carter explains. "By the second season, Glen and Jim were really coming up with their own stories and then bringing them to me, and I'd go over the board with them. This is how it worked all the way through their contribution in the fourth season."

Morgan and Wong's first episode upon returning, **"Home,"** would not only stir a firestorm of controversy but it would also become the only episode banned for repeat by the network. This shockingly graphic look at intergenerational inbreeding kicks off with the Peacock Brothers burying their infant brother/nephew as it gurgled. "I did, perhaps, the most awful shot of my career when I shot the baby's POV as it was placed in the hole, and the mud was being placed over the lens," Kim Manners says.

"That was one of the Standards and Practices notes, 'Make sure the baby sounds sick.'" —Glen Morgan

"That was one of the Standards and Practices notes: 'Make sure the baby sounds sick,'" Morgan explains. "If you had a healthy-sounding baby, then it would just seem like it was murder, and that was not going to be tolerated."

A running gag through the episode was the Peacock Brother's love of the old standard, "Wonderful, Wonderful," made popular by Johnny Mathis. "That was a Johnny Mathis sound-alike because Johnny Mathis wouldn't give us permission once he read the script," Manners laughs.

"I liked it when the song ran counter to what was going on," Morgan explains. "Certain songs have a creepy, icky quality that none of us have really openly acknowledged."

"That episode's so terrifying because you can really believe, if you're driving through a small town, that you might meet a family like the Peacock family," Frank Spotnitz says.

"Teliko" explores thorny issues of immigration and identity in the context of an African vampire fable. "The idea of a melanin-sucking vampire seemed like an interesting way to deal with race," Gordon says. "Once again, I did find a treasure trove in a lot of ethnic mythology." However, "Teliko" was a milestone in *The X-Files* history for another reason; it was the last episode in the old Friday night time slot. The show would run for the next five years on Sunday nights.

The fourth season of *The X-Files* coincided with the debut of Chris Carter's new series *Millennium*, a pitch-black exploration of violent crime and eschatology. The series starred Lance Henriksen as Frank Black, a former FBI agent who goes to work for the Millennium Group, a collection of former law enforcement officials who consult on serial murder cases and believe that the Apocalypse is drawing near. Carter used the same lessons learned on *The X-Files* for the new series.

"Even on *Millennium* I said the episodes are only as interesting as the villain," Carter explains. "It's the same thing. It's once again opposing forces. If you just have the force of good and then you have just a stock generic bad guy or 'evil,' if you will, it's gonna get boring really quickly."

However, the new show only added to Carter's crushing workload, leading the stars on his flagship series to worry about their own future. However, Carter had groomed a strong bench to handle the overflow. "Chris and I were the only two writers who were full time on *Millennium* and *The X- Files*,"

TOP LEFT: David Duchovny and Gillian Anderson between takes with their porcine costars in Morgan and Wong's shocking "HOME"—a pig sty, in and out; Kim Manners enjoying running the show on the set of "HOME," as Duchovny enjoys a laugh at the pigs' expense. A horrific discovery: the armless, legless Mrs. Peacock (Karin Konoval) is the matron of the murderous family's inbreeding program. "She was a tremendous actress, and she went through a lot of physical pain doing that role. And she never once complained," notes director Manners; **RIGHT:** "UNRUHE's" Gerry Schnauz (Pruitt Taylor Vince) prepares to "help" Scully; Pruitt on the set with Rob Bowman; Scully examines Mary Lafonte (Sharon Alexander), after she's been found wandering—post-icepick-lobotomy—on a country road, in "UNRUHE."

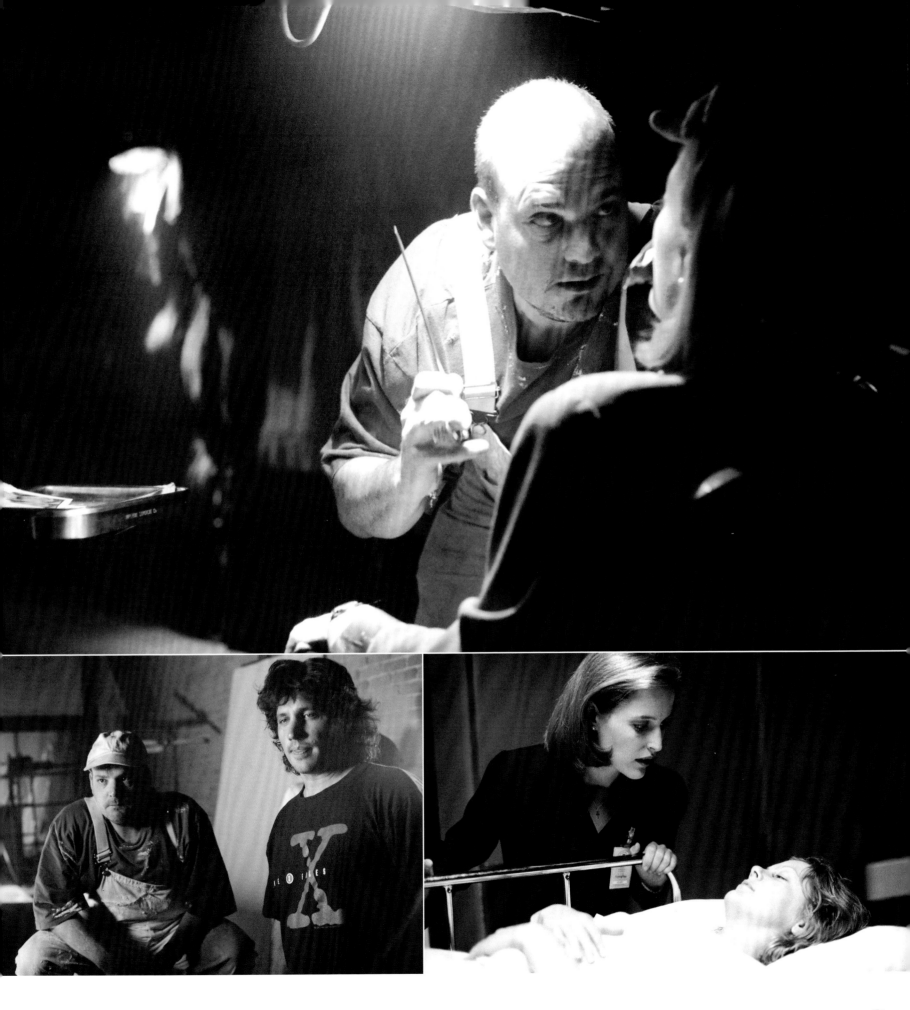

Spotnitz recalls. "That was the first year when Chris, because of time, had to spend less time at the boards, and more time rewriting. So, as a result, I started to get more responsibility in actually breaking the stories."

Vince Gilligan rose to the first division of *The X-Files* writers in season four. He wrote or co-wrote five of the most popular and groundbreaking episodes of the year. "I was really starting to feel I knew what I was doing on the show and that I had a future there," the writer says modestly.

Gilligan's **"Unruhe"** guest-stars Pruitt Taylor Vince as Gerry Schnauz,

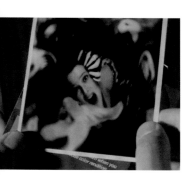

a psychotic who kidnaps and lobotomizes women he believes are possessed by demons called "Howlers." Photographs of his victims are imprinted with Schnauz's demonic hallucinations, as is a picture of Scully when she too is abducted by the madman.

One of the most indelible images of the series comes when Scully first meets Schnauz, who is wearing stilts while he works installing ceilings. "Plasterer's stilts have since been outlawed in a certain number of states, because they are insanely dangerous," Gilligan explains. "I remember our stunt coordinator came to me and said, 'You do realize how hard these are to walk in, don't you?' I'm just the idiot writer, and I'm like, 'Well, they can't be that hard, right?' And he said, 'Why don't we go out into the parking lot, and you put them on to see how hard they are.' And I got on those things, and I had six big guys standing around me ready to catch me if I fell. I sweated probably five pounds of water walking on those things out there."

The production crew used cutting edge technology for the spectral photos of demonic attacks. "Someone said to me, 'We're gonna Photoshop it,'" Gilligan laughs. "And I was thinking, 'What the hell does that mean?' It was 1996; I didn't know what the hell they were talking about."

Morgan and Wong's next offering was the reincarnation drama, **"The Field Where I Died."** A stirring exploration of the ecstatic nature of religious cults and the damaged nature of their followers, the episode nonetheless ran afoul of the large and extremely vocal contingent of *'Shippers*, a term for Mulder/Scully relationship enthusiasts. "'Shippers hated it, Glen Morgan laments. "I think it was the only episode *Entertainment Weekly* ever gave an F rating to."

The episode features a stunning performance by actress Kristen Cloke as a cultist suffering from a multiple personality disorder. At the time, Cloke and Glen Morgan had fallen in love, which inspired his script. "It was just my feelings about Kristen," Morgan recounts. "We got engaged about a week before she went up to shoot it."

"Sanguinarium" is a gruesome parody of America's mania for plastic surgery, equating the practice with the work of Satan. Written by Vivian and Valerie Mayhew who went on to produce *Charmed*, the episode also takes a positive view of Wicca, the nature-based religion, as well as neo-paganism. Twin Peaks star Richard Beymer guest stars.

Morgan and Wong would stir controversy again with **"Musings of a Cigarette-Smoking Man,"** an *Apocrypha*-like exploration of the villain's back story. Inspired by the DC Comics graphic novel, *Lex Luthor: The Unauthorized Biography*, the episode would tie the Cigarette-Smoking Man to the assassinations of John F. Kennedy and Martin Luther King. "You needed to show that this was about the most dangerous human alive," Morgan explains. "That was what I wanted to contribute to the show."

Directed by James Wong, the episode would introduce *The X-Files* fans to Canadian actor Chris Owens, who would later play a crucial role in the

"I think it was the only episode *Entertainment Weekly* ever gave an F rating to." —Glen Morgan laments

TOP LEFT: Imprinted precognitive photograph of Scully as the next victim in Vince Gilligan's "UNRUHE;" Mulder comes to Scully's rescue just before some unwanted brain surgery; Mulder and Scully follow Melissa Riedel (played by the versatile Kristen Cloke) for clues to her past life—and Mulder's—in "THE FIELD WHERE I DIED;" Mulder throws up his hands in an episode where he recalls a previous Civil War life; **ABOVE:** Mulder and Scully try to stop a mass suicide by cult members.

TOP LEFT: Kim Manners poses with one of his "SANGUINARIUM" co-stars who's had just a little too much "chemical peel;" The Cigarette-Smoking Man (William B. Davis) listens in on his own story in "MUSINGS OF A CIGARETTE-SMOKING MAN;" Who needs a face like that? Dr. Franklyn (Richard Beymer) gives new meaning to the expression "face peel," his discarded one lays waste on the clinic floor; Camera operators get a closeup of the Wiccan pentagram symbol in "SANGUINARIUM;" The new Dr. Franklyn.
RIGHT: Recreating history: JFK's assissination—executed by Cigarette-Smoking Man himself, apparently—in "MUSINGS OF A CIGARETTE-SMOKING MAN;" "Go ahead—make history"—an alien awaits a fateful death at the hands of Deep Throat; Deep Jerry Hardin, reprising his role as Deep Throat, who was killed off at the end of season one.

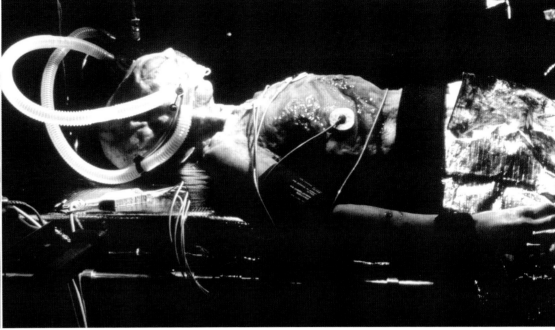

"Ken Horton was on my left, Chris on my right, and they were very clear:
'You can't kill Frohike.'" —Glen Morgan on writing "Musings"

mythology. "When William Davis saw me for the first time on the set, I was carrying a cigarette, and he said, 'You don't really smoke those things do you?'" Owens recalls. "And he went on to say, 'You're not tall enough,' in that dry delivery he has."

The running subplot of the episode is the Cigarette-Smoking Man's apparent ambition to become a novelist. "That's all based (on Watergate figure) Howard Hunt," Morgan says. "He wrote spy novels, but they say a lot of the material he was writing actually happened. But because they were crappy pulp spy novels, no one ever took him seriously." However, the script for "**Musings**" had one very important critic. "Bill Davis just hated that show," Morgan says, ruefully. "He was just killing Jim (James Wong), and it was his first time directing."

"It was bizarre in many ways because the writer and director hadn't been following the series," Davis counters. "So there were a lot of things in there that weren't true or weren't consistent with what had gone on before. I know Chris tried to patch it together."

The script called for the Cigarette-Smoking Man to kill off one of the Lone Gunmen at the end, in retaliation for divulging the villain's personal bio. This idea was not well received by the executive staff, and Morgan got called onto the carpet. "Ken Horton was on my left, Chris on my right, and they were very clear: 'You can't kill Frohike.'" Morgan remembers. "It was a big runaround, and we got into an argument."

"**Tunguska**" brings back both Alex Krycek and the Black Oil, which is found this time in the core of an extraterrestrial rock. Again the script presented scenarios far beyond the scope of an ordinary hour-long drama.

Again, Kim Manners was up to the challenge. "Chris was a task master," Manners explains. "We had some very talented directors come in to do an episode. They would shoot their episode and were never heard from again because Chris determined that it wasn't 100 percent excellent. If they delivered an almost-great show, that small percent missing was the end of their career on *The X-Files*."

Nicholas Lea also rose to the occasion, in a nail-biting scene where Krycek fights for his life while handcuffed to Skinner's balcony. "Kim

Manners is saying, 'Okay, we're going to put you on a platform, and we'll shoot you at such an angle that it looks like you're dangling, but you won't be,'" Lea recalls, "And I said, 'Wouldn't it be better to see my feet dangling?' So, they took it away."

These two-parters demanded extra effort. "The whole time, we were flying by the seat of our pants," Carter explains. "We never actually planned out an entire season at the beginning of the year. By season three or four, we knew what those two-parters were going to become; the tent poles of our order for that year."

Gillian Anderson explains that "Tunguska" inspired a running on set gag when Manners objected to the actors' attitude towards the story's main prop: "He was trying to remind us that what we were dealing with was from outer space, and we were treating it too casually. So right before we would shoot, he'd yell 'Rock from Mars!' and that became our running joke from that point on. Every time we needed to get it up for the scene, Kim would yell 'Rock from Mars!' and that would be his way of kind of sparking us into life again when we were just too exhausted."

Directed by Rob Bowman, **"Terma"** took the action to a Russian gulag, where Mulder was infected with the Black Oil during a vaccine experiment. The action was again at a high pitch. "We spent a lot of time shooting outdoors," Lea remembers. "You know, those scenes with the horses and everything? It was so much fun. Again, you feel like your life's a little bit in danger, but thrilling."

David Duchovny observed how the two directors would approach what was in essence two halves of a single script: "I think Kim was very attuned to the emotion of the relationship between Mulder and Scully. And Rob, I believe, was very much attuned to the action-flick action sense of the show."

"David was quite a sport because we put him in some very compromising positions," Manners says admiringly. "Putting him on those cold metal tables in Vancouver on a cold sound stage and covering him up—he was just about buck naked as I recall."

The action climaxed in a gruesome scene where rebels saw off Krycek's left arm. Nicholas Lea wishes he had taken the scene to the edge: "I always look back on that and think I should have been jerked by the movement of the guy cutting my arm, and I didn't. That's one thing I regret about that."

Vince Gilligan's stunner **"Paper Hearts"** features actor Tom Noonan as a devious serial murderer who psychically taps into Mulder's subconscious. The episode revisits Samantha's abduction as well as Mulder's days in the Behavioral Sciences unit. "Chris sets up early in this episode that Mulder had been an amazing criminal profiler," Gilligan explains. "So I was riffing on that

"Every time we needed to get it up for the scene, Kim would yell 'Rock from Mars!' and that would be his way of kind of sparking us into life again when we were just too exhausted." —Gillian Anderson

in 'Paper Hearts.'"

"I learned a lot from Tom Noonan," Gilligan says. "I learned that people don't think of themselves as bad guys. In the original draft, the character of Roche was much more mustache-twirlingly evil. There was one line where his character said, 'These little girls, I took them to a better place—at least for me.' And Tom Noonan said, 'I don't think Roche would say "at least for me." Roche really believed that he took them to a better place. That's how demented the guy was.'"

The episode would challenge Mulder on an emotional level, drawing him out of his usual detached, deadpan pose. Duchovny was keen for the challenge. Gilligan cites the star's impassioned performance as being among his best: "David was good in every episode, but I think he was just wonderful in that episode."

"El Mundo Gira" revisits themes of immigration politics explored in "Teliko," this time in the context of Crypto zoology. Rubén Blades guest stars in this horror tale dealing with the Mexican "chupacabra."

Fox tapped *The X-Files* for its prestigious post-Super Bowl time slot, and **"Leonard Betts"** would be picked over **"Never Again"** for the honor. "We

LEFT: Helmet won't help: A scientist at NASA's Goddard Space Center after being infected with the Black Oil, which he has just unleashed from a harmless-looking rock sample in "TUNGUSKA;" Kim Manners ponders an upcoming scene on the "GODDARD" set; Scully can't explain the condition of the infected scientist, who (below) cuts open the alien rock, unwittingly unleashing the Black Oil virus; Mulder, along with other prisoners, prepares to be infected by the Black Oil by Russian scientists trying to develop a vaccine. **ABOVE:** Nothing can penetrate this suit: Gillian Anderson on the "GODDARD" set. **FOLLOWING PAGE:** Director Rob Bowman makes his own "last looks" makeup adjustment to Gillian.

THIS PAGE, TOP: Almost had it: Mulder runs from an exploding truck after nearly retrieving the stolen space rock containing the Black Oil virus; "Comrade, we're all friends here in Tunguska"—The bespectacled scientist (Anatol Rezmeritza) in "Terma" jokes with David Duchovny during filming of Mulder's escape sequence; Scully is led to lockup, in contempt of the Senate, rather than further endanger Mulder; Scully testifies before a Senate counterterrorism subcommittee about the whereabouts of Mulder—and, on her own agenda, about the secretive Syndicate. RIGHT: Scully swears to tell the truth, no doubt with full intent to do so; Scully testifies; These hearings aren't all dry nuts and bolts testimony: Mitch Pileggi enjoys a light moment between setups; The Cigarette-Smoking Man has heard enough.

THIS PAGE, FROM LEFT: In a hopeful trade with convicted child molester John Lee Roche in "PAPER HEARTS," Mulder sinks a hoop for information; Performs his own stunts: Director Rob Bowman watches as his star makes his shot; Mitch Pileggi and Gillian Anderson have a laugh amid the abandoned buses of "PAPER HEARTS." The real "Chupacabras" that "came from the sky" in John Shiban's "EL MUNDO GIRA;" Mulder looks for clues in an immigrant encampment in Central California; "El Chupacabra," or "goat-sucker," makes an appearance.

RIGHT: I'll just grow another one: The decapitated head of Leonard Betts (Paul McCrane) is not quite dead. . . Kim Manners and crew enjoy a laugh at the expense of the decapitated head; Reel makes real: filming a rare onscreen date, this one between Scully and Ed Jerse (Rodney Rowland), with whom actress Anderson had become involved; . . . Or was that with Rob Bowman? The director and actress discuss the scene (BOTTOM RIGHT). CENTER RIGHT: I'll do it if you do it: Scully gets a tattoo—with a dangerous red pigment—in Morgan and Wong's final episode, the aptly-named "NEVER AGAIN."

"Gillian said to me, 'I really want to fall hard. I really want an intense kind of romantic or passionate relationship thing.'" —Glen Morgan

knew we'd get a huge audience," Gilligan says. "Chris really wanted to grab viewers who had never seen us before, and we knew the best way to do that would be with a really creepy stand-alone monster story." The episode also saw the arrival of Joel Ransom as primary cinematographer.

Played by Paul McCrane (*Fame, ER*), the title character is a genetic freak who relies on cancerous tumors for subsistence. Director Kim Manners advised McCrane to approach the role with utter emotional conviction. "Paul played it just that way, and it worked," Manners says. "I found that if you take the absurd and base it in the reality of human emotion, the audience is going to buy it as if it actually exists. You know?"

The episode became an *X-Files* milestone when it was revealed that Scully herself had cancer. "We had spoken to Gillian very early on and said we wanted to give her character cancer, and she was of course, I think, delighted—if you can be delighted about being given cancer," Carter said in 2001. "It was something new for her to play."

The final episode of Morgan and Wong's season four tenure, "Never Again," would be no less controversial than the others. Again taking aim at the Mulder-Scully relationship, the episode sees Scully having a fling with a recent divorcee whose new tattoo is driving him to murder.

"Gillian had called me and said that she'd heard a rumor that the character would fall for another guy," Morgan recounts. "She said to me, 'I really want to fall hard. I really want an intense kind of romantic or passionate relationship thing.' And I'm like, 'Thanks. You're going to get me in trouble.' She says, 'I'll deal with it.' And then I just got incredible grief."

Trouble arose with Carter when the script called for Scully enjoying a passionate night with her new beau. "That's the only time in the series that he rewrote me and took it out," Morgan says. "I think Chris thought that I was monkeying around with him, but I really wasn't. That was another case where I think they thought that I was out to sabotage the Mulder and Scully relationship, but I think that Gillian wanted to show that aspect of Scully."

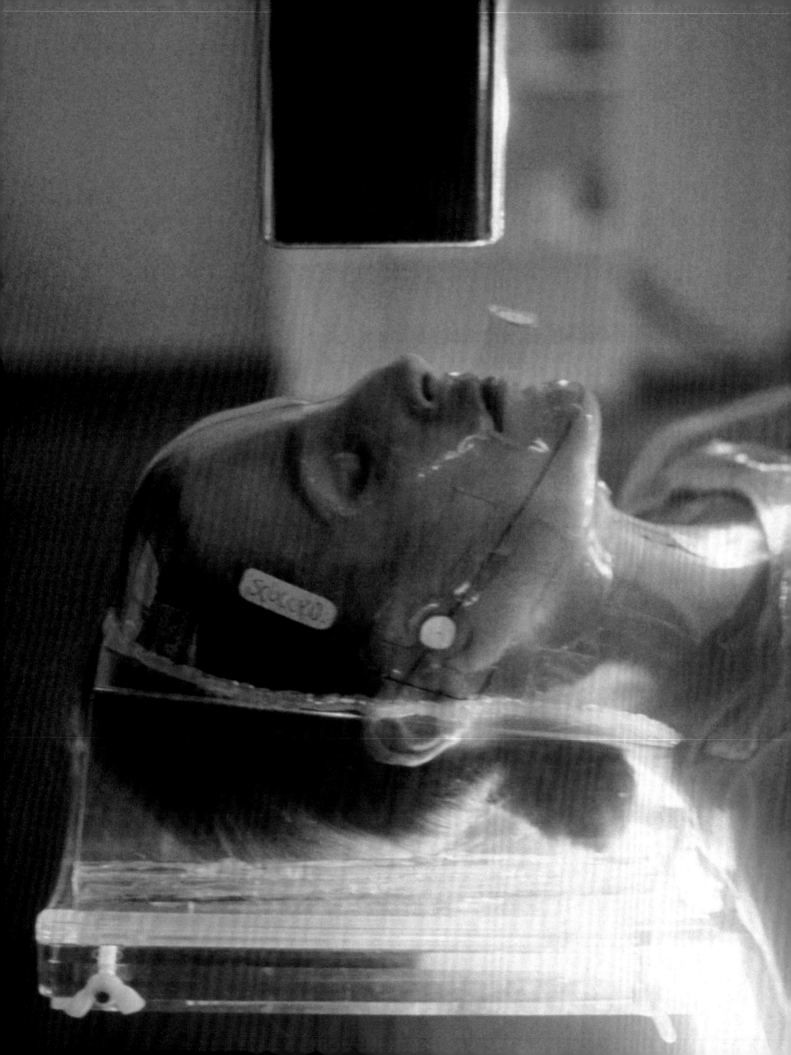

"For the first time I feel time like a heart beat.
The seconds pumping in my breasts like a reckoning;
the numinous mysteries that once seemed so distant
and unreal threatening clarity In the presence of
a truth entertained not in youth but only in it's
passage. I feel these words as if their meaning were
a weight being lifted from me. Knowing that you will
read them and share my burden as I have come to
trust no other. That you should know my heart, look
into it, finding there the memory and experience that
belong to you; that you are there is a comfort to me
now as I feel the tethers loose and the prospects
darken for the continuance of a journey that began
not so long ago and began again with a faith
strengthened and shaken by your convictions. If not
for which I might never have been so strong now as I
cross to face you and look at you incomplete. Hoping
that you will forgive me for not making the rest of
the journey with you."

    —Scully in opening scene from "Memento Mori" (4x15)

"Frank had told me before he gave me the script that he was giving me the most important script of the year. It's called 'Memento Mori' and Scully had cancer.'" —Rob Bowman

The voice of the tattoo was performed by Jodie Foster, who was close friends with both Gillian and the late casting director Randy Stone. Gillian would enjoy a real-life relationship with "Never Again" co-star Rodney Rowland, another *Space: A and B* veteran.

"Frank had told me before he gave me the script that he was giving me the most important script of the year," Bowman recalls. "'It's called **"Memento Mori"** and Scully had cancer.' I said, 'That's not going to work. It's too sappy, sitting around feeling sorry for yourself in a hospital.' He said, 'Trust me. It's going to work.' I said, 'I trust you, but it's not going to work.' I was wrong; he was right."

Frank Spotnitz explains the unlikely origins of the classic episode: "Darin Morgan had left the show but was going to contribute an episode. And we realized at the eleventh hour that it wasn't going to happen, and we were stuck with nothing," he says. "John, Vince, and I broke that story in maybe two days. We split up the acts, wrote it in probably another two days, and gave the crew something to prep before Christmas break. That was the worst ever. Chris ended up rewriting the script over the holiday. Ironically, I think that was the best mythology episode we ever did. It's my favorite one."

The episode features a heart-rending voiceover in which Scully apologizes to Mulder for her illness; in it the agent tries to come to grips with her onrushing mortality. "I learned from Frank that every episode should be about something other than just scaring the audience," Gilligan explains. "Every episode should have some greater point or theme to it. The theme might be 'courage.' The theme might be 'individual responsibility.'"

"I don't believe that entertainment should be propaganda," Spotnitz contends. "But I do think that storytelling is more interesting when there's something else going on underneath." I think the best episodes of *The X-Files* are about something. There's an idea driving the story."

Howard Gordon's **"Kaddish"** explores Jewish mysticism and the legend of Golem—a human figure made of clay and brought to life using the Kabbalah—in the context of a series of neo-Nazi crimes against an Hasidic community. "I was always compelled by the Golem mythology," Gordon says. "We had never really dealt with the horrors of anti-Semitism and the power of the word. And because I'm Jewish, it was something that was really compelling to me personally."

THIS PAGE, TOP LEFT: Mulder ponders his partner's future, and his relationship with her, in "MEMENTO MORI," the episode in which Scully is diagnosed with cancer; Scully receives an MRI to determine the extent of the disease; In an unused scene, Scully's brother, Bill (Pat Skipper), visits her in the hospital; Director Rob Bowman seen working with Skipper. **ABOVE**: The crowd listens to speeches on the indoor set of Howard Gordon/Chris Carter's "UNREQUITED;" Closeup coverage of David Duchovny trying to find the suspect; Now you see him; now you don't: Peter Lacroix as the occasionally invisible Nathaniel Teager.

ABOVE: A nervous Max Fenig (Scott Bellis) onboard a doomed jet aircraft in two-parter "TEMPUS FUGIT/MAX" with something they want—from above and from below; The impressive sequence required the construction of a complete airplane fuselage inside a North Shore Studios soundstage; Ellis is hoisted out of the plane aboard a mechanical boom to simulate his abduction (yet again) by aliens; The view from inside is startlingly frightening; special effects technician Fred Richards operates carefully-orchestrated movement of the fuselage to produce a realistic—and terrifying—sequence; Mulder and Scully survey the disturbingly-realistic crash site scene. **RIGHT:** Gillian Anderson with Hiro Kanegawa on the set of "SYNCHRONY;" "Last looks" gives makeup a chance to give a final touchup to Kanagawa as the defrosting Dr. Yonechi; Warmup takes a wrong turn as Yonechi spontaneously combusts; Scully says to Mulder in response to receiving her gift of an Apollo 11 key chain: *"I finally figured out why you gave this to me; this gift that you gave me for my birthday. I think that you appreciate that there are extraordinary men and women and extraordinary moments when history leaps forward on the backs of these individuals. That what can be imagined can be achieved, that you must dare to dream but that there's no substitute for perseverance and hard work and team work because no one gets there alone. And that while we commemorate that the greatness of these events and the individuals who achieved them we cannot forget the sacrifices of those who've made those achievements and leaps possible." "I just thought it was a pretty cool key chain,"* says Mulder in reply in "MAX."

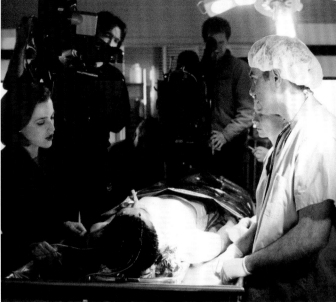

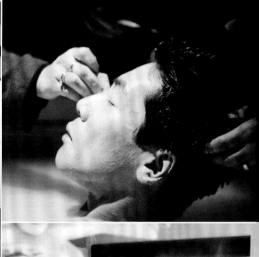

Gordon and Chris Carter then teamed up for **"Unrequited,"** another super-soldier story with a Vietnam veteran subplot. The X-File here deals with the vengeful subject of an invisibility experiment. "These stories come from scientific research," Gordon says. "If you move your finger you will see that you do have a blind spot because that's where the cortical nerves wind up bundling. So I said what if someone could actually create a field of vision where none actually exists?"

"Tempus Fugit" brings Max Fenig back for a nail-biting two-parter dealing with the aftermath of a military downing of a jetliner while pursuing a hostile alien craft. The show would reach a new technical plateau with an elaborate depiction of a crash site. "We wanted to make it as authentic as possible," said Carter, "and we had in a National Transportation Safety Board official who came down as our tech advisor and told us that we had recreated everything consistent with a crash site—absolutely believably—except for the smell." Carter added that the realism of the set got under the skin of the production crew: "It was the first time that his crew had been frightened by their work."

Carter tapped Rob Bowman to shoot the episode, which was rife with car chases and assassinations. "One of the things that Chris wanted me to do was make the show bigger," Bowman explains. "So I tended to spend a little bit more money with the unspoken promise that when I do make it a larger show and go over budget, he will protect me from the beatings of the studio production end."

The concluding episode, **"Max,"** focuses on the emotional aftermath of *Tempus Fugit*, and is directed by Kim Manners. "It's very important when you're slogging through a 24-episode season that the directors show up energized and positive and are helping to inspire the actors to believe that they're not just making the donuts," Duchovny explains. "Kim and Rob were guys that were very excited on set, and they were able to execute beautifully."

"Rob and I had the greatest competitive nature together," Manners laughs. "I would look at his dailies, and I'd say 'That dirty rat bastard' because he'd come up with a great shot, a great performance. He'd see my dailies, and he'd come down and go 'You son of a bitch.'"

"We had an National Transportation Safety Board official who came down as our tech advisor and told us that we had recreated everything consistent with a crash site—absolutely believably—except for the smell." —Chris Carter

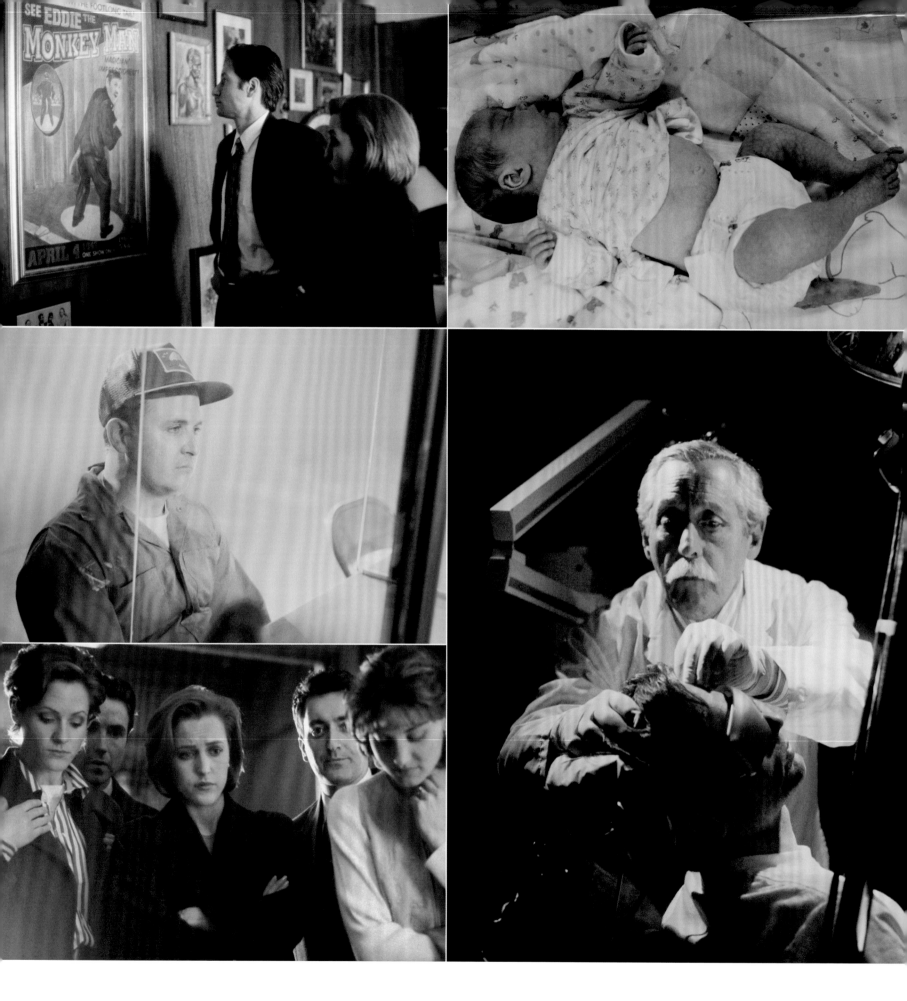

Howard Gordon's **"Synchrony"** is a sci-fi thriller in which a scientist travels back in time to kill his younger self. "One of the requirements of all these shows was finding something, whether it was a character or an idea, that was really worth taking to the next level creatively," Gordon explains. "In this case, it was 'How do you time travel in an *X-Files* way?' It's just that there's a guy who turns out to be you. In the end, I think it worked, but it's getting there that's really difficult."

Vince Gilligan's **"Small Potatoes"** features Darin Morgan as a lovelorn shape-shifter. "I considered myself a comedy writer before I ever got *The X-Files* job," Gilligan says. "I was just following in Darin Morgan's footsteps. And that was when I thought we should hire Darin Morgan to play Eddie Van Blundht."

After imprisoning the agent, Blundht impersonates Mulder in a bid to escape his dreary small-town life. The show is popular with fans for a sexy

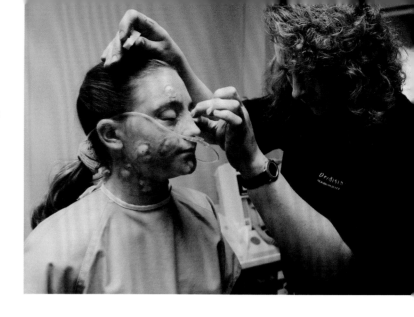

"I'd say 'Cut it; print it' and a kid would come running out crying, and the mother would say, 'Get back in there; you're working on *The X-Files!*'"   —Kim Manners

scene in which the faux Mulder calls on Scully—who is spending her Friday night immersed in scientific arcane—and nearly seduces her.

"I never thought about her really as being lonely," Anderson explains of her character's idea of a wild night. "I thought she was always quite content with her life and all the different interests that she has between medicine and science and the FBI."

"Zero Sum" is a shocking episode in which the Cigarette-Smoking Man uses Skinner to cover up an experiment with smallpox-carrying bees in exchange for a cure for Scully's cancer. "The hard thing for Skinner was that we had to keep him in the middle," Spotnitz says. "We had him tell Mulder not to bargain with the Cigarette-Smoking Man in order to save Scully's life. And then he himself struck a Faustian bargain with the Cigarette-Smoking Man and was in his debt for some time."

"Zero Sum" continues in the *X-Files* tradition of depicting the unthinkable with a disturbing scene where the Syndicate unleashes a swarm of the deadly bees on an elementary school playground full of young children.

"We had hundreds of thousands of bees that we had to release in a schoolyard full of kids," Manners recounts. "And their parents brought all these kids; there were probably sixty extra children. They released the bees, and we had paramedics standing by on the off-chance that someone got stung and would then go into anaphylactic shock. I'd say, 'Cut it; print it,' and a kid would come running out crying, and the mother would say, 'Get back in there; you're working on *The X-Files!*'"

"Elegy" delves further into the emotional fallout from Scully's cancer when the agents investigate an autistic man who sees visions of young girls before they are murdered. Christine Willes makes her first appearance as FBI psychotherapist Karen Kosoff in this John Shiban-penned thriller.

Howard Gordon's last script **"Demons"** begins with Mulder accused of murder after taking part in an illegal memory-recovery experiment and ends with the realization that the Cigarette-Smoking Man was actually his real father. "As the story developed, we developed a relationship between Cigarette-Smoking Man and Mulder's apparent father, and Cigarette-Smoking Man and Mulder's mother; then we started backfilling with an historical connection," William B. Davis comments.

OPPOSITE, TOP LEFT (left to right): Mulder and Scully prepare to meet the former "Monkey Man"—Eddie Van Blundht (Darin Morgan)'s father in Vince Gilligan's "SMALL POTATOES;" Looks just like his father: the result of some of Eddie's handiwork; The inglorious Mr. Van Blundht; Eddie did all this? An incredulous Scully upon finding out about Eddie's efforts; This won't hurt, and you'll remember everything: In a dangerous attempt at regression therapy in "DEMONS," Mulder allows Dr. Goldstein (Mike Nussbaum) to nearly lobotomize him while trying to learn of his past. **ABOVE:** A young extra has bee stings applied for the followup to the horrifying bee attack sequence in "ZERO SUM;" Scully checks for signs of brain damage in the openning scene of "DEMONS."

"As we were discovering the mythology, it was almost as if we were discovering something that had already been written, in a weird way. It was eerie at times." —Chris Carter

"It's an interesting development because it really was the development of the conspiracy," Carter explains. "The elements of the conspiracy were part of his development. But his back story became, of course, intertwined with Mulder's."

The episode has Chris Owens returning to the part of the young Cigarette-Smoking Man. It would be his first experience on a Kim Manners set. "When Kim directs, his favorite thing is, 'Kick it in the ass,'" Owens says. "Kim is very dynamic, and he loves to get right in there; he's very passionate. So the set would naturally be a little more boisterous that day."

"I felt like I had done my time," Gordon says of his decision to leave *The X-Files*. "It was a hard choice, but it was one I felt I had to make. It's always sad to leave, but I was extremely proud of the work I did, and extremely proud to have been part of it, and especially proud to have been part of it at its beginning. Everything comes to an end, and I applaud Chris for being there for the whole thing. Now having been at *24* for the whole thing, I appreciate even more how challenging it is. It requires a level of stamina that eludes most people."

"Howard wrote some very emotional stories," Manners says. "His approach was definitely from the heart, and he wrote some great stories. I was very sad to see Howard leave the series."

The season closed with Chris Carter's **"Gethsemane,"** which plays like Tom Clancy gone sci-fi. The episode opens with a hearing into the apparent death of Fox Mulder and then backtracks to unravel an elaborate conspiracy surrounding the discovery of a preserved alien corpse in the Yukon ice.

"Gethsemane" is heavily Scully-centric, showing the agent with her family, introducing Pat Skipper as Scully's older brother Bill and delving further into the course of her cancer. Kritschgau was named after a high school friend of Gillian Anderson's.

The episode also became a source of frustration for many online fans who preferred the beginning/middle/end nature of the stand-alone episodes. Carter was doing something unprecedented in television history—unfolding an epic story, a chapter at a time, spread out over several seasons of his program.

What was often frustrating in one episode at the time would pay off in 2005 when Fox bundled together the mythology episodes and released them in a series of DVD boxsets entitled *The X-Files Mythology*. The four sets—entitled *Abduction, Black Oil, Colonization,* and *Super Soldiers*—were best sellers for Fox Home Entertainment and were followed by reissues of the nine seasons.

LEFT: Mulder awaits the defrosting of a frozen alien corpse found in the Yukon in season four's closing episode, "GETHSEMANE." ABOVE: Toby Lindala's effects makeup team prepares the "corpse" figure; Lindala (in sweater at right) works on the "alien autopsy" version of the creature; No, that's not Frohike—it's Tom Braidwood at work at his "day job," as one of *The X-Files'* crack first assistant directors, watching Lindala work on the alien figure; Scully enjoys some short-lived time at home with family.

SEASON FIVE *VANCOUVER FINALE*

With *Fight the Future* in production and *Millennium* handed off to Morgan and Wong, Chris Carter prepared for what was originally planned to be the final season of *The X-Files*. Season opener "Redux" deals with the investigation of Mulder's faked death and Mulder's search within the Department of Defense (DoD) for a cure for Scully. Kritschgau then lectures Mulder on the history of the "UFO hoax," which draws upon actual historical events, such as Cold War-era radiation tests and Project Blue Book.

Inside the DoD, Mulder sees tables filled with what look like alien bodies and also a large number of unconscious pregnant women being experimented on. The episode ends with Mulder discovering a vial that could save Scully's life just as she collapses during an FBI hearing.

Kritschgau's lecture is well-researched. Mulder's process of discovery reflects Carter's own, and David Duchovny brings this into his perfor-

"I'm of the opinion that Mulder was Chris Carter's alter ego." —Kim Manners

mances. "I'm of the school of opinion that Mulder was Chris Carter's alter ego," Kim Manners says. "I think David understood that because David played Mulder as Chris plays Chris. Mulder stayed very calm, cool and collected and that's very much how Chris Carter is in real life." In **"Redux II,"** Mulder must deal with overtures made by Section Chief Blevins to name Skinner as a traitor and by the Cigarette-Smoking Man to quit the FBI and join the Syndicate. As a lure, the Cigarette-Smoking Man gives Mulder the microchip to cure Scully and sets up a meeting with another of the Samantha clones, whom Mulder believes to be real.

Scully's cancer and its aftermath subtly changed the nature of Mulder and Scully's relationship. "Theirs is an intellectual romance," Carter says. "That's what I'm interested in in life. It's the most potent kind of sexual energy or what I would call it the meeting of the minds. Everything else is easy and fleeting. Ephemeral. But that—I'll call it a soul connection—is the greatest romance."

"It was invented on the spot, which is partly why the series was so successful," William B. Davis says of the mythology. "It wasn't trying to follow a preset template. It was able to go with what was happening within the stories themselves and the characters themselves, and also within the audience's response to the stories. So it kept finding a life because of that. If you look for consistency, I think you're going to be challenged."

TOP LEFT: The Lone Gunmen's John Fitzgerald Byers waits out his time as his two compatriots bicker behind him; Guest star Richard Belzer with *The X-Files'* popular Lone Gunmen—Langly (long blonde hair, Dean Haglund), Frohike (short with glasses, Tom Braidwood) and Byers (in suit, Bruce Harwood) in their first "starring" episode, "UNUSUAL SUSPECTS." **ABOVE:** Have some doubt? Kritschgau (John Finn), in "REDUX," may just add fuel to the fire.

"The nature of Mulder and Scully's relationship...it's an intellectual romance. That's what I'm interested in in life. It's the most potent kind of sexual energy...the meeting of the minds."
—Chris Carter

"I've held a torch in the darkness to glance upon a truth unknown. An act of faith begun with an ineloquent certainty that my journey promised the chance not just of understanding but of recovery. That the disappearance of my sister 23 years ago would come to be explained and that the pursuit of these greater truths about extraterrestrial life might even reunite us. A belief which I now know to be false and uninformed in the extreme. My folly revealed by facts which illuminate both my arrogance and self deception. If only the tragedy had been mine alone. It might be more easy tonight to bring this journey to its end."
—Mulder, **Redux** (5x01)

"**Unusual Suspects**" was born of necessity. "The movie was still in production, so we knew in advance that we needed an episode that was without our two stars," Gilligan recalls, "So somebody suggested we do a Lone Gunmen episode. Frank, John, and I got into boarding it—and Chris as well. Once we realized that it could be an episode where we learn about the origins of these three characters, then it became an awful lot of fun."

The episode, which guest-stars Richard Belzer, tells of a mysterious woman named Suzanne Modeski who initiates the three weirdos into the world of crypto-politics. "I don't think I'd ever done an episode where I was the lead character," Bruce Harwood muses. "But I felt like the lead because it was my story about falling in love with this woman and then dragging these other two schmucks into the disaster that followed."

"I just loved the idea of Byers working for the government and being this very gung-ho pro-government guy," Gilligan says, "That's just a fundamental drama where you take a character on a journey and the journey takes him 180 degrees away from who he originally was."

"Up to that point they were sort of interchangeable in the information they delivered," Frank Spotnitz says of the Gunmen. "But then Vince, who loved the characters and really wanted a chance to dig more deeply into them, created a back story, and they became a lot more interesting."

"Vince Gilligan knew the hacker lingo," Dean Haglund says. "In fact, they met with real hackers. *2600* was a little news magazine and they had a monthly meeting at a phone booth by Union Station. Vince went to meet with them to get terminology and inspiration for the show."

The writer wanted the 1989 setting to be as authentic as possible. "I said to Ken Hawryliw, 'Find me the biggest cell phone you can find,' and he found this great old Motorola the size of a brick," Gilligan laughs.

"**Detour**" has Mulder and Scully stumbling upon the mysterious creatures known as Mothmen while on the way to a "team-building" seminar. Hints of the pair's developing romantic relationship are dropped as Scully shows up in Mulder's hotel room with a bottle of wine and then sings to Mulder to comfort him while he lies injured.

Like so many episodes, "Detour" ends with one of the monsters still at large. "We loved the endings that left the audience unsettled at the end," Frank Spotnitz says. "Nothing pleased me more than when I would talk to a viewer who said they really couldn't go to sleep that night, or they kept double-checking their windows and doors. It's scarier if you think he could still be out there."

"**The Post-Modern Prometheus**" was the most ambitious and elaborate comedy episode of the entire series. Filmed in black and white, Chris Carter threw *The Elephant Man, Mask, Frankenstein,* and *The Jerry Springer Show* into a blender and made it all come out *X-Files* style. Carter had originally cast Cher and Roseanne Barr to appear in the episode, but they were unavailable; Springer himself appears and John O'Hurley guests as the mad scientist Dr. Polidori.

Chris Owens, who appears as lovelorn freak, "the Great Mutato," recalls his somewhat unusual audition for Carter: "Chris said, 'Okay, did you ever see *Elephant Man?*' And I said 'Yes.' He said, 'What I'm looking for is dignity. He's got dignity. But he's definitely mutated.' So I tried something, and he said, 'Do it again with less autism.' It's the only time I've ever had that direction."

In the final scene, Mulder and Scully take the Great Mutato to a Cher concert; an impersonator was used for the role. "The makeup had taken seven hours, and then I had sat around for three or four," Owens recounts. "And now I was going to sit in the dark, and I could only see out of one eye. They put a big contact lens in. I got in the room, and everyone was standing around. Chris comes up to me, and he says, 'Can you dance?'"

ABOVE: Scully begins to get the picture in "REDUX;" Mulder discovers tables full of aliens corpses in a secret room at the Department of Defense—but are they real? Mulder pondering the state of things in "REDUX;" Scully, scared at sunset in the Florida woods in "DETOUR;" **RIGHT:** A childhood photo of a young Fox Mulder and his young sister, Samantha, before her abduction; A forest creature defends its territory in "DETOUR;" Duchovny in a lighter moment on the set.

"'Do it again with less autism.'" —Chris Owens on his audition for Carter

"Chris would come in and only direct every once in a while," Anderson says of Carter, "but every single time he pushed the boundaries and tried something completely new. And succeeded."

"Christmas Carol" is an emotionally-charged mythology outing that reveals that Scully's ova were used during her abduction to create a human-alien hybrid named Emily. The girl was then placed with a couple who are murdered when they refuse to continue with medical experiments performed on Emily. The episode features a series of poignant flashbacks, as well as Melissa reappearing in a series of spectral phone calls.

Lauren Diewold replaced another actress originally cast as Scully's daughter. Manners recalls the disastrous shoot with the original Emily. "We put her in front of the camera, and she just totally freaked out, and I couldn't get any work out of her," the director says. "I called Bob Goodwin and said 'We're dead in the water here, pal. This little actress is not cooperating at all.' We recast that role and started up again the next day."

The episode is a showcase for Gillian Anderson's startling acting chops. "It's great when you get a crew that really respects the work that's being done by the actors," Anderson explains. "That makes a world of difference

when you feel safe to go where you need to go as an actor, day in and day out. A crew is everything."

"Kitsunegari" is the sequel to "Pusher," featuring Diana Scarwid as Modell's similarly-gifted twin. Modell escapes from prison to protect his sister by diverting blame for her crimes to himself. Only Mulder realizes the plan, which prompts this classic Scully line: "That's one hell of a plan, Mulder. A serial killer makes us believe that he's guilty, in turn diverting the suspicion away from the real estate lady. Well, he had me going."

The twists and turns of the story didn't come easy to Vince Gilligan and Tim Minear. "When we were writing the ending for that episode, we had a real devil of a time coming up with the right one," Gilligan recalls. "I remember scouting that warehouse location with Dan and the crew, and we had not figured out the ending at that point, which is always a very bad feeling because we're on the tech scout with the crew and the director looks to you and says, 'Okay, now what's gonna happen?'"

"Schizogeny" guest-stars Sarah Jane Redmond; she played the demonic Lucy Butler on *Millennium*. The story deals with the ghost of an abusive patriarch possessing a tree orchard.

"Chinga" was based on a script written for the show by Stephen King. The story itself—which featured a murderous talking doll—was essentially a rewrite of the pilot episode of *Friday the 13th: The Series,* which in turn was based on an old *Twilight Zone* entry. The episode featured the gruesome violence and small-town sexual intrigue characteristic of King's novels but was heavily rewritten by Chris Carter.

"I was very excited to be able to direct a Stephen King piece, and when it was all said and done, there was very little Stephen King left in it," Manners explains. "The nuts and bolts were his, but that was really one of Chris' scripts."

"The biggest episode certainly that I ever directed was **"Kill Switch,"'** Rob Bowman says of the *X-Files'* foray into cyberpunk culture, "By the time it was done, it was 22 days. It was a great script. I loved doing it. But the madness that was there was this big movie back in Los Angeles where the director wasn't hanging around helping it. And there was a big, big script to

Chris Carter's ode to James Whale's Frankenstein: "THE POST-MODERN PROMETHEUS."
LEFT: Scenes from Graeme Murry's elaborate set, as Chris confers with the cast, including Chris Owens—shortly of Jeffrey Spender fame—in makeup; Carter describes a shot setup to first assistant director Tom Braidwood (back to camera), as David Duchovny looks on; Toby Lindala and team apply finishing touches to Chris Owens' makeup appliance; Carter watches a take on the "video assist" camera monitor. **ABOVE:** Which side do you believe? Lindala's fantastic two-faced makeup design for Chris Owens's sympathetic creature, The Great Mutato; Mulder and Scully come face-to-face—or rather, face to faces—with Mutato.
NEXT PAGE: Scully to the rescue: kickin' butt and takin' names in "KILL SWITCH."

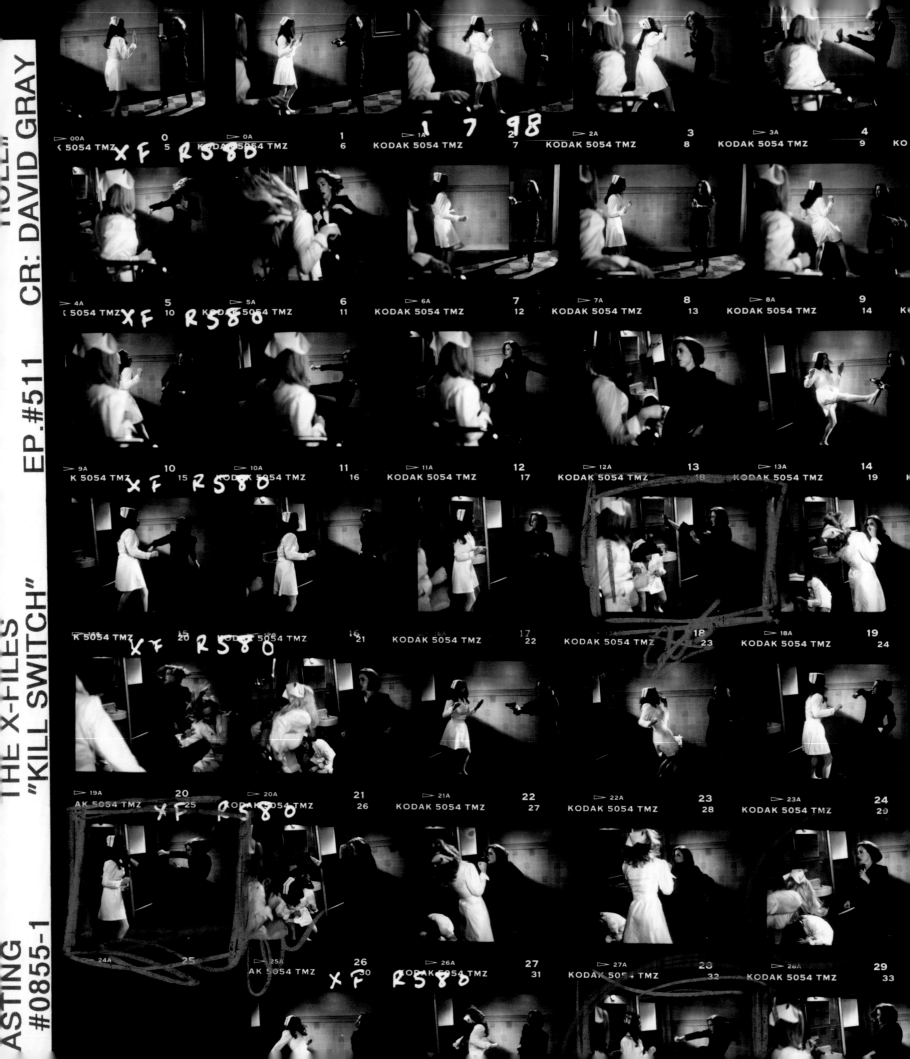

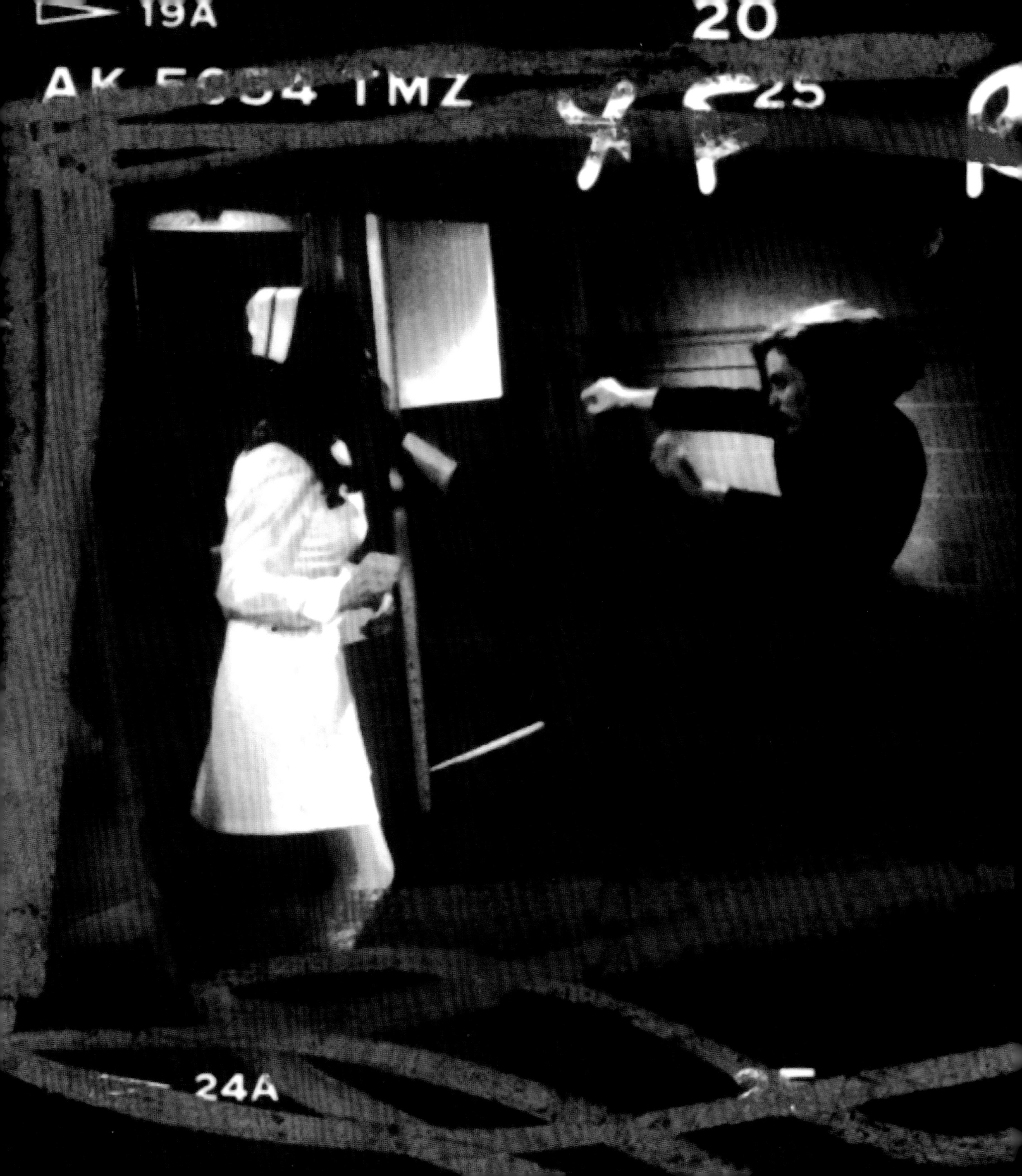
19A
20
TMZ
25
24A

be directed. William Gibson's script for "Kill Switch" came in huge. So Chris took a pass at it, and it was at least as big if not bigger."

The episode features a hilarious virtual reality scene in which Scully rescues Mulder from a pack of sexy nurses after his arms are amputated. Bowman recounts that Duchovny didn't quite appreciate his direction for Scully's karate showcase: "I say to David, 'You should be impressed with her karate skills.' And he says, 'But I don't have any arms all of a sudden.' I said, 'Oh, I know that. But you're also impressed with Scully's karate.' And he looked at me like I was brain-dead. 'But I have no arms. I've lost my arms. Why would I care about Scully's karate?'"

"When I read that scene, I was so happy," Anderson says. "I happened to be in good shape at the time and was just raring to get in there and be taking these half-naked nurses out with some karate chops."

"Chris read a farewell letter to the crew during the filming of **"Wetwired"** Bowman recalls. "It was a very difficult thing for Chris to announce to the crew that we now had to move to Los Angeles. That was a painful thing to do because all the good people in Vancouver had invested so much of their energy and patience and commitment above and beyond. "

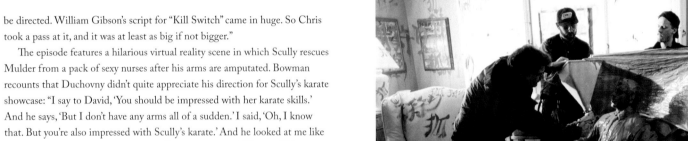

"When I read that scene I was so happy. I happened to be in good shape at the time and was just raring to get in there and be taking these half-naked nurses out with some karate chops." —Gillian Anderson

"It's my favorite episode of all time, and people make fun of me because of it," Gillian Anderson says of **Bad Blood.** She's not alone; Vince Gilligan's "he said/she said" vampire comedy is a perennial favorite among X-Philes.

"I think it was fun for David and Gillian to play because they got to stretch outside of their usual roles a little bit more," Gilligan notes. "They got to play it more for comedy and play it a little more exaggerated than they usually do."

"You never know whether the way you have to shoot something is actually going to end up inhibiting important performances," Anderson explains of the script's format. "It's hard to know whether that, in and of itself, will work and benefit the show. So the fact that it did work was very satisfying."

Luke Wilson appears as a country sheriff who's alternately a stud and a

TOP LEFT: Mulder discovers there's something different about Scully's daughter—born from Scully's stolen ova—in "EMILY;" Feeling kind of blue: Scully examines the body of a victim of Robert Modell's—or his sister's—who was forced to paint himself blue and then take a big sip, in Vince Gilligan/Tim Minear's "KITSUNEGARI;" Special effects team prepares the victim on set via airbrush. **TOP RIGHT:** Poor Mulder . . . The patient is prepared for a little limb removal by buxom blonde nurses in William Gibson/Tom Maddux's "KILL SWITCH." **BOTTOM RIGHT:** Just another day at the office as Mulder & Scully squat around a crime scene; Unbeknownst to him, Mulder looks closely into a future he will soon share—entrapped in a high tech world in "KILL SWITCH."

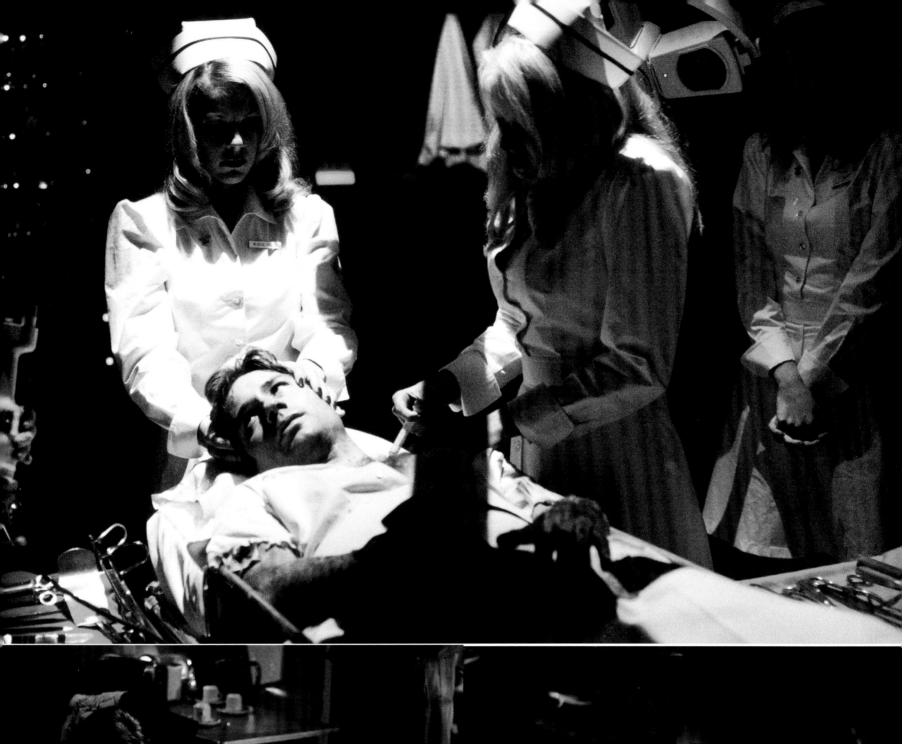

"I went to a bar next door and I was up at the front ordering a martini. In my ear I heard, 'I didn't know they served two-headed guys here.' I turned, and it was Chris Carter." —Chris Owens

bumpkin in the retellings. "I'd worked with him on a movie called **"Home Fries"** Gilligan says of Wilson, "and I'd asked him on the set if he would think about being in an *X-Files* episode. So I wrote that part with him in mind."

A highlight comes when Mulder and Hartwell have a hilarious discussion about *Rain Man*. "I'd love to tell you I wrote that, but I didn't. It was all ad-libbed," Gilligan laments. "His name was Sheriff Hartwell, and it would always sound like Fartwell," Duchovny laughs. "And that just goes to show what I think is funny."

Vince Gilligan explains that "Bad Blood" was nearly his last-ever episode on *The X-Files*. "We were out there all night, and we wrapped at sunrise, much like the vampires do," the writer explains. "I'd been outside without a proper jacket for 12 or 14 hours straight. I was shaking so badly from cold I suddenly feared for my life. I knew I had to get in the shower and get under the hot water, but I was shaking so badly that although I managed to get into the shower, I then fell right out of it. I was thinking, 'I'm gonna hit my head on the floor, I'm gonna be found here dead, and it's gonna be in *Variety*.'"

"Patient X" opens a two-parter that kicks the mythology into overdrive with some of the most terrifying imagery ever seen on television. The action centers around the emergence of a rebel alien force that use radioactive torches to immolate abductees being summoned by colonists. The rebels have mutilated their faces so that the Black Oil cannot enter through their orifices. Krycek, Marita Covarrubias, and the Syndicate are all drawn into the action, and the wife and son of the Cigarette-Smoking Man, Cassandra and Jeffrey Spender, are introduced as recurring characters. They are played by Veronica Cartwright and Chris Owens.

Rick Millikan says of Cartwright, "She's got a voice that adds a little creepiness and a little mystery that I thought played really well. She was just the perfect *X-Files* person."

"After I did **"Post-Modern,"** I was out at a movie theater seeing a film," Owens says. "I went to a bar next door, and I was up front ordering a martini. In my ear I heard, 'I didn't know they served two-headed guys here.' I turned, and it was Chris Carter. And he said, 'Have you heard the good news?' That's when I knew it was confirmed because my agent had said they might want to bring me on as a regular. And then to come in as Jeffrey, the prick."

"The Red and the Black" deals with the aftermath of an alien rebel attack on a group of abductees that included Scully and Cassandra. Krycek's plans to betray the group are thwarted as Marita is infected with the Black Oil. Scully undergoes hypnotic regression, and the horror of the rebel attack is relived. Mulder—whose belief in aliens was shaken by his encounter with Kritschgau—reverses course when he encounters the rebel aliens himself.

"It was a fine balance that we as actors, Gillian and I, had to walk. This was not a traditional television show in any way; week after week the slate was blank." Duchovny explains, "We had to carry certain knowledge of whatever this conspiracy was, whatever this mythology was from episode to episode, and therefore we had to make sure that our characterizations squared up with what we knew and what we didn't."

"David and Gillian liked those episodes, because they had personal stakes, which the stand-alones rarely did," Spotnitz explains. "So they were exciting because it means the actors were really going to be able to sink their teeth into

LEFT: Mulder and Scully on the hunt for vampires in Vince Gilligan's hilarious "BAD BLOOD;" There's two versions to every story: the agents examine the body of a victim; Luke Wilson as the bumpkin/stud Sheriff Hartwell. **ABOVE:** Of course you can trust her. . . Krycek and Marita in a romantic moment; Kim Manners and David Duchovny discuss a scene in Mulder's office; A hopeful Cassandra Spender (Veronica Cartwright) awaits the return of her alien benefactors with a fellow follower, few of whom would survive the night; Nicholas Lea as Alex Krycek; The rebel aliens want nothing to do with Cassandra and her friends, setting them all ablaze; Alex Shostock, Jr. as Dimitri, eyes sewn shut—in this case to keep the Black Oil in.
FOLLOWING PAGE: The aliens give Cassandra a lift, though she will be the only Earthling joining on this trip; "What's everybody looking at?" Chris Carter checks the overhead lighting rig aboard the bridge set.

ABOVE LEFT: Gillian Anderson chats on her cell phone as first assistant director. Tom Braidwood looks on, while Scully is in the hospital after her encounter with the faceless alien rebels in "THE RED AND THE BLACK;" Veronica Cartwright's Cassandra Spender is lifted away by aliens; Cassandra and fellow believers—including Scully—greet the visiting ship; Chris Owens as Jeffrey Spender; Chris Carter addresses the cast on the bridge prior to filming. **RIGHT:** Darren McGavin, the star of the *The Night Stalker*, the 1970s series which originally inspired Chris Carter to create *The X-Files*, finally makes an appearance, as Mulder's *X-Files* precursor, Agent Arthur Dales in "TRAVELERS;" Mulder with "MIND'S EYE" special guest Lili Taylor.

"I was supposed to direct "The Red and the Black," but we were prepping for the reshoots...so I couldn't do it. Reshoots meant you made a mistake and since I couldn't take it on, Chris had to direct this episode. He was so mad at me." —Rob Bowman

them. And invariably they had more physical resources than the stand-alone episodes."

"I was supposed to direct 'The Red and the Black,'" Bowman recounts. "I was supposed to do that, but we were prepping for the reshoots, I believe, of Mulder and Scully, so I couldn't do it. Reshoots meant you made a mistake and since I couldn't take it on, Chris had to direct this episode. He was so mad at me."

"Travelers" travels to the 1950s to explore the roots of *The X-Files* during the McCarthy era. Darren McGavin appears as Special Agent Arthur Dales, who first investigated the paranormal during the height of the Cold War. Real-life figures J. Edgar Hoover and Roy Cohn appear as characters in a thriller that suggests that the Red Scare was merely a cover for the unfolding alien conspiracy.

"Darren McGavin was Chris's inspiration for writing this series," Rick Millikan says. "He always had Darren in mind to use somewhere, and that was really his doing. He said 'I want Darren McGavin for this,' and he happened to be available, and we got him."

"Mind's Eye" is a psychic thriller written by Tim Minear about a blind woman who can see through the eyes of a murderer as he commits his crimes. Soon, she is accused of the crimes herself. Mulder and Scully realize that the killer is the woman's biological father. It was a rare television appearance for Lili Taylor, who had been known primarily for her work in independent film.

"All Souls" is a mystically-themed episode dealing with fallen angels, heretical priests, demonic assassins, and archangels. The episode has Scully investigating the strange deaths of a group of severely disabled girls who

may be Nephilim, the offspring of angels and mortal women.

The darkness of the story is balanced out by a bit of comic relief offered up by Mulder. "It was in the more straight ahead investigative shows, the creepier, scarier shows that I would try to make sure that we kept this kind of humanity alive through humor of it," Duchovny reveals.

John Shiban's script for **"The Pine Bluff Variant"** has Mulder working deep undercover infiltrating a neo-Nazi militia group who was being unwittingly used to test a toxic pathogen.

Vince Gilligan's telemarketing parody, **"Folie à Deux,"** finds Mulder where millions thought he always belonged—strapped to a hospital bed in the psychiatric ward. The story deals with a parasitic insect/vampire who finds suitable victims to zombify in the phone banks he manages. The creature disguises himself as a mild-mannered businessman, but soon Mulder sees through the deception. There was an eleventh-hour problem with this classic Monster-of-the-Week (MOTW) episode, however. "I remember the day before "Folie à Deux" aired, the special effects still weren't done," Gilligan recounts.

"The End" was the final episode filmed in Vancouver. Introduced are two pivotal new characters—a young chess prodigy named Gibson Praise (who might be biologically alien), and a former flame of Mulder's named Diana Fowley (who might be Mulder's ex-wife).

"There was something about that kid's personality that really came off on screen," Manners says of Jeff Gulka, the young actor who plays Gibson Praise, "He really exuded an intelligence that was pretty special. Chris saw what Bob Goodwin did with him and he knew that this kid was a special storytelling tool for the chronicle of *The X-Files*."

ABOVE: Even the devil needs a break: a made up extra sits between setups in "ALL SOULS;" Director Rob Bowman (far right) deep in thought on the set of "THE PINE BLUFF VARIANT;" Mulder under cover in "FOLIE A DEUX;" Captive Fox Mulder in "THE PINE BLUFF VARIANT." **RIGHT:** The big bug in Vince Gilligan's "FOLIE A DEUX" took a bit of post-production magic to make it believable; Hand that man some Raid: Skinner almost gets it from the mystery insect.

Fowley, who was portrayed by Mimi Rogers "was a character you were destined to hate because she was a competitor for Mulder's affection with Scully," Chris Carter said in 2003.

"If (a woman has) feelings for a man, and another woman also has feelings for that person, that's just something that you sense," Anderson says of the conflict between Scully and Diana. "She didn't make it easy on Scully. I think she was aware of her affect on Mulder and on the situation."

The episode begins in a massive arena, in which Vancouverites were invited to witness the filming of a chess match between Gibson Praise and a Russian grand master. "Thousands and thousands of fans showed up, and it was truly amazing. I had never done anything that big," says Braidwood, who gave the fans/extras their performance orders. The fans were then invited for a QandA session with their heroes. "We said hello, and then it was opened up for questions," Anderson recounts. "And somebody asked, 'Did you have your lips done?'"

The chess motif was carried throughout the story as the Cigarette-Smoking Man plays Mulder to a checkmate, using Jeffrey as a pawn. The episode ends with the X-Files office in smoking ruins.

"I used to go to conventions and try to convince everybone that I was the hero of the series and Mulder was the bad guy," William B. Davis explains. "I never succeeded, but I got a lot of laughs. But it's certainly true of how one plays the character. Nobody thinks they're evil."

And so ended the first era of *The X-Files.*

"I had never expected that the show would run five years," David Duchovny explains. "And at some point in the middle of the third year, Chris and I were complaining to one another about how tired we were. We were saying, 'Okay, we're going do five. We'll get out of here at five.' And then five came around, and no one was going anywhere."

"David loved the Vancouver crew as did everybody else," Kim Manners recalls. "But after five years being away from home, it gets a little old, so he just wanted to move the show back to Los Angeles for no other reason than to be in the comfort of his own home and environment. I could have kissed him because I was in the same boat. I was tired of being away from home. It's difficult to sacrifice not only home, but your family, your friends and everything else, to isolate yourself on location 1,200 miles away."

"It was a really hard thing to do; it was a very emotional thing to do," Chris Carter said. "A lot of these people had become my friends and everyone's friends. It wasn't fair in a way because they had helped put us on the map, and we had helped put them on the map, too, showing you could do a quality show up in Vancouver."

"They were really proud of what we were doing," Frank Spotnitz explains. "They couldn't believe what we were able to pull off on a television schedule. They'd never done anything like it before. A lot of them will never do anything like it again because it was just so insanely ambitious for television. So you can imagine how heartbreaking it was for all of us when we had to

"I used to go to conventions and try to convince everyone that I was the hero of the series and Mulder was the bad guy. I never succeeded, but I got a lot of laughs."
—William B. Davis

"Saying goodbye to the crew was really sad. I didn't expect to be as emotional about it as I was. I just could not stop crying all day long." —Gillian Anderson

leave because we really felt like we'd been partners in the show's success."

"It was sad to see it go—it had been a great ride—but we understood why it was going, and that was fine," Tom Braidwood says. "It was interesting to step away from that part of it and then simply go down to L.A. as an actor."

"We're very much a family and everybody was really close and played together and worked together. When we left, it was really hard saying goodbye to them," Mitch Pileggi says ruefully.

"It worked; it felt like home for that period of time," Gillian Anderson says. "Saying goodbye to the crew was really sad. I didn't expect to be as emotional about it as I was. I just could not stop crying all day long. They were good people."

Kim Manners says that the Vancouver period of *The X-Files* is now a distant memory. "Back then there were wonderful places to shoot, great locations with great character, old docks, old buildings, abandoned this, abandoned that, and the gray skies. For a show like *The X-Files*, it was custom made. Today, all the great spots we shot are gone, and they're all replaced with condominiums and office buildings."

"THE END" saw The *X-Files* final episode shot in Vancouver: **LEFT:** Jeffrey, let me fix your tie: rare pleasantries between Mulder and Spender as Chris Owens and David Duchovny share a joke on the set; "There's nothing to be afraid of." "You're a liar." The Well-Manicured Man prepares to take Gibson for a ride; Jeff Gulka as the young genius chess prodigy Gibson Praise; Scully struggles to take Spender's team briefing seriously; It was this big, I swear: John Neville and William B. Davis have a laugh together on set. **RIGHT (left to right):** Gillian Anderson takes a call as Bob Goodwin preps a scene from his last episode; Goodwin directs Chris Owens; "Hate to tell you this, Bill, but, uh. . . . no smoking." Chris Carter checks a shot; William B. Davis; Mimi Rogers as Diana Fowley; Mitch Pileggi awaits his turn, while David Duchovny and Mimi Rogers are otherwise occupied.

SPECIAL AGENT DANA SCULLY

While Dana Scully is not driven to discover whether aliens truly exist or intend to take over the Earth or even to explore the paranormal in general, she does have something else driving her: science. At least that's how it looks from the outside.

"It's interesting," says Chris Carter. "She is searching for the same thing that Mulder is, but by different means and ideologies. For Scully, the search for God is scientific. That's her God."

Though her initial assignment was to debunk Mulder's theories and, as her superiors would hope, deny *The X-Files* any basis in reality, she quickly finds the reality undeniable—though that doesn't stop her from explaining it away by any scientific means possible. "Like Mulder, she's single-minded and passionate in her pursuit of what she believes to be true," Carter explains, "but open-minded enough to follow a person like Mulder down the road of curiosity."

Constantly providing the counterpoint to Mulder's arguments. year after year, was a challenge for Gillian Anderson. "There were a couple of times when I put in a call to Chris in year five or seven, where I said, 'I don't know if I can do this anymore! I'm not sure I even believe a word coming out of my mouth at this point. How can I be arguing against all this when, in the last episode we shot, I saw this and this happen?' But his response was entirely valid—you've got to have that conflict between these two characters or it just falls apart."

Even David Duchovny understood the challenge for his colleague. "You've got to understand that week after week she comes back after seeing something that would blow her mind, really, and seems to go back to being the Scully that we met in the pilot. The same with Mulder, who can be abducted by aliens and have fish hooks pulling his face apart one week and show up the next week with barely a scar! But that's the nature of serialized television—the last week is erased."

Throughout the years, Mulder never lost patience with his partner, always allowing her to put whatever spin she might have on whatever he knew to be true. Or was it true? "She's never really wrong, because they always venture into the area of the unexplained," says Carter. "While Mulder may trump her by showing her something that is beyond the pale, it's never actually known for certain. And he wants that. As any doubter, which is what you need to be as a believer, you need to have someone to question your belief."

Sometimes even Scully herself, though, could see the ridiculousness of her always-plausible explanations. In season six's "Trevor" (Ep. 6x17), for example, after an obviously visible paranormal experience is explained away by Agent Scully—to which Agent Mulder reacts with a polite, acknowledging gaze—Scully responds, "Mulder, shut up!"

It doesn't help that, throughout nine years of *The X-Files*, Scully only sees an alien but a handful of times. She always seems to be turning her head at just the wrong moment. Even after being rescued at the South Pole by her partner from being used as a vessel for the birth of a hybrid alien being, Scully passes out just as the giant saucer breaks free from its snowy berth, as Mulder marvels at the sight. "I always miss everything. . . " she chuckles.

PART 3
FIGHT THE FUTURE

THE X-FILES AT THE MOVIES

The X-Files had become such a phenomenon that Twentieth Century Fox ordered up a feature film. Carter had intended to end the series at season five and turn *The X-Files* into a film franchise, but the series was immensely profitable for Fox, so those plans were shelved.

Preproduction on the film began at the same time that Fox launched *Millennium*. "That was the hardest year of the show because Chris and I were both working full time on *X-Files* and *Millennium*," Spotnitz reveals. "So, you can imagine, our summer vacation was spent breaking the story for *The X-Files* movie, and then in January, Chris went away for two or three weeks to write the script. We had to shoot during the summer vacation between seasons four and five of *The X-Files*. It was really brutal, really not a lot of fun."

Twentieth Century Fox ordered up
a feature film.

"It was an amazing time," Mark Snow recalls. "These guys didn't just fluff this stuff off. They were so into every frame of everything . I remember Chris telling me that period of his life almost killed him because he was running around like crazy from meeting to show. It was just insane."

Vince Gilligan revealed that *The X-Files*' creator had created an environment in which his producers were able to pick up the slack while Carter and Spotnitz were otherwise occupied: "The ship never steered itself. We had good

TOP LEFT: An early Texan, the first human to be infected by The Black Oil; Old friend: Director Rob Bowman ensuring that his alien is creepy enough; FBI bomb expert Darius Michaud (Terry O'Quinn) sticks around to make sure the bomb goes off; Bowman reviews a storyboard for the complicated explosion scene depicting the destruction of a Federal Building prior to filming; Scully stays in contact with Mulder while Michaud tries to gain entry; Duchovny shoots a closeup; Mulder and Scully run for their lives, captured by a Steadicam operator; Live action on-set explosion; A well-made miniature doubles for the Federal Building; Spectacular composited shot. ABOVE: Bowman watches some of the action on his monitor from the safety of an adjoining rooftop.

"I never believed the show would become that successful; you just hope it would stay on the air." —Rob Bowman

people steering the ship. But as he was able over the years to delegate more and more, and as the show sort of found its rails, a set of rails that it ran on smoothly, then he was able to delegate and step back a little more."

Carter tapped his main mythology man Rob Bowman to direct the feature. "It was a show we liked doing, and I never believed the show would become that successful," Bowman shares. "You just hope it would stay on the air. Lots of good things happened as a result of hard work over the course of several years. That result was going to be that we'd earned the right to make a movie."

"It was gutting to not let the Vancouver crew shoot the movie because they deserved to work on it," Bowman laments. "I felt bad about it; I know Chris felt bad about it. But it was just that the practicalities of it didn't line up. So we had to hire movie people. The disappointment in that was the movie doesn't mean much to a working feature crew. The Vancouver crew had really grown and, I felt, earned the right to do it."

The pressures to deliver a blockbuster to Fox wore heavily on everyone from Carter on down. "It was a rough experience for Rob because Chris was right there and had his finger on the pulse all the time," Kim Manner reveals.

"It was nothing I had to concern myself with. That was more something the writers had to board out," David Duchovny counters. "For me it was either

ABOVE: Mulder and Scully arrive in Texas looking for clues; Bowman and buddies: the director shows his young cast their shot—the boys have just discovered the buried caveman remains, and the Black Oil has discovered them—on a playback monitor; Bowman and Carter discuss a scene; Carter and Duchovny review a shot; **RIGHT:** One of the boys has found the caveman's skull; Prepping a shot for an evacuation pod; Chris Carter; The Black Oil has discovered one of the intruders; A scientist prepares to administer a vaccine to an uncovered alien: good luck; You can stay with your alien friend. . . A camera operator captures the scientist's point of view before he is trapped inside with his attacker. **FOLLOWING PAGE:** David Duchovny listens to Bruce Harwood tell a tall tale as the Lone Gunmen prepare for their appearance in "FIGHT THE FUTURE."

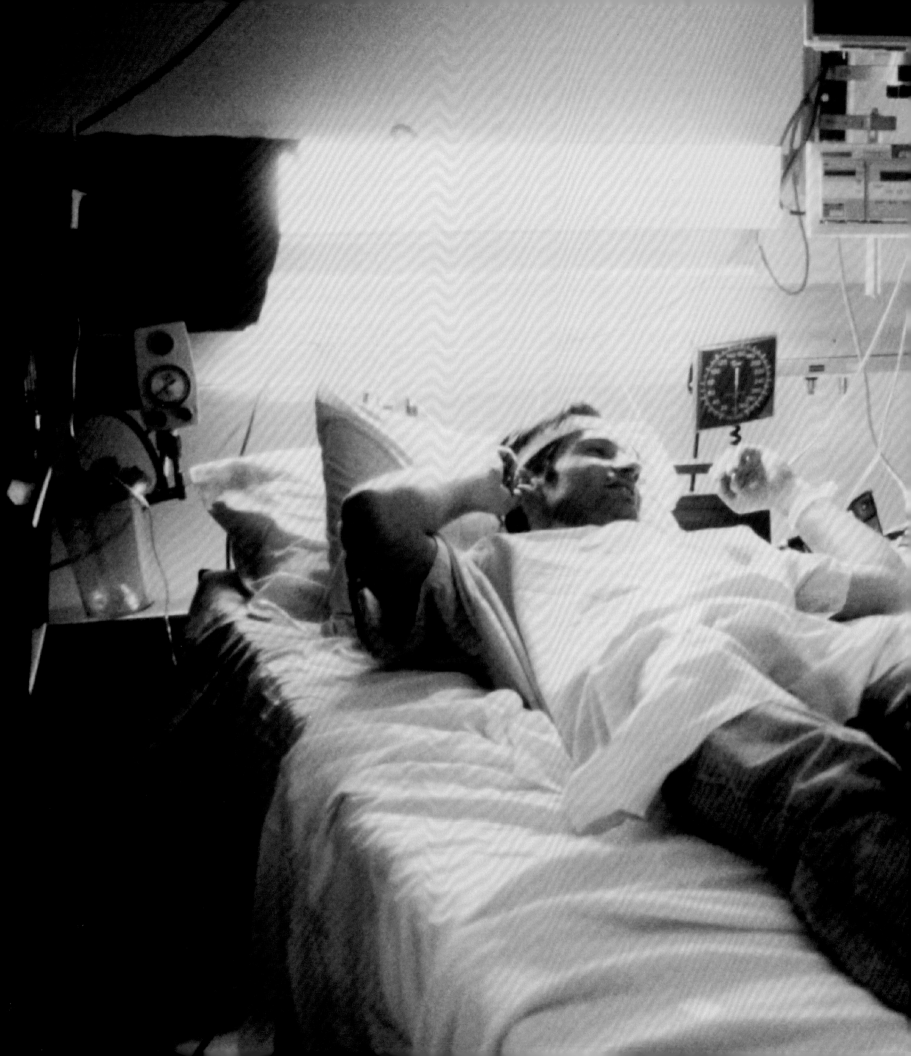

"I never wanted to make the FBI the bad guy. I always saw the characters at the FBI as being, not the ultimate bad guys but the middle men."
—Chris Carter

this or some other movie that I might be able to do on my hiatus. But that was just twenty-two months of all *The X-Files*, all the time. But I was really happy with how the film turned out, so it was all worth it."

"When the movie was released, we felt an obligation—expectations were going to be huge that things were going to be revealed in the movie," says Spotnitz. "What we finally revealed in the movie was that the Black Oil was a virus that has been around since before man was around—alien in origin— and has taken over the universe. And ultimately that's what colonization on Earth would be, was this Black Oil infecting all of us. And that's why the bees were being bred, to carry the Black Oil."

Rob Bowman observes the obvious parallels between the Syndicate's deal with the aliens and the wholesale importation of German spies and scientists into the United States with Operation Paperclip. "To me, all those characters are patterned after post-war Nazi criminals," the director says today.

These themes informed the drama of the series from the very beginning. "I never wanted to make the FBI the bad guy. I always saw the characters at the FBI as being, not the ultimate bad guys, but the middle men," Carter said. "The people above them, represented by the Cigarette-Smoking Man, were the people who were pulling the strings, the puppeteers, if you will."

Although Martin Landau was tapped to be the feature's marquee guest star, it was John Neville's turn as the Well-Manicured Man who stole the show.

Frank Spotnitz reveals that the Syndicate figure "was actually a character of conscience, a good guy working in a bad organization. That's another thing that was important to the show; no institution is monolithic. Everything, even the alien conspiracy and certainly the government, is peopled by both individuals of integrity and people who are corrupt."

"It's so sad that when he finally figures it out and stands up for the right thing, he gets killed," Spotnitz continues. "Again, it speaks to my understanding of the world. I believe that happens. I don't believe life is full of happy endings. There are a lot of good people who meet unjust ends."

The other breakout star of the film was Mark Snow and his epic soundtrack. Snow notes that *Fight the Future* "was basically a huge mythology episode. And the music had to be a little bit more traditional. That's why the big orchestra thing worked so well," Snow recalls. "I knew the synth couldn't carry this kind of thing."

"This was really a lot of fun for me because they had only known me as this guy who sits in a room and plays the keyboard and pushes buttons," Snow continues. "They didn't know that years before I met them my whole thing was conducting and writing it out, the whole bit. They saw me up there conducting this 85-piece orchestra, and they really flipped out. They didn't know I could do that."

Snow didn't have any time to rest on his laurels, however. "I did the movie and then the next thing—boom—I was back on the series," the composer remembers.

The X-Files: Fight The Future premiered on June 19, 1998, and would go on to earn $186 million dollars worldwide.

LEFT: Two giant bee domes await investigation in a cornfield grown especially for the sequence; The bees are released—real ones; Mulder and Scully look aside as a camera crane captures the shot from above. RIGHT: Scully looks for clues in the morgue after the Federal Building bombing; Mulder studies up in his apartment; FINALLY. . . almost: The long-awaited kiss is just about to happen, save for a single bee; The deleted kiss; Closeup of an injured Gillian Anderson post-bee sting.

FIGHT THE FUTURE

147

LEFT: Duchovny and Landau shoot a scene outside the characters' meeting place; "Step in, Mr. Mulder"—The Well-Manicured Man awaits a fateful conversation with Fox Mulder; John Neville and David Duchovny in the limo set; The real leader of the Syndicate: Rob Bowman poses with John Neville, Jeffrey De Munn (Bronschweig), and William B. Davis; Bronschweig adds the German touch. . . ; Bowman and Carter discuss the Syndicate meeting sequence on set. **RIGHT:** A disgruntled Mulder spills his guts to barmaid Glenne Hedley.

"So, what do you do?"

"I'm a key figure in an ongoing government charade, a plot to conceal the truth about the existence of extraterrestrials. It's a global conspiracy actually, with key players at the highest levels of power and it reaches down into the lives of every man, woman and child on this planet. So of course no one believes me, I'm an annoyance to my superiors, a joke to my peers, they call me Spooky, Spooky Mulder who's sister was abducted by aliens as a kid and now chases after little green men with a badge and a gun shouting at the heavens that the fix is in, the sky is falling, and when it hits, its going to be the shit storm of all time."

"Well, I'd say that does it. Spooky."

"Does what?"

"It looks like 86 is your lucky number."

"You know one is the loneliest number."

TOP LEFT (clockwise): The creepy, spectacular interior set for the buried alien ship; Scully after being freed by Mulder as a host for an incubating alien; The two escape inside the Fox Studios frozen soundstage; A Panavision camera captures the scene as Mulder and Scully flee the ship prior to its departure; The former host body has served its purpose in the film's opening: a newborn alien is on the loose; Miniature effects crew prepares to shoot the detailed model for the shot. Mulder emerges from one of the ship's vent tubes during his escape; Gillian Anderson reviews a shot of her escape with Rob Bowman. **ABOVE**: Composite shot depicting the enormous scale of the alien craft; Miniatures artist puts the final touches on a maquettes design for an alien; "Now, open wide, and then spit." David Duchovny plays dentist with an alien mockup; Gillian Anderson takes a moment to relax—and warm up.

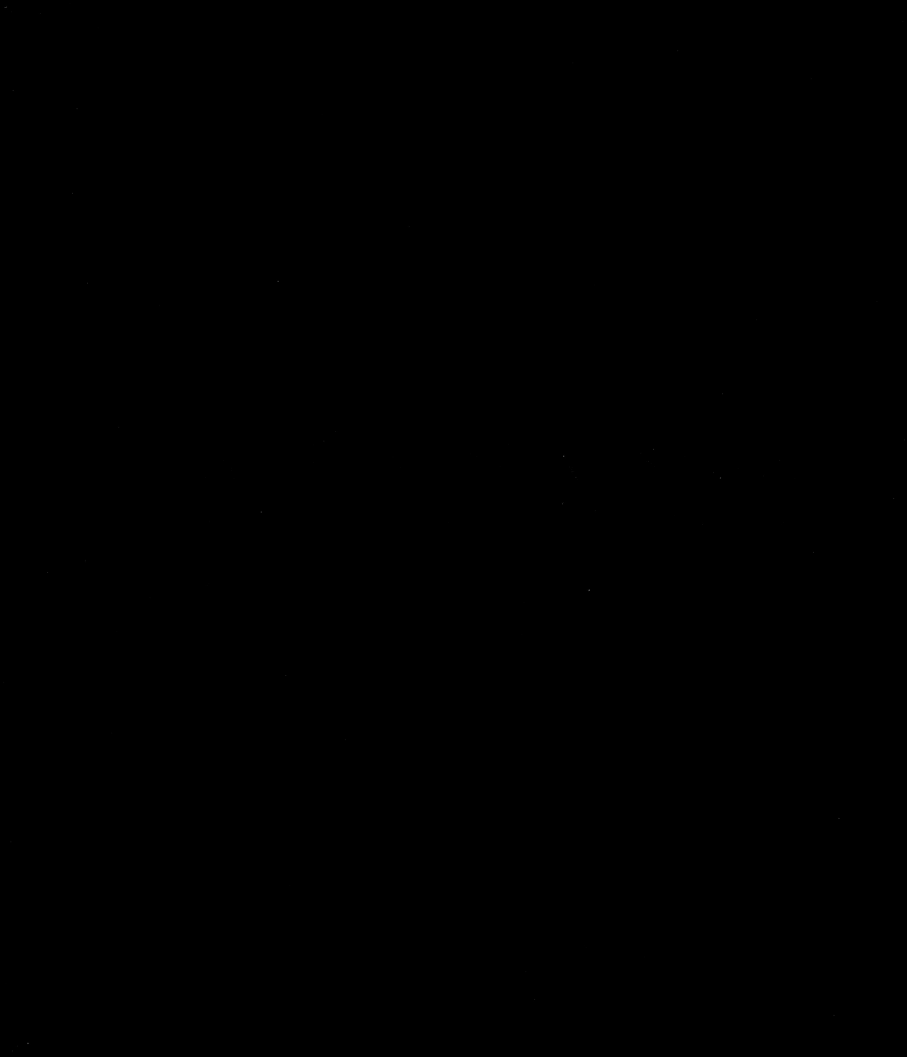

PART 4

NEW BLOOD, NEW MYTHOLOGY

TOP LEFT: Mulder and Scully watch news footage of the first exploding head case in "DRIVE;" Gibson Praise is brought in to read the mind of the hiding alien in "THE BEGINNING;" Mulder and old flame Diana Fowley (Mimi Rogers) go alien hunting; Gibson undergoes a little brain surgery—never mind that he's awake; The nasty, hardened Patrick Crump (Bryan Cranston) keeps Mulder on his toes—and the gas pedal in Vince Gilligan's "DRIVE." The episode won new L.A. director of photography Bill Roe his first Emmy for the series; Mulder and Scully, now on routine terrorism follow up patrol, about to hop in their high performance Ford Taurus in "DRIVE."

SEASON SIX THE X-FILES *MOVES TO HOLLYWOOD*

The move to Los Angeles was challenging, as it would require assembling a new crew from scratch. On the downside, production costs would increase dramatically and the moody atmosphere of Vancouver would be gone. The benefits however, would include the built-in infrastructure and sizable talent pool of Hollywood, offering new perspectives and inspiring new directions. "I just took the opportunity to use things that we didn't have in Vancouver," Chris Carter reflects.

Kim Manners felt the move helped him creatively. "I actually think that the show grew by leaps and bounds once it got to L.A.," the director says. "Part of that is psychological because I was a happier human being. There were certain challenges in L.A. that had to be overcome, one of which being the sun. Chris and Frank were up to the task and wrote some very, very interesting story lines."

Rob Bowman explains that the show's popularity was a boon in status-conscious Hollywood: "What helped us was that we came to L.A. with an established show, a show that people liked, and certainly a show that film-

we never had days off. Everything felt like it lightened up a bit. It all felt a bit easier."

"The crew went through a big learning curve because they suddenly realized that they weren't just doing a one-hour episode of television; they were doing features," Kim Manners explains, adding that the new team "rose to the occasion brilliantly."

"They did their best to make it as creepy," Dean Haglund explains, "but Chris really had an appreciation for the drabness—days get dark around three or four o'clock (in Vancouver)—and they really utilized that kind of

"The crew went through a big learning curve because they suddenly realized that they weren't just doing a one-hour episode of television; they were doing features." —Kim Manners

makers liked." Nonetheless, Bowman was ambivalent about the move. "I've left behind all the people who helped birth the show," the director laments.

Gillian Anderson recalls that the producers would have to make adjustments for the climate. "There was a lot more material that was shot inside, because shooting outside was prohibitive to the mood of the series," Anderson says. However, there was one immediate benefit to shooting in Los Angeles: "I don't know whether they just brought in more characters, or whether it was because less time was taken redoing material due to rain and snow days, but it seemed like we had more time off once we moved down south," the actress states. "In the first year in California, I think I had more days off than I ever had in five years of the show combined. In Vancouver

heavy atmosphere in the show unlike any other show up until then. So there was an abrupt mood shift when the show came down to L.A."

The financial issues raised by working in Los Angeles would be extremely challenging. "At the time, the exchange rate between Canadian and U.S. dollars was pretty dramatic," Bruce Harwood explains. "Somebody told me that the cost per episode doubled, even tripled, once they moved. So it knocked the show around a bit."

"Everything in Los Angeles is more expensive across the board," Vince Gilligan elaborates. "The deals with the unions are more expensive, and taxes are higher. It became apparent very quickly to me that we were no longer going to have things such as the nuclear submarine descending through the

ice and trains exploding in the middle of the woods."

Season-opener **"The Beginning"** had Mulder and Scully testifying to the events seen in *Fight the Future* to a review panel, who promptly take the X-files away from the team and install Jeffrey Spender and Diana Fowley in their place. Mulder and Scully are then assigned to desk duty under Assistant Director Alvin Kersh, played by James Pickens, Jr. (now seen on *Grey's Anatomy*).

"Ultimately, we created another character in order to put pressure on Skinner, and that was Kersh," Frank Spotnitz says. "Mitch Pileggi was not in the original design of the series but was so good and appealing that we found ways to incorporate him and keep him alive throughout the life of the series."

Defying orders, Mulder and Scully travel to Arizona to chase a killer alien, whom the Cigarette-Smoking Man is assigned to find before they do. The alien takes refuge in a nuclear reactor core and Gibson Praise is brought in by the Syndicate to lure him out.

The sun-soaked teaser notwithstanding, most of "The Beginning" was set at night. To help create a new atmosphere for the show, cinematographer Bill Roe was brought on board. Before joining *The X-Files*, Roe worked mainly as a camera operator but quickly distinguished himself in his new role. "I think it was exciting for Bill to work on a show where lighting mattered," Bowman offers.

"Bill helped to make the show moody and atmospheric when sometimes we didn't have atmosphere—or at least not free atmosphere," Chris Carter. "But it was also Corey Kaplan as the production designer and Michael Watkins who hired these people onto the show. It was a stroke of good luck hiring the right producer in Los Angeles, who in turn selected the right people for us."

Vince Gilligan says of Roe (and Bartley before him), "There's a certain kind of director of photography (DP) who, if you called them an artist, they would probably just shrug and say, no, I'm a technician. I'm not sitting here thinking about art. They come across like meat and potatoes guys, but they are truly artists."

Chris Carter noted that Roe's previous occupation gave him an added advantage when it came to shooting. "Bill Roe not only lights the scene but sets the shot with the operator," Carter explains. "The operator has a tremendous amount of input, but Bill does both where John simply leaves the camera work to the operator."

Two other crucial additions to the team were John Vulich, who was in charge of special effects makeup and Cheri Montesanto-Medcalf, who would go on to win three Emmy Awards for "Outstanding Makeup for a Series" for her work on *The X-Files*.

The season's first stand-alone was Vince Gilligan's **"Drive"**, which finds Mulder speeding to a naval station in San Diego with Patrick Crump, a belligerent redneck adversely affected by a military experiment. Mulder discovers that if he stops the car, Crump's head will explode. Vince Gilligan says of Crump, "I wanted to take Mulder's paranoia to its full measure with a character who lives in a trailer and really thinks the government is out to get him 24/7."

"'Drive' is a rip-off of *Speed*, Gilligan admits, adding "and it is a rip-off

of the best episode of *Homicide: Life on the Street*, where Vincent D'Onofrio, one of the detectives, spends the entire hour talking to a guy trapped under a train in Baltimore, and this trapped man's a real asshole. And yet, when they finally move the train off of him, and he passes away—you feel so bad for the guy. I loved that idea, and I wanted to borrow that dynamic."

With **"Triangle,"** Chris Carter once again pushed the envelope of series television in a comedic stand-alone in which Mulder travels back in time while searching for a lost ship in the Bermuda Triangle. Carter would draw upon the continuous-take format of Alfred Hitchcock's *Rope* for inspiration. "I said 'Wouldn't it be great since we have 44 minutes of programming time if we just did an episode where we did four 11-minute takes and put it all together?'" Carter recalls. "And everyone looked at me like I was nuts."

Frank Spotnitz says that Carter was constantly looking to innovate, and to this day, "tries to be as ruthless as he can, not just with the people that are working for him, but with himself, in terms of defining a clear, compelling and interesting story, and then executing it as best he can. He's very competitive, with himself and with others. He really wants to succeed and looks at every script as an opportunity to do better than he's ever done before. He's tireless—I mean, he was often the first person there in the morning and the last person to leave at night."

"One thing I really liked about *The X-Files* was that they were always challenging themselves," Chris Owens says. "Chris would write an episode in

TOP LEFT: May I cut in? Chris Carter works with his cast aboard the Queen Mary during the ballroom sequence in "TRIANGLE," as Steadicam operator Dave Luckenbach—one of the true stars of the episode—prepares to capture the shot; Mulder deals with his Nazi-era counterparts—including Scully; Chris Owens, Chris Carter, David Duchovny and William B. Davis enjoy a light moment aboard the Queen Mary while shooting the episode. **ABOVE:** David Duchovny and Michael McKean reenact Harpo Marx's mirror gag from Duck Soup in "DREAMLAND;" The Lone Gunmen pose with McKean and a copy of their prized newsletter. McKean would also appear in the short-lived Lone Gunmen spinoff series; A post-surgery Gibson Praise; McKean's slimy Morris Fletcher has unwittingly swapped bodies with Fox Mulder and likes the change; Kim Manners directs Duchovny in a convenience store sequence in "DREAMLAND;" Mulder drives home the message to a soldier whose body has been swapped with that of an old Navajo woman; A young Fox Mulder and sister Samantha in home movies from "DREAMLAND;" L.A. director of photography Bill Roe. "Bill not only carried on the good work of the cinematographers in Vancouver," says Frank Spotnitz, "he expanded it."

"From the moment "How the Ghosts Stole
Christmas" started, it was fun; from sitting
in the car and having the conversation about
Christmas to the nonstop bickering to 'What
are we doing out here?'" —Gillian Anderson

which we're going to do **"Rope"** without any cuts, seemingly. A great challenge for a cast and crew."

"Chris had some really strange ideas about how to shoot it," Braidwood remembers. "It was really tough for William because he had to learn all this German. Chris really wanted to do these 10-minute shots on Steadicam, and it was just brutal for William, because if he made one mistake we would have to start again."

"Maybe we shouldn't try to do two clever things at once," Davis offers. "I think it worked fine, but it was a struggle to do it. Because it's one clever thing to have us all speaking German and a second to try to do everything in great long 10-minute takes."

"I had gone to school in Germany for a couple years, so I did speak some German," Mitch Pileggi recounts. "I told Chris that what I was saying didn't make any sense with what we were doing. He said, "Just say whatever you would say." So I was able to write my own German dialogue in that."

"I never quite understood whether it was going to work or not," Gillian Anderson says of the episode. "When we finally saw "Triangle" after this new way of filming everything, a style which we'd never attempted before, as well as trying new scenes … trying this, trying that and to see that it actually worked in the end; that was terrific,"

In keeping with the try-anything spirit of season six, Vince Gilligan, John Shiban, and Frank Spotnitz unleashed **"Dreamland,"** a two-part comedy adventure in which Mulder switches bodies with a man-in-black named Morris Fletcher, played by comedy legend Michael McKean. Mulder is then trapped in Fletcher's miserable suburban household while Fletcher revels in Mulder's bachelor lifestyle, going so far as to attempt to seduce Scully. Shiban noted in 2002 that with all of the horrors Mulder had faced "the scariest thing to do with this guy was to put him in a house with a wife and two teenagers."

"Everything he was, we owe to Michael McKean," Gilligan says of the Morris Fletcher character. "We wrote some funny lines, but that was the extent of our input into it. He just really made that character come alive and was so watchable and so charismatic despite being such a shit." Fellow *Saturday Night Live* vet Nora Dunn played Fletcher's harridan of a wife.

The episode featured an updating of Harpo Marx's mirror-image routine from *Duck Soup,* which he and Lucille Ball had recreated on *I Love Lucy* . "I said 'Let's just really go for it,'" Duchovny remembers. "Let's make it that thing from the Lucille Ball show where she and Harpo see each other in a mirror. So it was on my shoulders to figure out this choreography. We hired a choreographer, and whenever Michael and I had 10 minutes, we'd go, and we'd try to do our little dance. And ultimately it was going to be the thing that only played in one take. It's about 97 percent right which is pretty good, and I think it's a funny little gag."

The X-Files' first haunted-house caper, **"How the Ghosts Stole Christmas,"** began as a sop for anxious Fox executives. "We kept promising we were going to do an episode that would save them a lot of money," Chris Carter said, "So we did one that took place in one room." Ed Asner and Lily Tomlin were cast as the ghosts who psychoanalyze their victims to death. Carter's script, with its dense and insightful dialogue, made the episode a fan favorite.

"Before Chris was ever a writer, he made pottery," Frank Spotnitz explains. "That's one of the things he did, and he would do it over and over and over again. It's that repetition and desire for perfection. You can see the flaws and blemishes very clearly as a potter, and he's exactly like that as a writer. He is focused on beauty and perfection and symmetry."

Gillian Anderson says what she enjoyed about the episode "was the crazy repartee between Mulder and Scully throughout the whole thing. Just the nonstop bickering, which was the focus of Ed and Lily's characters; they were trying to psychoanalyze us and our relationship." The actress adds, "From the moment that episode started, it was fun; from sitting in the car and having a conversation about Christmas to 'What are we doing out here?'"

TOP LEFT: Edward Asner and Lily Tomlin guest star as a pair of ghosts in Chris Carter's "HOW THE GHOSTS STOLE CHRISTMAS;" You can't shoot a dead person, but an irritated Scully may soon try. Note red insert appliqué on Tomlin, later replaced in post production with a see-through hole, evidence of her demise; Director Rob Bowman works with actor Bruce Campbell in David Amann's "TERMS OF ENDEARMENT;" All she wanted was a devil of a baby: Mulder and Scully discover a mass grave of "reject" babies that just didn't have the demon stuff in "TERMS OF ENDEARMENT." **ABOVE**: Kim Manners directs David Manis in "THE RAIN KING;" Doctors tend to Skinner, infected with blood-stopping nanobots in "SR 819," Krycek's mechanism of controlling the Assistant Director; Krycek in disguise; Gillian Anderson with actor Geoffrey Lewis as Alfred Fellig in Vince Gilligan's fascinating "TITHONUS;" A victim whose death Fellig was able to foresee; Scully listens to Skinner's dying words in "SR 819;" Victoria Jackson (of *SNL*) on set with David Duchovny and Gillian Anderson in "THE RAIN KING."

"Terms of Endearment" was a *Rosemary's Baby* parody featuring B-movie icon Bruce Campbell as a demon desperate to conceive a human son. David Amann's script was originally not as lighthearted as it became, but the end result would be another fan favorite episode.

Jeffrey Bell's "The Rain King" featured *Saturday Night Live's* Victoria Jackson in a love triangle with Mulder and a telekinetic meteorologist who can control the weather.

"SR 819" deals with the Syndicate's latest—and final—attempt to control *The X-Files*; Skinner is intentionally infected with deadly nanobots, which Krycek activates by remote control. Writer John Shiban got the idea from the 1950 film *DOA* in which a man is poisoned and tries to find his killer within 24 hours.

"My original pitch was that it was Mulder who gets infected," says John Shiban, adding that Chris Carter responded: "The audience knows we're not going to kill David Duchovny's character. Why don't you make it Skinner?"

The episode was hard for both Skinner and Mitch Pileggi. "Skinner had no love for Krycek, and so to be under his control was almost unbearable. Then, as an actor, enduring the prosthetics that were involved," Pileggi says. "It looked good, but it was a real pain to deal with. After a couple episodes of that, I went to them and I said, 'Can we please resolve this nano thing?'"

"Tithonus" guest-starred Geoffrey Lewis as a crime photographer who is unable to die. Scully is sent to New York to investigate him and has her own encounter with the Angel of Death.

"Our stars were always completely professional," Gilligan explains, "But at a certain point, you get kind of tired of playing the same character week

in and week out. That episode seemed to reinvigorate Gillian a bit. She really liked Geoffrey Lewis and the two of them had this kind of simpatico. They had chemistry together."

In a stunning turn of events, Chris Carter and Frank Spotnitz suddenly did away with the entire Syndicate story line in a sweeps-week two-parter. "Two Fathers" and "One Son" have the alien resistance beating back colonization and destroying the Syndicate. Chris Carter reflects. "You can look at the show as pre-'Two Fathers/One Son, and post-'Two Fathers/One Son.'"

Kim Manners puts it this way, "I've said for years that the show really resolved itself, if you will, by accident. The whole story line of the Syndicate and the bees and the aliens and the chips in the neck, they all seemed to just accidentally fall into place and create an intriguing, mysterious story line that eventually got so mysterious and so intriguing that Chris had to blow it up, because he couldn't deal with it anymore."

The action opens with the rebels sabotaging a medical experiment in which Cassandra Spender is made fully alien. After the credits, the Cigarette-Smoking Man narrates the entire story of the Syndicate conspiracy to Diana Fowley. "I learned from Rob that with the Cigarette-Smoking Man there were two characters," Kim Manners ponders. "There was the Cigarette-Smoking Man, and there was the cigarette."

As the Syndicate begins to unravel, the Cigarette-Smoking Man enlists Krycek and Spender to try and clean up the mess. When Spender talks back, the Cigarette-Smoking Man responds with the back of his hand and tells him that he pales in comparison to Fox Mulder. "It's the classic father-

son scene," Chris Owens observes. "If you take away the aliens and all the
conspiracy and what have you, it comes down to trying to do your best for
your father to fulfill his dreams of you."

Krycek then takes Spender under his wing. Frank Spotnitz says of
Krycek, "The thing that I really liked about his character was that he was
sort of the bastard son of the Cigarette-Smoking Man—not literally, but
he wanted to be his protégé. He wanted to be respected, and the Cigarette-
Smoking Man looked at him as a punk, as a thug."

When the Cigarette-Smoking Man finds himself staring down the
barrel of Mulder's Sig Sauer, he reveals the sacrifices the Syndicate members
were forced to make by the alien colonists. "The kind of parallel that I've
used, and Frank's used, is Vichy France," Davis says. "We made a deal with
the conquerors—in this case the aliens—that seemed to be the best we
could get. They're going to take over. Yes, you could fight them futilely, and
no one would survive, or you could make a deal with them—which is what
the French did with Hitler. And that's fine until Hitler—or the aliens—start
to squeeze you."

As the conspiracy unravels, Spender searches for his mother at the
abandoned Fort Marlene and finds a ravaged Marita Covarrubias, who has
been subjected to vaccine tests for the Black Oil. "It's not often you'll find a
beautiful actress who's willing to let herself be painted up as a zombie and
destroy her looks. But she went headlong into that," Bowman marvels. "I
thought it was terrifying to put a face to the consequences of the testing.
This is what it looked like."

The Syndicate members and their families are then called to a rendez-
vous with the colonists at an abandoned hangar. But instead they find
themselves facing the radioactive torches of the alien rebels. "I love the
mythology episodes because of the power swings back and forth," Bowman
says, "and that these men were not just power-hungry villains, but they were
also scared and afraid of their own demise."

With his life's work in ruins, the Cigarette-Smoking Man guns down
Jeffrey Spender when the agent turns against him. Owens learned of his
character's demise in the usual fashion when Carter phoned the actor to
discuss his latest script. "I remember Chris Carter telling me, 'You're going
to go out a hero, of sorts.' I thought, 'Go out a hero? I'm going already?'"
Owens laughs. "And the next thing I knew, I got the script, and there
it was."

Following the momentous two-parter, **"Agua Mala"** brings back Darren
McGavin as Arthur Dales as the agents battle with a Lovecraftian sea
monster washed ashore by a Florida hurricane.

"Monday" features a *Groundhog Day*-type conceit in which Mulder
repeatedly experiences a disastrous bank robbery. The robber's desperate
girlfriend—played by the late Carrie Hamilton (daughter of Carol Burnett)
—is the only person aware of the time-loop and tries in vain to warn
Mulder.

"Monday" was the biggest rush job of any single episode I ever had a
hand in," Gilligan recounts. "We had probably about six days to write that
episode, and I just thought it was going to be a disaster. Frank and John
came up with the basic idea for the episode, and then we all sat in a room
and tried to hammer it out, and damned if it didn't come up with a really
great idea for a show."

Kim Manners had to deal with the new challenge of a monotonous story.
"I literally approached it in my homework as if it was four different episodes
of television, and I tried to totally ignore the fact that it was the same story,"
Manners explains.

"Arcadia" is a parody of the gated-community phenomenon, in which
an evil patriarch uses a muck-monster to punish residents for breaking the
strict community guidelines. The episode became a hit with the Shippers for
its depiction of Mulder and Scully posing as the ideal suburban couple.

Gillian Anderson says of the episode, "It was just very funny to be

The demise of the Syndicate in the spectacular two-parter, "TWO FATHERS" and "ONE SON"
LEFT: Gillian Anderson and TV veteran Veronica Cartwright on the set of "TWO FATHERS;"
Bowman enjoys a story from his guest star. **RIGHT:** John Vulich's burn makeup design
for Nick Tate's Dr. Eugene Openshaw; The beginning of the end: rebel aliens begin
the fiery destruction of the Syndicate; A "1970s snapshot" of Bill Mulder and the
Cigarette-Smoking Man; Nice lapels: the 1970s versions of Bill Mulder (Peter Donat)
and the Cigarette-Smoking Man; The Syndicate prepares to close the deal with the
"nice" aliens, unaware of the doom that awaits them; Rob Bowman talks with his young
stars in "ONE SON"—the small "grays" were all performed by young girls; The 1970s
Cigarette-Smoking Man; The girls are outfitted with their costumes—plus tennis shoes
at former Tustin Marine Corps blimp hanger used as the soundstage in "ONE SON."
Veronica Cartwright as Cassandra Spender—Cigarette-Smoking Man's former wife, and
Jeffrey Spender's mother.

Cassandra was beginning to realize her
role in the greatest science project that
man had ever known. She was the center of
fifty years of work, the key to all of our
plans. Something even my colleagues didn't
realize yet. I killed to keep them unknowing.
I killed Dr. Oppenheimer so they wouldn't
discover her, when it was Cassandra I should
have killed. Cassandra needed to die. I
couldn't do it; with all the blood on my
hands, I couldn't kill the mother of my own
son. The woman I never even loved.

My colleagues never knew; focused as they
were on the new threat, the faceless alien
rebels who burned our doctors alive but my
colleagues had become old men. Blind to the
fact that the faceless rebels already held
their upper hands. That they'd used their
powers of disguise to infiltrate our group.

If Mulder hadn't known of his father's
history with me, he was fueled now with
names, dates, certainties. I couldn't stop
him any longer. Stop him from hearing of our
sins. His father's and my own. The truth was
out there. Fatally exposed. I had one last
hope. One chance to preserve my legacy.

I've trusted no one. Treachery is the
inevitable result of all fears. Every man
believes he has his own good reason. I have
little doubt my son's disloyalty to me.
Certainly he led Mulder and Scully to us.
His mother must know by now her central role
in the grand plan. And she's as much alien
as human. Do you wonder why I've chosen you?
You've never betrayed me. And now I need
someone to trust."
-Cigarette-Smoking Man to Agent Diana Fowley
in Two Fathers

LEFT: The Cigarette-Smoking Man prepares an offering of peace to the gray aliens in 1973 "ONE SON;" A gray accepts; Burn 'em like this: first assistant director Stephanie Herrera gives direction to the Faceless Men prior to the torching of The Syndicate; Spender comes upon a tortured Marita Covarrubias, now the subject of alien virus vaccine experiments; A young "gray" extra, sans her alien mask, awaits her turn on set; The rebel alien disguised as a nurse; The alien fetus—the soruce of the alien genome for the Syndicate's experiements; Frozen in time—a scientist who has seen better days; Cigarette-Smoking Man puts an end to his disappointment, putting a bullet into son, Jeffrey.

"It's the classic father-son scene.
You take away the aliens and all the
conspiracy and what have you, but it
comes down to trying to do your best
for your dad to fulfill his dreams of
you." —Chris Owens

TOP LEFT: Duchovny with Carrie Hamilton in Vince Gilligan's "MONDAY;" The mostly unseen garbage monster in "ARCADIA;" The return of Morris Fletcher in "THREE OF A KIND;" Agent Scully is eerily drawn to writer and Mulder neighbor Phillip Padget (Jonathan Hawkes) in "MILAGRO;" Meet the Petries: Mulder and Scully go under cover in a little-too-controlled community in "ARCADIA;" Kim Manners and David Duchovny confer on the streets of downtown Los Angeles in Monday; Manners directs Scully in a key scene from "MILAGRO;" Manners shows actor Darren Burrows how to add just enough terror. **RIGHT**: Kim Manners enjoys a gag between actors Duchovny and Hawkes on the set of "MILAGRO;" Have a light ma'am? A tipsy Scully has no problem attracting suitors in "THREE OF A KIND;" Dean Haglund gets serious. . . sort of, in same episode.

"It was just really funny, that shot of the two of us standing in the driveway with our Izod shirts on and the little gray sweaters."
—Gillian Anderson

portraying these completely normal, straight-up, Stepfordy-Wife-type characters, and at the same time having Mulder making jokes, all the while I'm trying to keep a straight face and hold it together. It was just very funny, that shot of the two of us standing in the driveway with our Izod shirts on and the little gray sweaters."

"Alpha," a werewolf story, features *Dirty Harry's* Andrew Robinson as research scientist suffering from lycanthropy. The episode also features Mulder facing the heartbreak millions of people have suffered through over the past two decades when he actually meets his Internet pen pal, in this case veterinary scientist Karin Berquist.

"Trevor" told the story of a convict who develops the ability to pass through solid matter after being struck by lightning. He escapes prison and tries to regain the son who gives the episode its title.

"Milagro" is ostensibly about a murderous "psychic surgeon" called to life by an obsessive novelist but is actually a meditation on the relationship of a creator to his creation. Frank Spotnitz devised the original story after contemplating how the characters of Mulder and Scully had become real people to him. Spotnitz, John Shiban, and Chris Carter worked on the script that had Scully fascinated by the attention given to her by the troubled writer. The episode shifts in and out of reality and includes a very steamy scene in which Scully is seduced by the lovelorn scribe.

David Duchovny's script for **"The Unnatural"** again flashed back to the career of Arthur Dales, this time investigating an out-of-this-world slugger on the 'Roswell Greys' baseball team. Duchovny recounts that the script was inspired by a newspaper story about Joe Bauman, who had hit 72 home runs while playing for the minor league Roswell Rockets. "I just remember thinking, 'Oh, Roswell, that's kind of coincidental,'" Duchovny says. "Then I noticed at some point that the famous Roswell incident was the same year that Jackie Robinson broke the color line. So I thought, 'Well, this is a very interesting set of coincidences.'"

The episode marked David Duchovny's debut as both writer and director. "It was just a wonderful experience and something I'm forever grateful for, to be able to cut my teeth directing in such a safe environment," Duchovny says today, "and yet it was difficult. Difficult because it was ambitious, but also safe in that these people were all going to do their jobs, and the show was going to get made, and it was going to look like an X-File even if I just showed up and drooled for 24 hours a day."

"Darin's comedy episodes actually opened up a whole new sub genre," Chris Carter observes. "And David Duchovny was fueled by those episodes as well."

"Three of a Kind" is the sequel to season five's "Unusual Suspects." The Lone Gunmen try to gatecrash a defense contractors' convention and find that Suzanne Modeski has taken up with a sleazy gun runner played by yet another *Saturday Night Live* alumni, the late Charles Rocket. Vince Gilligan co-wrote the episode with John Shiban. "To be brutally honest about it, I never saw myself as a Mulder type, this good looking, adept, smart guy," Gilligan says. "I always saw myself as one of the Lone Gunmen. Those guys more closely represent the rest of us. They're struggling along, and they're scared, but they're still heroic."

"I'd worn my wedding ring when I first played the part, so I imagined a married life for Byers," Bruce Harwood says, noting "Unusual Suspects" complicated matters. "They did this whole back story where Byers had this lost romance kind of thing. So I took my wedding ring off, and said, 'Okay, Byers wasn't married in 1989,'" Harwood continues. "And then they brought the character Suzanne Modeski back in season six, and that was supposed to be in the present. So I had to redo my back story; I said Byers had been divorced."

Haglund got his chance to play serious when Langly is set up as a Manchurian Candidate-type assassin. "It always shocks me because I always think I was playing it as serious and dramatic, and then you hear, 'Oh, you

"The show was gonna get made, and it was gonna look like an X-File even if I just showed up and drooled for 24 hours a day." —David Duchovny

TOP LEFT: Writer/director David Duchovny at work on his "THE UNNATURAL;" Walter Phelan as the alien baseball player; Rob Bowman drops by to offer a little guidance; The director views a little playback to check his work; Time for a Kleenex: Mulder trapped underground by the hallucinogenic plant life in "FIELD TRIP;" The Cigarette-Smoking Man ponders the next conspiracy in Biogenesis; Gillian gets "gooed up" on the set of "FIELD TRIP;" Kim Manners gives some direction to Mitch Pileggi in same episode. RIGHT: Anderson chats with African "tribesmen" extras in "BIOGENESIS;" The camera photographs Scully's discovery at Malibu's Leo Carillo State Beach; "BIOGENESIS's" Dr. Merkmallen is found in Dr. Sandoz's apartment. . . but not in one piece.

guys are so hilarious,'" Dean Haglund exclaims. "And I'm thinking 'Am I really that crappy as a dramatic actor?'"

The Lone Gunmen actors not only worked together, they played together, too. "We just enjoyed each other's company; it was fun to hang out together," Tom Braidwood says. "The other guys were always complaining that I was the one that was the most recognizable; I don't know if that's true."

"Field Trip" was a trippy tale in which the agents are trapped in the hallucinatory spell of a massive killer fungus. "That was a fun one for all of the mind games we got to play on the audience," Gilligan says. "Things get progressively weirder as each act occurs. By the end of it, you're probably thinking 'What the hell am I watching?'"

"Oh, my God, that was so sick," Anderson says of the shoot. "I remember being covered in yellow goop and then being pulled through the earth, and then being covered in a layer of dirt on top of that. It was kind of fun and kind of just completely disgusting at the same time."

"Biogenesis" took the mythology in a completely new direction. With the Syndicate killed off, Carter and Spotnitz dove into the arcane world of "Ancient Astronaut Theory," which posits that the gods and angels of ancient mythology were in fact alien colonists who genetically engineered the human race.

The case centers on a graphite rubbing taken from the surface of an alien spacecraft discovered of the coast of Africa. The agents are stunned to discover that the writing on it is nearly identical to an ancient Navajo script. The radiation embedded in the rubbing activates the Black Oil virus dormant within Mulder, and the case soon captures the attention of the Cigarette-Smoking Man and Diana Fowley. The episode ends with Scully standing on a beach staring in disbelief at the alien spacecraft.

In 2002, Chris Carter said of "Biogenesis," "I actually met a man very early on during the course of *The X-Files*; I told him what I was doing, and he told me he was one of people responsible for leading the U.S. project to map the human genome. I became very interested in what he was telling me and suddenly realized this was exactly what I wanted to do with the show. So we decided to tie that in with the alien mythology."

SEASON SEVEN *CLOSURE*

The seventh season of *The X-Files* would in some ways be the most difficult of the series. Duchovny and Anderson were exhausted from six years of extremely hard work and, with the Syndicate storyline wrapped up; it was unclear where to take the mythology next.

Millennium had been cancelled at the end of its third season and Ten Thirteen's new series, *Harsh Realm*, would be cancelled after only three episodes, amidst a running battle with Fox over production budgets. HBO's new series *The Sopranos* was airing opposite *The X-Files* and was drawing away viewers and critical accolades.

With David Duchovny playing out the final year of his contract, there was serious discussion among senior staff about whether this season would be the last. "Everyone was a little anxious—mostly me—about how to approach these episodes as if they were the final *X-Files* stories we would ever tell," Chris Carter confesses.

"**The Sixth Extinction**" picks up where "Biogenesis" left off. Mulder remains in intensive care while Scully is in Africa, researching a prehistoric alien ship upon which are written scientific formulas and religious texts that defy explanation. Skinner contacts Michael Kritschgau to help him cure Mulder, who has developed psychic powers as the result of the Black Oil virus being reactivated. After a series of disturbing visions, Scully returns home.

In "**The Sixth Extinction: Amor Fati**", the Cigarette-Smoking Man kidnaps Mulder and takes him to a secret medical facility in the Pentagon where he has genetic material extracted from him. While under sedation, Mulder experiences a series of dreams where he leads a normal, suburban life with Diana. Back at the FBI, Scully confronts Diana regarding Mulder's whereabouts. Her conscience pricked by the Cigarette-Smoking Man's deteriorating mental state, Diana secretly delivers a pass-card to Scully, who rescues Mulder from an abandoned operating room. The episode ends with both Mulder and Scully profoundly affected by their exposure to the radiation from the alien spaceship. Mulder then confides to Scully that, through his ordeal, she was his "touchstone."

"Everyone was a little anxious—mostly me—about how to approach these episodes as if they were the final *X-Files* stories we would ever tell."
—Chris Carter

LEFT PAGE (upper right): Mulder and Scully burst in on "HUNGRY" man Rob Roberts (Chad Donella); "REMAINDER." Images from "THE SIXTH EXTINCTION" and "THE SIXTH EXTINCTION II: AMOR FATI"; Scully tells Mulder of her find, which she hopes will have all the answers; In Africa, Scully begins to put the pieces together from rubbings of the surface of the discovered alien craft; The Cigarette-Smoking Man and Agent Fowley observe the Christ-like Mulder, complete with crown-of-thorns; In a delusional state, Mulder dreams of a peaceful life with Diana Fowley—and his grown sister, Samantha (Megan Leitch), safe and sound; Agent Fowley finds the disabled Mulder has seemingly changed hospital rooms by himself. RIGHT: I want what you have: the Cigarette-Smoking Man prepares to receive Mulder's alien virus immunity.

It began with an act of supreme violence. A big bang
expanding ever outward; a cosmos borne of matter and gas;
matter and gas. Ten billion years ago. Whose idea was this?
Who had the audacity for such invention? And the reason?
Were we part of that plan ten billion years ago? Are we born
only to die? To be fruitful and multiply before giving way
to our generations? If there is a beginning, must there be
an end? We burn like fires in our time, only to extinguish,
to surrender to the element's eternal reclaim? Matter and
gas. Will this all end one day? Life no longer passing to
life. The earth left barren like the stars above. Like the
cosmos. Will the hand that lit the flame let it burn down,
let it burn out? Could we too become extinct? Or if this fire
of life living inside us is meant to go on, who decides? Who
tends the flames? Can he reignite the spark, even as it grows
cold and weak?"

-Scully in New Mexico with Dr. Sandos from **Biogenesis** (6x22)

"I came in search of something I did not believe existed.
I've stayed on now in spite of myself; in spite of
everything I've held to be true. I will continue here as
long as I can; as long as you are beset by the haunting
illness which I saw consume your beautiful mind. What is
this discovery I've made? How can I reconcile what I see and
what I know? I feel this was not for me to find, but for you.
Make the connections which cannot be ignored. Connections
which for me deny all logic and reason? What is this source
of power I hold in my hand? This rubbing, this simple
impression taken from the surface of the craft. I watched
this rubbing take its hold on you, saw you succumb to its
spiraling effect. In every illness, lies its cure.

-Opening Monologue for **The Sixth Extinction** (7x01)

"It was a tough scene. Frank and I had spoken on the phone about the dialogue in the wrap-up scene...you couldn't deny the fact that Scully killed Donnie Psaster in cold blood. How do we deal with that?" —Rob Bowman

Co-writer David Duchovny based the dream sequences—in which Mulder is tempted by a conventional suburban life—on Nikos Kazantzakis' The *Last Temptation of Christ*.

"So they finally did an episode which said I was Mulder's father," William B. Davis says of "Amor Fati's" stunning teaser. "The fans didn't believe it. Part of the mystique of it was that everybody had their own idea of what was going on."

"It happened naturally that Mulder and Scully were on a quest to find this thing that was set up in the first two episodes," Carter says of the mythology, "But it just worked out that those stories became the most personal. And those were the quest stories. They became the running story through the otherwise disconnected stories."

Gillian Anderson discovered this after her close encounters with the paranormal in the "Sixth Extinction" episodes. "There were a couple times when I put in a call in to Chris in season seven saying, 'I don't know if I can do this anymore. I don't even believe a word coming out of my mouth anymore," the actress remembers. "How can I be arguing against all this when in the last episode we shot this other story line happened?' I was having that conversation constantly and his response was 'You've got to have that conflict between these two characters or it just falls apart.'"

Vince Gilligan's "**Hungry**" is a tragicomic parody of the self-help movement, in which a guilt-ridden mutant tries to twelve-step his appetite for human brains away.

"I was very proud of it because it felt like a very different kind of *X-File* episode to me," the writer says. "It had a completely different point of view on it. It was from the point of view of the killer. When we were coming up with the story, we were thinking a lot about *Crime and Punishment*."

Gilligan found that his director didn't share his enthusiasm for the script at first. "I remember Kim saying, 'Oh, buddy, I don't like this episode. Don't like it at all. I think it's a loser,'" Gilligan recalls. "I remember getting really offended. I have to say maybe it's best to give Kim episodes he really doesn't like because I think he directed the hell out of that episode."

Millennium, a controversial crossover with the now-cancelled series, teams up the agents with Frank Black to thwart a plot by members of the Millennium Group to bring about the Apocalypse. *Millennium* star Lance Henriksen was unhappy with the episode, believing it wasn't an appropriate end to his characters' story.

Vince Gilligan explains that tying up the dangling threads of the *Millennium* series was beyond the reach of an *X-Files* episode: "It wasn't about the plot as much as it was about getting these guys down in the basement of this creepy old house with these zombies climbing up out of the ground, and having to be shot in the head."

If Henriksen was unhappy, *The X-Files* fans were ecstatic about Mulder and Scully's long-awaited kiss as the New Year began at the end of the episode.

Part of the inspiration behind the episode was all of the media hype predicting the end of civilization once the year 2000 began. "In the run up to the turn of the year, all these so-called experts were on every news outlet you could find talking about how once that clock kicked over to 2000, suddenly, computers everywhere would go dead and lock up, planes would fall out of the sky, satellites would rocket to Earth and buildings would explode," says Gilligan. "I am proud to say I never bought into any of that Y2K BS for a minute!"

"**Rush**" is David Amann's take on the DC Comics superhero, the Flash,

ABOVE: If I only had a brain: the shark-like Rob Roberts (Chad Donella), sans faux ears, seeks help in Vince Gilligan's "HUNGRY"; Frank Black (Lance Henricksen) makes a return from the canceled Millennium; "Do you have dry or oily hair?" Donnie Pfaster (Nick Chinlund) also makes a creepy return in "ORISON". **RIGHT**: Scully battles Pfaster in Gillian Anderson's biggest fight scene of the series; Ricky Jay as The Amazing Maleeni; In autopsy, Scully finds Maleeni's decapitation a little too clean cut; In Signs and Wonders, David Duchovny came face to face with real slithering reptiles; Scully doesn't quite buy Maleeni's magic; Willie Garson as the very lucky Henry Weems in "THE GOLDBERG VARIATION".

"David didn't want to cry. Instead he said, 'Just watch what I do; trust me.'" —Kim Manners

ABOVE: Walk-Ins Welcome: Mulder and Scully go to "Santa's North Pole Village," looking for clues to the disappearance of a young girl; The ghost of Kathy Lee Tencate's (Kim Darby) six-year-old son visits her in prison; In one of the most emotional scenes of season seven, the spirit of Samantha finally puts her brother's heart to rest in "CLOSURE"; David Duchovny's perfectly underplayed reaction surprised—and gratified—director Kim Manners; Mulder reads Scully entries from his sister Samantha's diary; Psychic Harold Piller (Anthony Heald) leads Mulder to the place where Samantha grew up in seclusion. **RIGHT:** Appropriate help: The Lone Gunmen assist Scully in helping Mulder defend himself from a killer video game character in "FIRST PERSON SHOOTER"; Mulder in action—and in costume.

in which a group of high school student are mysteriously granted the power of super-speed.

"The Goldberg Variation" is another lighthearted, high-concept outing in which a hapless janitor's preternatural luck is combined with a series of plot contrivances inspired by cartoonist Rube Goldberg's fanciful machines. A young Shia LaBeouf guest stars.

"The seventh season, for my money, was one of our best because we took more storytelling risks than in previous years," Vince Gilligan states.

Written by *Millennium* show-runner Chip Johannesen, **"Orison"** featured the return of Donnie Pfaster, who kidnaps Scully after breaking out of prison with the help of a vengeance-seeking minister. The episode climaxes with Scully shooting Pfaster down in cold blood.

"There's a slo-mo scene where Mulder comes in the room with Scully and guns are drawn," Mark Snow explains. "They're looking around, and I do these big boom single hits with a lot of reverb. There's nothing else but that. Sometimes that is really effective."

"It was a tough scene," Bowman recounts. "Frank and I had spoken on the phone about the dialogue in the wrap-up scene with Mulder and Scully. Even though she shot him in the heightened state, you couldn't deny the fact that she killed Donnie Psaster in cold blood. How do we deal with that?"

"The Amazing Maleeni" is a puzzle-piece of an episode in which two magicians are running a con on Mulder and Scully. The episode features real-life magicians Ricky Jay and Jonathan Levit. "That episode started with Frank, because he—for several years—had wanted to write an episode about magicians," Gilligan explains. "Frank was a fan of the TV show *The Magician* with Bill Bixby so I believe that was part of it, but Frank is interested in the idea of magic and the idea of fooling people who wish to be fooled."

"There was no choice other than Ricky Jay as far as we were concerned," Gilligan states, "He was not looking forward to the idea of playing a magician because I think he felt that magicians were never portrayed very realistically in movies or television shows."

"Signs and Wonders" is a theological exploration of the nature of evil against the backdrop of snake-handling Fundamentalist churches. The episode featured an incendiary performance by Michael Childers as a back-woods minister. "The actor that we cast for that show had done theater work

exclusively, and was, in fact, the son of a preacher," Manners says. "He had gone to church as a child and handled snakes."

In **"Sein Und Zeit"**, a small girl mysteriously vanishes from her home and Mulder goes to investigate. A strange line left in her ransom note harkens back to an old case, and Mulder infuriates Skinner by publicly exonerating the missing girl's parents. After Mulder's own mother commits suicide, he learns from the mother involved in the earlier case that "walk-in" spirits (which were first explored in "Red Museum") took her son, knowing that he was about to suffer a violent death.

"Closure" introduces Harold Piller (played by Anthony Heald) as a police psychic who offers to help Mulder find the missing girl. as well as his sister.

Piller leads Mulder to the home where the Cigarette-Smoking Man lived with Samantha and Jeffrey. Mulder discovers Samantha's diary hidden in a wall and learns that Samantha had been subjected to horrible medical experiments. At the age of fourteen, she had run away and sought refuge in a hospital. As an enraged Cigarette-Smoking Man came to get her, the walk-in spirits took her away. The story's beautiful denouement has Mulder encountering Samantha's spirit as she and the spirits of other children play in the starlight, finally putting an end to his search.

"In the script, it called for his sister to run up and hug him, and Mulder was to start crying," Manners recalls. "David didn't want to cry. I said, 'David, you're finally realizing that your sister is, in fact, dead. We've come a long way to get to this answer, and it's a very emotional time for Mulder.' He said, 'Just watch what I do; trust me.' And, he held that little girl actress—there was a beatific smile on his face that was absolutely astounding. I printed it, and I said to him after the sequence was shot, 'You were absolutely right, and I learned something here today.'"

"We needed someone to bring a visual style to an episode that would deal with ethereal beings in a literal way—we had to SEE these things," Carter explained, "Kim gave it a look that turned out to help communicate the deep emotion—the music also helped in telling the story of Mulder coming to terms with what had happened to his sister."

As Carter notes, the drama of "Closure" is greatly enhanced by the soundtrack, in which Moby's elegiac hymn "My Weakness" blended in seamlessly with Mark Snow's score. "As the seasons went on, I was getting a bit tired of simply *whoosh* and *shooo* and things like that so I started to

> "I took it to Chris, and said, 'I have an idea for an episode and I want to direct it.' He responded, 'Well, if you write one and it's any good, then you can direct it.'" —Gillian Anderson

write more melodies," the composer explains. Kim Manners was especially taken with Snow's score for "Closure. "Mark was nearly half of *The X-Files*," Manners states. "His music was pure storytelling, you know? He could ratchet tension like nobody else."

"X-Cops" was based on an idea Vince Gilligan had for years. "I went to Chris and said, 'I have this great idea,'" Gilligan remembers. "Let's have Mulder and Scully be on *COPS*. Everybody looked at me and rolled their eyes."

"Chris's big issue was that it was too goofy, but another big issue he had was how to shoot it," Gilligan explains. "I said, 'You'd shoot it on video. If it's going to be Mulder and Scully on *COPS*, it's got to look like an episode of COPS.'" To reach that goal, *COPS* producer John Langely came aboard to consult.

"I wanted the same editing style, I wanted the same fonts for the legends that pop up," Gilligan recounts. "So, we referred to John Langly's crew for all of that information. Our camera operators—and, even Michael Watkins himself—operated the camera for a lot of the shots, but also (*COPS* cameraman) Bertram van Munster shot quite a bit of it because we wanted it to look in every way, shape, and form as much as possible like a real *COPS* episode." It looked so much so that Gilligan says "Fox got nervous, and they said we have to put some kind of a notification here at the start of the episode so that people don't tune in and say, 'Oh, shit. *The X-Files* has been preempted this week by *COPS*.'"

"It was interesting to make the adjustment to playing something more real than you might play for television," Gillian Anderson says. "It's a different way of playing something, and the whole side story of Scully getting pissed off at the camera crew. That was fun."

"First-Person Shooter" was William Gibson and Tom Maddox's second script for the show. The story has the Lone Gunmen call on Mulder and Scully when a Silicon Valley startup they were consulting for begins to experience freak deaths within their virtual reality game.

Bruce Harwood says the action sequences were challenging to the actors: "It's pretty difficult on a set when the stuntmen come up to you and go, 'Don't worry, you'll be safe. Nothing to worry about. Okay. Everyone put their safety glasses on .'"

"Theef" tells the story of an Appalachian mountain man named Oral Peattie who uses witchcraft to get revenge on the doctor who treated Peattie's daughter after a deadly accident. *Space: Above and Beyond's* James Morrison guest stars. The story was another John Gilnitz creation—written by Frank Spotnitz, John Shiban, and Vince Gilligan. "I think I was enlisted for the fact that I'm Southern, and they thought I was the closest thing they had to a hillbilly on the staff," Gilligan laughs.

"En Ami" was based on a story by William Davis in which the Cigarette-Smoking Man uses Scully to help him obtain secret medical technology. "The initial idea it came from was, 'Hey, guys, how many seasons have we done? Seven? And I still haven't had a scene with Gillian Anderson,'" Davis laughs. "So it originally came from their response, saying 'Alright, let's do a story about Scully and the Cigarette-Smoking Man.' That initially prompted the episode."

"It was, to some degree, a marriage of my work and Chris's work," Davis explains. "I developed the concept and the story line, but, in the end, a lot of the dialogue belonged to Chris."

Sadly, "En Ami" would be Rob Bowman's final bow on *The X-Files*. "Artistically I felt like I couldn't help any more," the director explains. "Financially, was it the right decision? It's hard to say. I wanted to make movies. And I would not have made *Reign of Fire* if I had stayed on the show. I wanted to make that movie. So my feeling was, 'At this point, I'm probably more of a problem than a solution.' My responsibility to build up the show was no longer needed; they didn't need me to figure out how to make the show 'look' any more. It was all figured out."

"Chimera" has Mulder investigating the mysterious murders of women linked to an adulterous sheriff. David Amann's script is an insightful commentary on suburban repression and self-delusion, which made a major comeback in the conservative late '90s.

In **"all things"**, threads of synchronicity run through an exploration of Scully's pre-*X-Files* life. It would be Gillian Anderson's first script for the show. "At one point enough people had said to me, 'Are you ever going to write and direct an episode?' since David had done either one or two by then," Anderson explains. "I had a conversation with my manager and said, 'I keep being asked this question, and it has never even crossed my mind. I don't necessarily even have a desire to do one.' But all of a sudden I just had this idea for a storyline. And the next day I took it to Chris, and said, 'I have an idea for an episode and I want to direct it.' He responded, 'Well, if you write one and it's any good, then you can direct it.' And so I started to write."

"Kim (Manners) was a great mentor during that period of time," Anderson recalls. "And he taught me important things to know in terms of where to put the camera, etc. Every weekend I would go home and run my own prep, diagram out every single scene, and plan out where the camera was going to be."

"Brand X" played upon themes popularized in Michael Mann's tobacco-industry exposé *The Insider*. Future *Saw* star Tobin Bell plays a chain-smoker with an addiction to an experimental kind of cigarette with a particularly deadly kind of secondhand smoke.

David Duchovny's **"Hollywood AD"** is a comedic farce in which an

FROM UPPER LEFT: The cast's turn: A dolled-up Scully in William B. Davis's "EN AMI"; The secrets to the universe go overboard; First-time writer/director Gillian Anderson lines up a shot with former flame Dan Waterston (Nicolas Surovy) in her "ALL THINGS"; Mulder with his beloved Scully in all things. Sniper Zombies are everywhere in David Duchovny's hilarious *X-Files* sendup, "HOLLYWOOD A.D."; The Cigarette-Smoking Pontiff (Tony Amendola) holds "Scully" (Tea Leoni) captive while zombies abound; David Duchovny's real-life Scully—his wife, Tea Leoni—along with DP Bill Roe's brother, Tim Roe pose with their director; The director checks his shot; Anderson discusses a shot with camera operator for "ALL THINGS". FOLLOWING PAGE: Scully with a grown-up Billy Miles—a character who is about to start a great deal of trouble.

abrasive producer makes his own *X-Files* movie, casting Garry Shandling and Tea Leoni as Mulder and Scully. The dense script also dealt with the pursuit of the "Lazarus Bowl," which contained the voice of Christ and could raise the dead.

Duchovny explains that the original idea for "Hollywood AD" was "this silly science fiction idea of somebody's voice being recorded like a phonograph, except in pottery. It was just Jesus's voice, but it would have all of these kind of superhuman qualities to it. But I didn't know what the caper was. Even the funny X-Files had to have a strong caper in the middle of them. We always called it 'the caper' just because it sounded so old Holly-wood. Just like every joke has a gag, every show has a caper."

"David's pretty relaxed and casual about his directing," Anderson says admiringly. "I think he goes back and forth between being a perfectionist and being quite lackadaisical about it. I think ultimately he just wants to have fun, too."

The episode holds a hidden message from *The X-Files* star. "In the last scene between Mulder and Scully, they're sitting in the fake graveyard talking about how they're gonna be remembered," Duchovny remembers. "And as silly as the episode is, to me that was really my coded farewell."

"**Fight Club**" is a frenetic comedy in which twin sisters, sired by a preter-naturally angry man, leave destruction and chaos in their wake. Comedienne Kathy Griffin guest stars.

"**Je Souhaite**" is a fable about a jaded hipster genie who is discovered by two idiots (played by Kevin Weisman and Will Sasso) whose wishes backfire on them disastrously. "That's one of the stories that's been told more times than you could count, but it's one that writers always come back to because it's just an endlessly fascinating thought experiment," Vince Gilligan states. "What *would* you do if you had three wishes? I imagine we've all thought about that from time to time."

The episode also marks writer Gilligan's first go at directing. "I was beyond nervous," he remembers. "I was having hysterical diarrhea for weeks leading up to when I knew we were going to start production." According to Gillian Anderson, Gilligan seemed to get a lot more comfortable once he was on set. "I remember Vince being pretty relaxed, kind of calm, and just kind of himself," the actress states. "I didn't get a sense that he was particu-larly worried or nervous."

As the seventh season came to a close, Michelle MacLaren came in

as line producer. "Michelle had been the line producer on *Harsh Realm.*" Gilligan says, "A line producer is the person who's responsible for spending the finite amount of money you have in your budget so that it goes as far as it can possibly go and so that you get as much on the screen as you can. It's a very high-stress job, and there's a lot of politics involved, and there's a lot of people who will be made unhappy because money doesn't stretch forever. She was one of the best line producers I ever worked with because she was there 100 percent for the filmmakers, and as a result, she very often made Twentieth Century Fox unhappy."

In season-closer "**Requiem**", Mulder and Scully return to Oregon, where a spaceship crashes while bounty hunters are rounding up past abductees. Sheriff Billy Miles and Teresa Hoese reappear from the pilot episode, as well as the Alien Bounty Hunter. "There was some pretty strong sentiment inside and outside the show that it was time to call it a day," Spotnitz said in 2005. "So we very consciously went back to the pilot and to the characters of that episode."

The Cigarette-Smoking Man, now stricken with terminal cancer, sends Krycek and Marita to find the ship in order to strike a new deal with the aliens, but the pair decide to betray him instead. With Scully experiencing fainting spells, Mulder and Skinner leave her in Washington, D.C., and return to Oregon. Mulder is then abducted himself. When Skinner returns to Washington, Scully reveals that she is pregnant.

Nicholas Lea enjoyed the scene where Krycek attempts to do away with the Cigarette-Smoking Man. "That's one of the character's great moments, when I get to push Bill Davis down a set of stairs," he beams. Davis says of the Cigarette-Smoking Man's apparent demise, "In a sense, he has nothing to lose because his life's burned out. So death doesn't have the same terror that it would to a young happy chap."

The episode features some snuggling action between Mulder and Scully, which seems nearly pornographic in the context of their long, chaste courtship. However, Gillian Anderson notes these displays of affection were sprinkled throughout the series. "Someone had sent me some of these YouTube clips that people put together of all the intimate moments between Mulder and Scully," the actress explains. "And a few things hit me; one was just the amount of tenderness there was between them. The looks of understanding into each other's eyes and the clarity that we were there for each other; and then there was the number of times we actually did touch hands, or kiss on the cheek or forehead or even on the lips at times. There was a lot of that."

When "Requiem" wrapped, David Duchovny's contractual obligation to Twentieth Century Fox was fulfilled. The future of the series seemed more uncertain than ever. "David's part in the show and future of the show were uncertain as we wrapped; would he come back completely or would he come back part time?" Carter recounts.

"I was kind of a free agent after season seven, and to me, there was not much else to do in terms of the character," Duchovny says today. "So it was really about me wanting to pursue other parts of my career as a writer, director, and actor."

"Je Souhaite" is one of those stories that writers always come back to because it's just an endlessly fascinating thought experiment." —Vince Gilligan

OPPOSITE LEFT: New Co-Executive Michelle MacLaren on the set of her Season Nine episode, "JOHN DOE" with an unknown grip and 1st Asst. Dir Barry K. Thomas. MacLaren replaced line producer Michael Watkins late in Season Seven and would see the show through to completion. **ABOVE**: Comedienne Kathy Griffin guest-stars as a good/bad pair of sisters in "FIGHT CLUB"; Scully on a visit to Frank McGee's Bob Damfuse—the sisters' father; A "tech scout" aboard an aircraft carrier (for "REQUIEM", for an unused location) with the L.A. crew: (left to right): Crew member from the carrier, Transportation Co-Captain Greg Wallace; Director Kim Manners, Location Manager Ilt Jones, Production Designer Corey Kaplan, Stunt Coordinary Danny Weselis, Co-Executive Producer Michelle MacLaren, unknown carrier crew member. Wally (Transportation Co-Captain), Kim Manners (Director, Executive Producer), Ilt Jones (Location Manager), Corey Kaplan (Production Designer), Danny Weselis (Stunt Coordinator), Michelle MacLaren (Co-Executive Producer), Crew member from carrier; Cigarette-Cigarette-Smoking Man dying of—you guessed it—cancer in "REQUIEM"; Mulder finds Scully passed out in the forest from. . . pregnancy; Mulder and Scully examine the body of the "wish I was invisible" Anson Stokes (Kevin Weisman) in Vince Gilligan's genie tale, "JE SOUHAITE"; Don't you wish you could just get your boss to shut up? Paul Hayes as Jay Gilmore, formerly Anson Stokes' boss; Mulder reaches into the field of the cloaked alien ship just seconds before his abduction.

CREATOR CHRIS CARTER

Chris Carter was born on October 13, 1956, and raised in the working-class suburb of Bellflower, CA. After college, Carter landed a job with Surfing magazine, as editor and feature writer, but it wasn't until his wife—herself a screenwriter—encouraged Chris to try his hand at a script that he began to pursue a career in Hollywood in earnest. His initial efforts caught the eye of Jeffrey Katzenberg, who was then an executive at Disney and it was during that period that he began to make a name for himself. However, it wasn't until he landed a development deal at Twentieth Television that he would conjure up a concept that would, unbeknownst to him, change the face of television.

This idea of Carter's for a series about a pair of paranormal investigators did indeed catch the eye of Twentieth Television President Peter Roth, but his first pitch was unsuccessful. He came back to Peter with some revisions – including the addition of an alien-abduction hook which was inspired by a statistic he had stumbled upon suggesting that 3% of Americans claimed to have had personal encounters with extraterrestrials. Roth accepted the pitch, the script was written and sold to the fledgling Fox network

"Chris tries to be as ruthless as he can, not just with the people that are working for him, but with himself," writer/producer Frank Spotnitz says. "He really wants to succeed, and looks at every script as an opportunity to do better than he's ever done before."

Actress Annabeth Gish concurs, adding that Carter was "very polite, kind, but has a raging intensity underneath." But that intensity didn't overpower others working for him. "You could argue Chris out of an idea," writer/producer Vince Gilligan remembers. "And that philosophy filtered down amongst the rest of us, that the best idea should win the day. It should never be about who's got the most seniority." That working philosophy would permeate the creative process for The X-Files for the life of the series.

A meticulous attention to detail was applied to every stage of production. "Every script that came out of Chris' camp, was done with such careful strokes," director Rob Bowman says, adding, "You were really swinging hard in every episode." Complacency was not tolerated, and creative autonomy was the watchword. "Once the show became a hit, Chris' approach was, 'We're going to make this show the way we want to make it; budget be damned, schedule be damned,'" producer/director Kim Manners says. The show would raise the bar not only for sci-fi shows, but for all TV drama. The mandate was to create a "mini-movie" every week, and that visual sophistication would carry over to Carter's other series (Millennium, Harsh Realm, The Lone Gunmen) and would influence later dramas including CSI, 24 and Lost.

Carter was very much a hands-on producer, involved in every step of the creative process. "I would get phone calls from Chris and he'd want to make sure that before we started an episode that we had a conversation," actress Gillian Anderson remembers. "Chris was very specific about how he wanted things," actor Mitch Pileggi said, adding, "All the writers understood that."

Carter hung in there with every episode, start to finish, right down to the making of the show's stunning musical scores. "He was very, very encouraging, and it made your confidence level go way up," composer Mark Snow recalls. "I could really go 'out there' with some of my work."

Many fans have not been aware that Carter had to go to bat with skeptical executives to get some of the most popular X-Files episodes such as "Beyond the Sea" and "Humbug" (to name a couple) produced, and it was that willingness to push the envelope that set the show apart from all of its imitators. "What I think is wonderful about The X-Files is that it's like four or five different TV series," actor David Duchovny notes. "And yet it is one. That's what I always thought was the real strength of the frame that Chris was able to develop."

SEASON EIGHT *THE NEW X-FILES*

With David Duchovny at the end of his contractual obligation, *The X-Files* now faced its most serious challenge since the move to Los Angeles. "It was tough to pull out, because I didn't want the show to end," Duchovny explains. "I worked up a compromise with Chris where if I appeared in half of season eight, they would be able to take it in this next direction, and eventually we would spin it off into movies."

To fill the void, Carter created a new character, Special Agent John Doggett, though the idea of Doggett was definitely *not* to replace Mulder. "The fans were going to have a reaction to anyone that we brought in, so we didn't want someone who would be considered to be a love interest," Carter explained. "What we got from Chris was that Doggett was a meat-and-potatoes cop, and he did not believe in the paranormal," Vince Gilligan recalls. "But he was not some stooge of the Cigarette-Smoking Man or part of the greater government conspiracy either."

Robert Patrick, best known for his portrayal as T-1000 in James Cameron's *Terminator 2* had read for *Harsh Realm* and was now looking for a meaty TV role. He had a connection to *The X-Files* through his brother Richard, whose band *Filter* had contributed a song to the *Fight the Future* soundtrack. "I had done *The Sopranos*, and it's pretty much where the idea to do television came from for me," Patrick recounts.

"We had considered Christian Slater, but that wasn't going to happen," Rick Millikan says. "We looked at Patrick Dempsey, Lou Diamond Phillips; we looked at D.B. Sweeney; we looked at Dominic Purcell, Bruce Campbell, Hart Bochner. Esai Morales. We looked at Craig Sheffer …"

Robert Patrick got the job as soon as he entered the audition room.

"When Robert walked in the door, I think we all just said, 'This is him. This is John Doggett,'" John Shiban recalls. "If you're going to ever walk into the lead role on a television series, this is a great show," Patrick says today. "The character was me, and there was just no way I WASN'T going to do it."

"He is great, and he brought the right kind of energy," Gillian Anderson exclaims. "It wasn't the same, and it was never going to be the same, but this direction was as good as it could get without being the same." A vocal minority on the newsgroups wasn't as thrilled with the choice. "To be honest with you, I wasn't the kind of guy that ever checked out the internet," Patrick says. "People were in an uproar when it was announced I was doing the show, and it really made me go, 'Wow.'"

"Within" introduces Special Agent Doggett, who is assigned as task force leader in search of Mulder. Skinner and Scully are under suspicion, as associate director Kersh believes that there is some larger plot at work.

Aware of the opposition that Patrick would be facing among some in the fan community, Carter wrote a scene in which Doggett attempts to deceive Scully into thinking that he knew Mulder. Scully realizes the deception and indignantly hurls a cup of water into Doggett's face. "It's my favorite scene I ever shot," for the series, Patrick says today. "I couldn't think

TOP LEFT: May I offer you a drink of water? Scully meets her new partner in Robert Patrick's Agent John Doggett in the Season Eight opener, "WITHIN"; In an iconic *X-Files* image, the aliens have their way with the abducted Mulder, unbeknownst to his friends on Earth, thanks to some spectacular makeup by John Vulich; Kim Manners goes over the all-important meet-and-greet scene with Patrick and Anderson.

of a better way to introduce this character, and it says so much. And it actually helped me, I think."

"Robert Patrick did a great job, he was a great guy to work with — and talk about a handicap to come into a series like that," Braidwood says. "He made his own character out of it, and I think one of my favorite scenes, still, of all the years, is when he and Scully first meet."

"Without" brings the action to the Arizona desert. Scully and Skinner, the FBI and the Alien Bounty Hunter are all searching for Gibson Praise, who has taken refuge in a school for the deaf. It was a bad time to be shooting in the desert. "The whole sequence with Gibson Praise out in the desert happened to take place during an incredible heat wave," Paul Rabwin recalls.

"My wife was going to give birth to my son, and I had told them that when we started," Patrick remembers, "There were some helicopters that were involved in the shots, and they had put it out to me that they were willing to, at the drop of a hat, fly me and get me there. It really endeared those guys to me even more."

"Patrick is great, and he brought the right kind of energy. It wasn't the same, and it was never going to be the same, but it was about as good as it gets."
—Gillian Anderson

When the Kim Manners-directed two-parter was completed, Robert Patrick recalled that "Chris screened it at the Academy of Television Arts and Science out there in North Hollywood, and they put them back-to-back, and they held it up on the big screen like a feature film. It really made me feel proud, because a lot of effort went into those two episodes."

With Rob Bowman gone, Carter's other star director handled both episodes. "Kim Manners is just an incredible director," Patrick marvels. "He's one of my favorite people. He's got amazing energy; he understands not only what he wants to do with the camera but what is going on with the actor."

"Patience" begins a run of back-to-basics stand-alones that return to the darkness and intensity of the earlier season. Written and directed by Chris Carter, "Patience" has Scully and Doggett investigating a series of murders by a human-bat hybrid, reminiscent of the '70s Batman villain, Man-Bat.

Scully and Doggett meet a recent widower who has been hiding for 40 years from the creature, along with his recently deceased wife. "This is where it starts to toy with my willingness to believe in the paranormal and strange happenings," Patrick explains. "You've got a guy that's a bat, which is sort of out of the norm."

"Roadrunners" features an uncharacteristically brutal Vince Gilligan script about a desert-dwelling cult that believes a parasitic slug is the second coming of Jesus. Scully investigates on her own and is taken hostage by the cult. In one harrowing scene, Scully is seized by the cultists and pleads for her unborn child's life while the slug burrows into her back. She then writhes in agony as the slug moves up her spine toward her brain.

"It was a fun scene to shoot," Anderson recalls. "That was exhausting, though, struggling on that bed for so long. Not hogtied, but tied down, my arms to the headboard and my legs to the footboard." It wasn't fun for everyone. Paul Rabwin recalls that he had "cameramen start to lose it" over the gruesome effects. Scully is then rescued by Doggett.

"I wanted to have this gangbusters episode, one that showed how Doggett was a good guy; someone to be counted on and who could be trusted by

OPPOSITE TOP LEFT: Agent Doggett comforts a shaken Scully after her confrontation with an alien replicant of A.D. Skinner; Doggett has a hard time convincing Skinner and Scully that he has just seen Scully's missing partner; Mulder—or is it?—with Gibson Praise (Jeff Gulka); The faux Mulder will survive this fall from a cliff, as will that broken arm—another fine makeup effect; A desert-hot Chris Carter gives Anderson her marks. **ABOVE LEFT:** On the set of "ROADRUNNERS", Gillian Anderson and cast work out her induction as host to the slug; The REAL killer—Cesar Ocampo (Danny Trejo)—from Steve Maeda's "REDRUM"; Doggett checks out the body of a fellow agent killed during surveillance on a cult group in Pittsburgh in Frank Spotnitz's eerie "VIA NEGATIVA"; Doggett and Skinner visit the mass suicide scene; Scully and Doggett at an accident scene —car vs. pedestrian—where the victim walked away but the car didn't in Jeffrey Bell's "SALVAGE"; Scully and Doggett discuss the evidence with Joe Morton's Martin Wells in "REDRUM"; Doggett and Skinner find yet another victim in "VIA NEGATIVA". The episode featured top notch acting by Patrick, as a terrified Doggett unable to tell if he is awake or dreaming.

TOP LEFT: Robert Patrick enjoys a laugh on the set of "SALVAGE"; A subway patron from Medusa who didn't complete his ride; An expert horror makeup job by special effects makeup artist Clinton Wayne; Doggett meets his own informer character, Knowle Rohrer, in "PER MANUM"; The Soul Eater (played by Jordan Marder) from "THE GIFT"; Doggett "rescues" a cured Marie Hangemuhl, healed by the Soul Eater; The rarely shaken Agent John Doggett from "MEDUSA".

Scully," Gilligan explains, adding that Scully "apologizes for not trusting him and for cutting him out of the loop. And he says, 'You're right; you screwed up.' Apparently, the fans were really angry at how, in their mind, condescending Doggett was and how their heroine, was suddenly being dressed down by this interloper."

Robert Patrick offers his interpretation of the exchange: "The whole essence of the scene was, 'Look, I'm here for you. I've got your back. We're partners now.' And you give that the weight of a Marine saying to someone, 'I'll jump on a grenade for you, so you can trust me.' The idea was to really reassure the fans that the show was continuing on."

"Invocation" is a harrowing ghost story in which a kidnapped boy returns home ten years after his abduction—but has not aged. The case has a deep personal resonance with Doggett, as a psychic reveals that the agent's own son was kidnapped and murdered some years before. "A very important arc, because you start to see the vulnerability of the Doggett character, what drives him," Patrick says. "That's where we first realize something's happened to him. There's a tragedy that's involved with him."

"Badlaa" — known to fans as the infamous "Butt Genie" episode — is a thriller about an Indian fakir who, seeking revenge on employees of a company responsible for a deadly chemical accident, crawls into his victims' bodies through their rectums.

John Shiban recounted the development of "Badlaa" in 2003: "My original idea was a beggar with no legs who can actually shrink himself and climb inside your ear, and Chris Carter—and this is why he's Chris Carter—said 'No, no, no! I know what's even better.'"

"The Gift" is a Doggett solo outing that focuses on the Native American myth of the Soul Eater, a healer who eats his sick victims and regurgitates them healed. Doggett investigates and discovers that Mulder sought out the Soul Eater to cure his brain disease. Doggett is later killed by an angry mob and resurrected by the creature, which allows the long-suffering Soul Eater himself to die.

Frank Spotnitz explains his approach to morality tales like "The Gift": "If you're going to depart from literal reality as most of us know it, if you're going to go into the supernatural—as a writer you have to ask yourself

"There are characters who can be powerful as absent centers, as Mulder was through the eighth and ninth seasons." —Chris Carter

"Redrum" is a *Twilight Zone*-type thriller guest starring Joe Morton as a corrupt district attorney accused of murdering his wife, who is living his life in reverse time. "Joe Morton is a fantastic actor," Patrick says. "We never worked together in *T2*, but we're in that movie together. And Joe was *The Brother from Another Planet* (the 1984 John Sayles sci-fi film).

"Via Negativa" teams Skinner and Doggett to investigate psychic murders involving a drug cult. During their case, Doggett begins to experience disturbing hallucinations. "We were clicking on all cylinders on that one," Patrick says proudly.

"We were eager to get Skinner out from behind the desk, and we were always looking for opportunities to get him out of that office and get him into the field," Spotnitz says. "Seasons eight and nine were actually really liberating because, with Mulder gone, it was a lot easier to create opportunities for Skinner."

"It was a big hole when Mulder was gone," Pileggi says. "But I thought that Robert came in and did a wonderful job. He brought a really good energy to the set, and it was a lot of fun getting to know and work with him."

"Surekill" deals with a pair of brothers—one blind, the other with superhuman vision—who go into the drugs-and-murder business. Robert Patrick's biker buddy Michael Bowen guest stars, which gave the already energetic actor a boost on the set.

"Robert was like an Energizer Bunny," Anderson recounts. "He was just *wound* and wouldn't unwind until the day was done, no matter how long the day went. So that picked up the energy of the series, in a sense."

"Salvage" focuses on a worker at a disposal facility seeking revenge after being infected with a nonbiological disease that turns him into metal. It was around this time that Patrick recalls feeling comfortable in his new role. "We started seeing our numbers. Our numbers were good, and everyone was happy," Patrick recalls.

'Why? What's the purpose? What's the reason?' And, if you don't really have a point or a reason, your story's probably not going to be very good."

Gillian Anderson says today that she appreciated the time off that these Doggett-centric episodes offered her. "I had a very strict schedule with my daughter. She was in school up in Canada, and I was determined that they respect that I would work for three weeks and then have two or three weeks off to go and be with her. So they agreed to that, and that was important to me. I'd never had that before on the show."

"Medusa" follows Doggett through the Boston subways system as he tries to find the source of a deadly contagion before an impatient police chief gets the trains rolling again. "There was a huge budget on this one," Patrick marvels. "They got us in there, and we did it, and they built a huge subway tunnel set on a soundstage. It was the biggest damned thing I'd seen in my life."

For the second half of season eight, *The X-Files* would essentially become a serial drama, with the return of Mulder, the introduction of a new agent and the drama surrounding Scully's pregnancy.

The first installment was **"Per Manum"**, which introduces the character of Duffy Haskell (played by Jay Acovone), a man with a dubious history who reveals that Scully's obstetricians are also involved in the experiments implanting alien fetuses into woman seeking fertility treatments.

As Doggett and Scully investigate Haskell's claims, Mulder appears in a series of flashbacks dealing with Scully's prior attempts at conceiving. "There are characters who can be powerful as absent centers, as Mulder was through the eighth and ninth seasons," Carter says.

The episode also features the introduction of Adam Baldwin as military intelligence operative Knowle Rohrer, who would become Doggett's Deep Throat—and his Cigarette-Smoking Man. Robert Patrick says of Baldwin: "Every once in a while, you come in, and there's somebody raising the bar up there a level, and I remember him being like that."

Throughout the episode, we see Doggett begin to figure out Scully's secret, culminating in an emotionally powerful scene in which he confronts Scully about keeping her pregnancy from him. "You could tell that he really cared about Scully, but you didn't get the sense that he wanted to take advantage of that," Anderson says of Doggett. "I think they did themselves a huge favor by casting him as that character. And I think that they really mapped out the course of the relationship with Doggett very carefully and very thoughtfully."

"It took several episodes to grow comfortable with each other. Chris chose not to bring someone in who would be buddy-buddy with Scully, because I think that would have offended the audience," Kim Manners explains.

"**This Is Not Happening**" brings back a whole host of characters from the mythology—including Fox Mulder. Doggett, Scully, and Skinner travel to Montana after one of the original abductees from the pilot episode is found left for dead. The young UFO buff Richie Szalay reappears, following UFO reports and looking for his missing friend Gary. Jeremiah Smith also resurfaces, now in league with a UFO cultist named Absalom. Together they are helping to heal the mutilated abductees and prevent an alien virus from transforming them into Body Snatcher-like replicants.

Anticipating Gillian Anderson's possible departure at the end of the season, Annabeth Gish was introduced as Special Agent Monica Reyes. Stumped by the bizarre nature of the case, Doggett brings Reyes onboard because of her specialty in investigating ritual crime. "This is very significant because it's the first glimpse that I would possibly look for something that's a bit unconventional to help solve a case," Patrick says.

"As much as Robert Patrick was unlike Mulder, we needed someone who was equally unlike Scully." —Chris Carter

Reyes' presence on the show would complete the gender role reversal Carter had created with Mulder and Scully. "As much as Robert Patrick was unlike Mulder, we needed someone who was equally unlike Scully," said Carter. "With Monica they wanted an external kind of radiance," Gish explains. "Chris really wanted Monica to be a sunny force, which is hard to play sometimes. But it's a natural instinct for me; I can find happiness in the midst of darkness."

John Shiban explained in 2005 that "It was a big challenge to deal with David Duchovny's departure in season eight, and, in a way, we brought in both Doggett and Reyes to kind of get both sides of Mulder's personality."

The casting process for Reyes was unconventional. "I got a call from my agent. He said they were looking for a new female in *The X-Files*," Gish recalls. "The first time it wasn't even a reading. It was just a meeting with Chris and Frank."

"It came to Daphne Zuniga, Annabeth, and Stacy Edwards," Rick Millikan remembers, "Nobody had any material. It was all just meeting people. I didn't know what Chris was really looking for."

The preemptive online attacks against Robert Patrick were obviously fresh in everyone's minds. "Chris advocated my not getting too familiar with anything." Gish says today, "His thing was 'Don't go online.' I'm sure he was just trying to safeguard me from the criticisms they all knew would come my way."

"This Is Not Happening" ends with Mulder's body found in the woods and Jeremiah Smith beamed aboard a hovering ship before he can revive Mulder.

Following this episode, *The X-Files* went on a five-week hiatus and *The Lone Gunmen* spin-off series premiered in that time slot. The series was a

OPPOSITE TOP LEFT: Absalom (Judson Scott) watches as Jeremiah Smith (Roy Thinnes) heals a woman abandoned by the aliens after experiments in "THIS IS NOT HAPPENING"; Meet Agent Reyes: Annabeth Gish's first appearance as Special Agent Monica Reyes; Doggett introduces Scully and Skinner to their new colleague. **ABOVE:** Scully doesn't know whether to be elated or scared after Mulder is found semi-alive in his coffin; Scully and Skinner attend Mulder's burial; A bloated Billy Miles pulled from the sea returns to life; The Black Oil is nowhere near the pipeline in Steve Maeda's "VIENEN". Scully discovers that attempting to keep Mulder alive with life support only helped incubate the alien virus which was trying to transform him into a Super Soldier; The Lone Gunmen bow their heads at the funeral of Fox Mulder; Even Kersh and Doggett pay their respects.

SEASON EIGHT

In this episode Mulder might have been a Greek chorus of sorts, designed to help the audience feel at ease with Doggett.

labor of love for Spotnitz, Shiban, and Gilligan, and would air in the good ol' Friday night at nine slot, but sadly, it would not be renewed for a second season.

Tom Braidwood recalls how he heard of the plans for the series: "I got a call from Dean. He said, 'You should go down and get the daily *Variety*.' So I did, and there was this article about how Fox had let it slip that they were going to do a *Lone Gunmen* pilot for a potential *Lone Gunmen* series, and that's the first we had heard about it." Bruce Harwood says this was par for the course with Ten Thirteen. "They always left it to the last minute to let us know," Harwood laughs.

"That came about because we were all fans of the characters," Gilligan recounts. "We thought there was enough interest there for a spin-off to *The X-Files*. And, unfortunately, in the long term, there wasn't."

"We loved doing that show. The crew loved it. The actors were having the time of their life," Spotnitz says, lamenting. "It was a joy from beginning to end. I think it was just too late in the life of *The X-Files*. The wave had already crested. If we had done it three or four years earlier, it probably would have turned out differently."

"Deadalive" opens with Billy Miles (from the series pilot) being pulled out of the ocean by a fishing crew. When it is discovered that Miles is miraculously still alive, Skinner has Mulder, who was buried earlier in the episode, exhumed. Mulder's coffin is opened, and we see that he, too, is still alive, albeit imperceptibly. "That's a photo double with a mask of David Duchovny," Cheri Medcalf said of the exhumation in 2003, "It was a brilliant job because no one knew that."

British director Tony Wharmby joined the team in time to helm "Dead Alive". Robert Patrick says of Wharmby, "He's a wonderful man. Very articulate, knew his way around, what he wanted to do, and how he wanted to tell a story. You really felt like you were part of something."

It is then discovered that an alien virus is gestating inside both Miles and Mulder. In a memorably gruesome scene, Miles rises from his deathbed, showers away his bloated flesh, and emerges as an alien replicant. Krycek resurfaces, offers Skinner a vaccine (which he had stolen from the Russians in "Terma") to prevent Mulder's metamorphosis, and demands that Skinner

ABOVE: Mulder and Doggett finally come to an understanding in "VIENEN"; Mulder just can't stay away from the office—even if he no longer works there; Agent Mulder. RIGHT: The Black Oil pours from an oil worker in "VIENEN"; Resting comfortably: a pregnant Scully takes it easy; Mulder bears a gift for his pregnant friend in "EMPEDOCLES"; Doggett and Mulder working together; "ALONE"'s Salamander Man (Jay Caputo); Caputo as the Salamander Man suit is being developed; Doggett follows the trail in "ALONE". David Duchovny, Robert Patrick, writer Steven Maeda and director Rod Hardy watch playback of an oil derrick scene on the set of "VIENEN"; Robert Patrick with his "ALONE" writer/director, Frank Spotnitz.

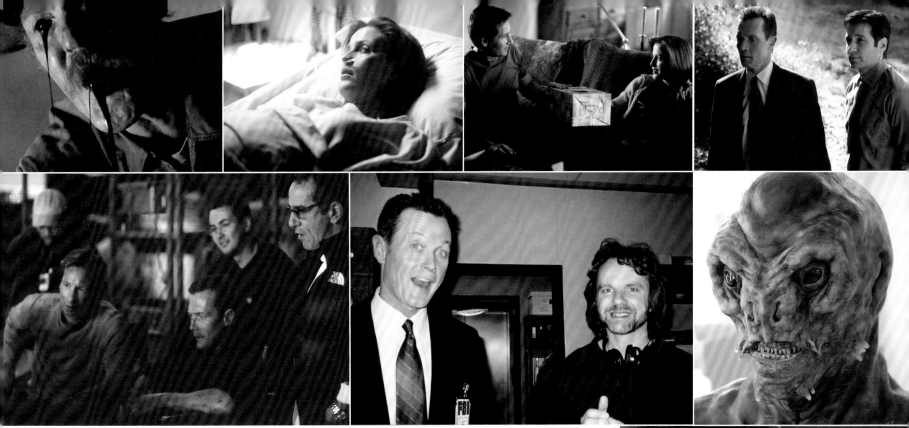

terminate Scully's pregnancy in return. It later will be revealed that Scully's baby is prophesied to play an important part in the alien colonization.

"You have to feel for a bad guy on some level," Nicholas Lea explains. "You have to understand why he's doing what he's doing. If he's just twirling a mustache, then that's boring. And, you know, the same thing is true for a hero. The flawed heroes, in my mind, are the only good ones."

"Three Words" is a trademark *X-Files* thriller that delves into the emerging phenomenon of the new human-replacements. Following the death of one of his followers, Absalom escapes from prison and kidnaps Doggett at gunpoint in order to prove the growing conspiracy to him. After Absalom is killed by a death squad, Mulder is set up for assassination by Knowle Rohrer.

As the season wound down, Mulder was refused readmittance to the FBI, and the drama began to focus on establishing the new agents. "I completely thought it was correct that they should be trying to focus elsewhere, and that, since I was going to come back for the second half of season eight, if you were to refocus on whatever Mulder's up to, you'd be in the same lousy situation at the beginning of season nine," Duchovny says today.

"Empedocles", which focuses on the idea of evil as a contagion, reintroduces Monica Reyes and deals with back story of the murder of John Doggett's son. Monica acts as peacemaker between Mulder and Doggett, and glimmers of Reyes' attraction to her future partner are revealed. "We're not going to try to duplicate it, we're not going to try to regenerate that magic chemistry," Patrick says of the emerging dynamic. "However, I will say that Gillian and I had our own chemistry that was unique unto itself, and likewise with the addition of Annabeth. It was different."

"Vienen" teams up Mulder and Doggett to investigate an outbreak of the Black Oil virus on a drilling rig in the Gulf of Mexico. Robert Patrick sees the episode as way to have Mulder give Doggett his blessing and pass him *The X-Files* baton. "That's how clever those guys are; they are aware of what's going on in the audience's head," Patrick says admiringly. "In this episode, Mulder might have been a Greek chorus of sorts, designed to help the audience feel at ease with Doggett."

Written and directed by Frank Spotnitz, **"Alone"** teams Doggett with a

"We call it the miracle of life; conception, a union of
perfect opposites. Essence transforming into existence,
an act without which man would not exist and humanity
cease to exist. Or is this just nostalgia now? An act of
biology commandeered by science and technology? God-like
we extract, implant, inseminate and we clone. But has our
ingenuity rendered the miracle into a simple trick? In the
artifice of replicating life, can we become the creator?
Then what of the soul? Can it too be replicated? Does it
live in this matter we call DNA or is its placement the
opposite of artifice, capable by God? How did this child
come to be? Let's set its heart beating. Is it the product
of a union or the work of a divine hand? An answered
prayer? A true miracle? Or is it a wonder of technology and
the intervention of other hands? What do we want to tell
this child about to be born? What do I tell Scully? What do
I tell myself?"

-Mulder from **Essence** (8x20)

> "The tears were just rolling down their faces, and the whole crew stood there and watched this in silence. It was truly one of the most emotional experiences I've ever witnessed in my life." —Kim Manners on the final scene between Mulder and Scully

temporary partner, the ditzy Leila Harrison, who idolizes Mulder and Scully from her accounting department perch. Mulder, now a private citizen, must rescue Doggett and Harrison when they are abducted by a shape-shifting reptilian. "She was the fan of The X-Files being let in to be a part of The X-Files, and to go through it with them," Patrick says of the Leila character.

Patrick was pleased with Spotnitz's first turn at the helm. "You're talking about some incredibly intelligent individuals, and they were very willing to let you, as an artist, discover what they were trying to do with the role," Patrick says. "That's a wonderful environment to work in."

The season would come to a close with two more entries in the ongoing mythology.

In **"Essence"**, the alien genetic experiments unveiled in "Per Manum" are revisited. Billy Miles returns as a full-fledged Super Soldier, and begins killing off doctors connected to the old Syndicate conspiracy. Duffy Haskell also resurfaces, acting as handler for a spy (played by Frances Fisher) who is posing as Scully's nursemaid. As the threat of Billy's transformation is revealed, Alex Krycek reappears and explains the new phase of alien colonization.

Nicholas Lea explains the evolution of Krycek's motivations: "Toward the end, he realizes that it's possible that the world could completely go down the tubes—then he's got a stake in trying to keep that from happening. That's when he starts giving the information to Mulder so that he can use it."

"Existence" has Reyes secretly taking Scully to Doggett's hometown in Georgia to give birth away from any threat, conspiracy, or alien. Back at the FBI building, Skinner, Doggett, and Mulder themselves deal with the new alien threat, later battling with Knowle Rohrer and Agent Crane, who themselves are Super Soldiers. Throwing in his lot with Knowle, Krycek betrays Mulder but is killed by Skinner. Super Soldiers arrive at Scully's hideout to attend William's birth, recognizing his alien origin but uncertain what it means for the future colonization.

A memorable moment in the episode has Reyes serenading Scully with her karaoke rendition of a whale's mating call. "Chris gave me a tape of whale songs, which was hysterical to be playing in my trailer," Gish recalls. "I'll never forget, either, that as I'm delivering the baby, they were putting cottage cheese and grape jelly in my hands as special effects of afterbirth."

Extra money was budgeted for the special effect of the bullet that kills Krycek, "When they came to me and told me that I was the one that was going to kill Krycek, I was elated," Mitch Pileggi remembers. "Not because I wanted Nick to go away or anything, it was just from a character standpoint; Skinner just wanted to kill Krycek so bad."

"Krycek really was just a creep, and you really should just hate him," Spotnitz says. "And yet there's something about Nick Lea and the way he plays it that you sort of liked him. I didn't want to see him die. I was hoping he would find a way to squeak through, as amoral as he was."

"It's a great visual effect, and it's a great scene to be able to play, getting shot in the head," Lea says. He adds, "But there was some kind of groveling going on in the end," though Krycek's impromptu Russian arm surgery in "Terma" would prove his downfall. "That was my thing, to try to grab the gun, but I couldn't because my fake hand wouldn't work."

The episode ends with Scully returning home. She and Mulder kiss as they hold William, portrayed by none other than John Shiban's then-newborn son Jerry.

"It was really a special moment to have him brought on set and to have Mulder and Scully, the characters who I had lived with so long to be holding this little baby," Shiban said proudly in 2003. "Here we were giving everyone what they had longed for, what they had been teased about and cheated out of in the movie," Carter said of the kiss. "We gave the real thing here. It was hot."

David Duchovny was now finished with Fox Mulder. It was unclear if either Chris Carter or Gillian Anderson would themselves be back the next season. Carter vowed to return if Anderson stayed on. The actress was offered a generous incentive by Fox to stay another year and took it.

"It was clear that he was done," Anderson says of Duchovny. "And it was obvious that it was better that he was happy with where he wanted to be, and that would benefit everybody."

TOP LEFT: "ESSENCE/EXISTENCE": Frances Fischer plays Lizzy Gill, recommended by Scully's mom as a nursemaid, but with an agenda of her own; Super Soldier Billy Miles; Krycek tells the team about the unstoppable Super Soldiers—sound familiar Robert?; Nick Lea in the makeup department prepares for his final shot of the series; The demise of Alex Krycek; Reyes sings whale songs to Scully in the safety of a mountain hideaway; Skinner with a very pregnant Agent Scully; Robert Patrick chats with Kim Manners on the fertility clinic set; Mulder and Doggett plan their visit to the fertility clinic; Losing one's head: the result of crossing paths with Billy Miles.

SEASON NINE *THE TRUTH AND THE END*

The "Nothing Important Happened Today" two-parter is a typically eventful season-opener. Following a battle with Knowle Rohrer and Agent Crane at the FBI building at the end of season eight, Mulder goes underground. Doggett and Reyes take over the X-Files office while Scully cares for her newborn son. And an anonymous tip reveals a conspiracy to add chemicals to drinking water to aid in the gestation of the new human-alien hybrids.

An old Marine buddy of Doggett's named Shannon McMahon enters the mix, played by none other than Xena herself, Lucy Lawless. "I had seen her at a couple different functions, and she had come up to me and told me she was a fan of the show," Carter said of the actress. "So when we approached her, she was game." The cast and crew, particularly Robert Patrick, enjoyed working with Lawless. "We did a little mouth-to-mouth resuscitation underwater," Patrick jokes, "I think I blew take after take on that."

Also introduced was FBI Assistant Director Brad Follmer (who took his name from Chris Carter's assistant), who was brought onboard to help flesh out Monica Reyes' back story. British actor Cary Elwes played Follmer, bringing a certain ambiguity and aloof quality, fitting for the role.

With Gillian Anderson hanging in for one more season, the new skeptic/believer paradigm would be complicated for the writers. "What became trickier was writing for Annabeth Gish's character," Vince Gilligan notes. "With three characters, you want three different points of view and that's not always possible in any given argument."

The Super Soldiers conspiracy formed the basis of the mythology in this season, which was intended to bring an action/adventure feeling to the show, more in keeping with the new Doggett character. "What's so terrifying about those situations is that the attacker is without a conscience," Spotnitz says of the Super Soldier episodes. "There's no appeal. There's nothing but escape or be destroyed."

With Chris Carter and Gillian Anderson set to exit at the end of season nine (Carter didn't come back aboard until this season opener was in preproduction), the intention was to ultimately wrap up the Mulder and Scully story line and introduce more supernatural elements into the show, had there been a season ten. "We kind of felt 'This is a new series; this is a new beginning,'" John Shiban comments. But for a lot of fans, these new elements—and the new characters—were (somewhat unfairly) seen as an unwelcome intrusion.

"David Duchovny had left the show for his own personal reasons," Gilligan says. "Robert and Annabeth were *hired* to play these roles. It's not like they came in and took the job away from David, but, boy, you couldn't

"I had a secret crush on Annabeth. I'm a happily married guy, but she's quite an eyeful," Patrick laughs, adding, "and on Gillian, for that matter!"

TOP LEFT: What cadaver? A.D. Brad Follmer thought he'd caught Reyes and Scully performing an unauthorized autopsy at the lab in Quantico in "NOTHING IMPORTANT HAPPENED TODAY"—only problem is, no body. . . ; Scully explains to students at the FBI Training Academy in Quantico, Va. what an X-File is in "DAEMONICUS"; Writer/director Frank Spotnitz works with his cast in the Quantico lecture hall; Settled right in: Scully and new colleague, Monica Reyes; Super Soldier Shannon McMahon (Lucy Lawless) gives Doggett a little breath of fresh air in "NOTHING II"; Shannon gives Scully the low-down on her baby, William; Kim Manners gives direction to Robert Patrick on the Quantico lab set in "NOTHING".

"There's some burning within Gillian that really comes across on screen. She is brilliant, and she brings so much; the camera loves her."
—Kim Manners

tell that from reading the exchanges on the Internet. It was as if people took it very personally that Mulder was no longer in the show and took it out on Robert and Annabeth. I felt sorry for them because they were just giving it 110 percent and doing a great job."

But the cast and crew would find themselves struggling with thornier issues than fan discontent. Exactly two months before the premiere of the new season, the world was shaken by 9/11, the worst terrorist attack on American soil in history. Production of the show was thrown into chaos by the attacks, and the sudden shift in the country's mood may well have sounded the death toll for the series.

In fact, the Internet would soon be ablaze with conspiracy theories dealing with the fact that, just a few months earlier, the pilot episode of *The Lone Gunmen* featured a scenario where a cabal of war profiteers had commandeered a jet airliner and were planning to fly into the World Trade Center and blame it on terrorists. "On September 11, after the shock of what actually happened wore off, it suddenly dawned on me: this is like life imitating art," Vince Gilligan recalls.

The production of the occult thriller **"Daemonicus"** would coincide with the 9/11 attacks. Robert Patrick recounts that September morning: "The day before we were going to shoot that episode, the World Trade Center happened. And because I worked nights, my wife woke me up, and she said, 'I can't deal with this by myself. You have to get up.' And I went in, and CNN was on, and we watched as the South Tower went down. And I said, 'What the f**k's going on?' And she said, 'They think it's terrorists.'"

The plot of "Daemonicus" deals with a demon-possessed mental patient named Professor Josef Kobold, who was orchestrating a series of ritual crimes in order to trick the authorities into aiding in his eventual escape. On location at the University of California-Los Angeles (UCLA), Patrick found himself unable to focus on the demanding scenes with James Remar, who played Kobold. "It was the first time that I couldn't do my lines. Usually I would show up, and they'd always put the camera on me first because I'd nail my dialogue, and then they'd shoot the other people," Patrick remembers. "I really took a lot of pride in showing up prepared. And I couldn't do it. The dialogue was all about demonic possession, and it just was freaking me out."

"4-D" is an innovative science-fiction thriller about a psychopathic mama's boy who travels through dimensions to kill women. "We increasingly found ourselves

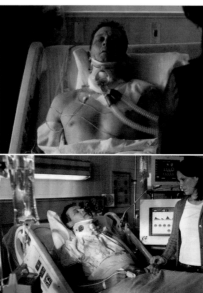

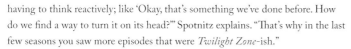

having to think reactively; like 'Okay, that's something we've done before. How do we find a way to turn it on its head?'" Spotnitz explains. "That's why in the last few seasons you saw more episodes that were *Twilight Zone*-ish."

In this episode, Reyes cares tenderly for a Doggett in another dimension, who's been paralyzed by a gunshot wound. "I came up with the shaving idea," Patrick says. "I'd read *The Diving Bell and the Butterfly*, and I believe there's a part of that in the book where the character gets shaved, and I thought, 'Wow, that's really an intimate kind of moment.'"

The episode also dealt with the developing relationship between Reyes and Doggett, who were less emotionally reserved than their predecessors. Still, the attraction was as tentative and unspoken as ever. "Chris was never big on the flamboyant big performance," Gish says. "So everything had to be held back regardless." Patrick enjoyed the flirtatious undercurrents. "I had a secret crush on Annabeth. I'm a happily married guy, but she's quite an eyeful," Patrick laughs, adding, "and on Gillian, for that matter!"

"Lord of the Flies" marked the return of the comedy episode, revisiting themes of genetic grafting experiments from "Travelers" in a humorous context. Jane Lynch guest stars as the overprotective mother of a human-insect hybrid.

I had a hard time with that episode," Patrick says. "I couldn't deal with some of the material. As an actor, I found some of it to be a little silly. Kim Manners directed this one, and I needed help; I relied on him a lot."

Though **"Trust No 1"** opens with a heart-wrenching montage of stills from earlier episodes showing tender moments between Mulder and Scully, Carter and Spotnitz's script is a prescient, cautionary tale about Orwellian surveillance. Terry O'Quinn returns as a Super Soldier who offers Scully secret information in a ploy to lure Mulder out of hiding.

Responding to fan complaints that season eight didn't deal enough with Mulder's abduction until Duchovny returned to the show, episodes such as "Trust No 1" would deal with Mulder's disappearance, which in and of itself didn't always sit well with the fans either. "The only thing that I thought we didn't do right during seasons eight and nine was that a lot of the shows were about Mulder, and I thought it was a mistake to make a series about a man that wasn't standing in front of the camera," Manners says today.

"John Doe" is a showcase for Doggett, who wakes in a dusty Mexican village with his memory erased. The story has the agent battling a drug cartel, and

TOP LEFT: Reyes tries to stop the cycle of skinning-alive deaths from continuing, as they have for generations, in David Amann's shocking "HELLBOUND"; Director Kim Manners and Robert Patrick go over a scene from the episode; Reyes views one of the dead; You've got a little mustard there, John: a tender scene between Reyes and Doggett in "4-D"; "I'm supposed to be dying in a hospital, but I'm here, too?" Kim Manners tries to help clarify the complicated storyline; Doggett takes a daring leap of faith—for a flatfoot: the only way out is to kill me; Welcome home, John.
RIGHT: The dashing Dr. Rocky Bronzino (Michael Wiseman) is caught in a web of intrigue in Thomas Schnauz's "LORD OF THE FLIES"; Not much there: a teen's brain appears to have been eaten away by flies; Doggett isn't going anywhere easily in "JOHN DOE"—even if he doesn't remember his own name; Co-Executive Producer Michelle MacLaren takes her turn behind the camera, directing Robert Patrick in the gritty "JOHN DOE", an episode which once again showcases Patrick's talents; Nestor (Ramón Franco) taunts Doggett, an amnesiac trapped in Mexico; Who's watching whom? Doggett and Reyes on surveillance for whomever has been following Scully in "TRUST NO 1"; The new *X-Files* team in action; MacLaren reviews lines with her cast.

Bill Roe borrowed motifs from Steven Soderbergh's *Traffic* for the set up. The village was constructed out of whole cloth especially for the shoot. "Every day I showed up, it was a mini-movie," Patrick says. "The budgets were incredible, the crews were incredible, the writers, everything was just wonderful."

The episode was directed by Michelle MacLaren. "It was the first time she had ever directed, and she did a great job," writer Vince Gilligan beams. "She really rose to the occasion and really did her homework."

MacLaren was fortunate that her "day job" as co-executive producer included prepping episodes with directors — a group that fortunately included Kim Manners and Chris Carter. "Kim taught me how he breaks down a script and prepares his shot list," she recalls. "The most powerful thing he said to me was that he imagines the show all cut together and sees the movie in his head and really visualizes it. That was a great help to me." Carter also offered his experience to his producer. "He said, 'Make sure the camera is always telling the story,' which was great advice."

The ongoing post-9/11 turmoil influenced Patrick's approach to his work. "I was really affected by what was going on outside the soundstages, and it might have helped me out quite a bit," he explains.

David Amann's **"Hellbound"** is an extremely explicit occult thriller about a serial killer who skins his victims alive. The subplot of the episode deals with reincarnation and the idea of karmic justice. The makeup for the victims was of a level of detail and sophistication never before seen on series television. "I have to give credit to Sheri Medcalf and the special-effects makeup guys," Patrick notes. "They literally did a 36-hour day to pull some of that off."

In **"Provenance"**, the first of a mytharc two-parter, the extent of William's powers are revealed when an FBI mole tries to murder him. The agent had been investigating a cult conspiracy revolving around a spaceship unearthed in Canada. Featuring Neal McDonough as the murderous FBI agent Robert Comer, "Provenance" returns to themes of ancient astronauts

and human origins explored in the **"Sixth Extinction"** two-parter.

Director Kim Manners noted that Gillian Anderson wasn't simply playing out her string in season nine; she still very much exuded the magnetic power she brought to the series. "There was something about Gillian that was very sexual," Manners says. "There's some burning within her that really comes across on screen. She really is brilliant, and she brings so much; the camera loves her."

"Providence" deals with the FBI manhunt after the UFO cult kidnaps William and asks for Mulder to be killed as ransom. Comer reveals that the cult believes that William will play a crucial role in the final alien invasion of Earth. "The baby's the Messiah. I don't understand any of it," Robert Patrick jokes. "I'm Episcopalian; I don't get it."

Chris Carter took the reigns and opened the proceedings with a harrowing flashback detailing Super Soldier involvement in a Gulf War firefight. "I think actually that Chris has directed some of our best episodes," Anderson says today. "He's very even tempered, and he's quiet and gentle and quite nice to have as a director, because that energy can't help but pervade the rest of the set as well. He's got a clear vision, and he's good at communicating that." Annabeth Gish agrees, "Chris Carter is very meticulous, in his directing and everything. He knows exactly what he wants."

"Audrey Pauley" sees the return of "Oubliette" guest star Tracey Ellis, who plays a mentally-handicapped nurses' aide whom Reyes encounters in a dreamlike state after the agent is involved in a serious car accident.

"Without sounding selfish, "4-D" and "Audrey Pauley" are my two favorite episodes," Gish explains, "because they are stand-alone episodes about Reyes and Doggett. Wonderful acting challenges, and the stories were fantastic."

This was another difficult shoot for Robert Patrick; during production he learned that director Ted Demme had died at the age of 39. "One of my close buddies died while I was making that episode, so I was kind of raw. I remember being a little worried about bringing too much emotion to it,"

BELOW LEFT: Meet the new boss: Doggett in the X-Files office—not always a popular sight for die-hard fans; Annabeth Gish and Robert Patrick pause between takes as the new investigative team on The X-Files. **RIGHT:** Provenance/Providence: That's not how you hold a baby, Tom: Kim Manners shows his former 1st Asst. Director what he's looking for in the scene; Cinematographer Bill Roe and director Chris Carter plan out shots for the scene in which Scully's mysterious baby is the lone survivor of a UFO cult experiment gone wrong; The only ones left we can trust: Scully turns William over to the Lone Gunmen—but even they can't protect him; Chris Carter directs Annabeth Gish in a hospital sequence where the agent visits the unconscious undercover man, Robert Comer; Scully's mysterious baby is the lone survivor of a UFO cult experiment gone wrong.

"One day you'll ask me to speak of a truth of the miracle of your birth, to explain what is unexplained and if I falter or fail on this day know there is an answer, my child, a scared imperishable truth but one you may never hope to find alone. Chance meeting your perfect other, your perfect opposite, your protector and endangerer. Chance embarking with this other on the greatest of journeys—a search for truth's fugitive and imponderable. If one day this chance may befall you, my son, do not fail or falter to seize it. The truths are out there and if one day you should behold a miracle, as I have in you, you will learn the truth is not found in science or on some unseen lane but by looking into your own heart and in that moment you will be blessed and stricken...for the truest truths are what hold us together, or keep us painfully, desperately apart."

-Scully's letter to her son William **Trust No One** (9x08)

"If we're going to get Burt Reynolds to do an episode, I want to create something specifically for him." —Chris Carter

Patrick remembers. "I felt safe with Kim; he knew I was going through a tough time."

"**Underneath**" tells the story of a deeply religious cable TV technician who shape-shifts into a brutal killer. The episode explores Doggett's background in the New York Police Department and revives themes explored on the *Millennium* series. Robert Patrick relished a chance to work again with his friend, Arthur Nascarella, who appeared in "Underneath" as Doggett's former partner. "I stole his New York accent in *Copland*, and I stole it to do *The X-Files*," Patrick explains, "but I got him cast in *The X-Files* show."

Chris Carter scored again with "**Improbable**", a humorous and innovative exploration of numerology and number mysticism featuring Burt Reynolds in the role of God. "I heard that Burt was really interested in doing an *X-File*," Robert Patrick says. "So somewhere in season nine, I said to Chris, 'Hey, Chris. What about Burt Reynolds coming to do an *X-File*?'" Carter was sold on the idea. Patrick adds, "Chris said, 'If we're going to get Burt Reynolds to do an episode, I want to create something specifically for him.'"

Carter's script returned to the metaphysical, spiritualist aspect of Reyes' character, which had been overlooked since "Existence." "I remember learning my lines and thinking, 'Oh, my God. I've got to memorize

this,'" Gish recalls. "It's scary. Like physics unified theory, all of that."

The cast and crew alike loved working with Reynolds, and the screen legend was treated like royalty on the set. "He had a great time, and he loved working with everybody," Patrick says. "Burt's the kind of guy who doesn't leave to go to his trailer between setups; he sits on the set. He loves making movies."

Gillian Anderson recounts that there was quite a waiting list of stars wanting to do *The X-Files*. "There were a few people over the years who wanted to be on the show, like Whoopi Goldberg. At one point, we were trying to get Tom Waits onto the show. Bruce Springsteen at one point wanted to."

Chris Carter speaks of the importance of the humorous novelty episodes, particularly in the pitch-black season nine: "It is the melody. There are the downbeats, and then you need that relief in the tension. And it makes the characters likable. Scully was always the straight man until she started getting her own comedy episodes."

"**Scary Monsters**" features the return of Leila Harrison, who refers the X-Files team to a psychotic young telepath who can create the illusion of giant killer insects. The show was significant for *The X-Files* cast and crew

OPPOSITE LEFT: Annabeth Gish with actor Stan Shaw in Steve Maeda's eerie "AUDREY PAULEY"—director Kim Manners's 50th *X-Files* episode; Scully watches over the comatose Monica Reyes **ABOVE:** Checkers it is: Film and television icon Burt Reynolds with Scully and Reyes in Chris Carter's classic, "IMPROBABLE"; Who's playing God now? Carter and Reynolds; God enjoys the beauty in numbers while Scully and Reyes while away the time playing checkers; Carter directing Reynolds on the back lot street at Universal Studios; Robert Patrick endures another chuckle from his friend Burt; The affable Reynolds joins the gang for a photograph at Universal on February 15, 2002.

"And he said, 'Walk with me. I wanted you to be the first to know; this is going to be the end.'" —Robert Patrick on Chris Carter

for another reason during its production; Chris Carter announced that *The X-Files* would end with this season.

Robert Patrick recalls when he heard the news: "We were halfway through season nine, and Chris came on the set and watched me shoot a scene. And he hadn't done that since the first scene I had shot. And when the scene was over, I said, 'Is everything all right?' And he said, 'Walk with me.' And we walked to my trailer, and in this very calm, Chris Carter way, he said, 'I wanted you to be the first to know; this is it.' I said, 'What do you mean this is it?' And he went, "This is going to be the end.'"

Patrick was devastated. It was then that he noticed that Fox's new series *24* was being heavily promoted by the network even though its ratings were not significantly better than *The X-Files*. "I was asking people, 'Boy, it seems like you're spending a lot of money promoting this *24*. What's going on with our show?'" Patrick recalls. "I vaguely remember getting the feeling like we had been abandoned by Fox. That's probably one of the reasons why Chris decided not to do it."

The home stretch of season nine would be dedicated to wrapping up the various story lines and mythologies, since the original intent was to begin work on a feature film later on in 2002. "Chris had told everybody well in advance that this was going to be the last season. So there was quite a buildup for the last half of the season to this final episode," Michelle McLaren recalled. "And we all knew we were part of something really, really big."

With the controversial **"Jump the Shark"**, threads unresolved from cancellation of *The Lone Gunmen* were wrapped up, ending in the trio's death. Michael McKean returned as Morris Fletcher, who found himself contending with a new X-Files team uninterested in UFO lore.

"*The Lone Gunmen* was still kind of an open wound for me," said Gilligan, who co-wrote the episode with Frank Spotnitz and John Shiban. "I was still very disappointed that it had been cancelled, that Fox had not given it another season."

Gilligan notes that Doggett "wasn't a comedian, but it was fun getting to write dry, sarcastic repartee whenever he'd be faced with some supernatural bugaboo or whatever." Neither was Doggett impressed with the Lone Gunmen. "I was impressed with those guys as actors. They had a real great energy," says Patrick. "But let's just say they weren't Marines."

The script had the Gunmen sacrificing themselves to prevent the outbreak of an engineered bioweapon. "*The Lone Gunmen* was so different from *The X-Files*, it was very hard to bring it all together, but I was glad we were killed off in the end," Bruce Harwood says. "Dean said it's either that or we walk off into the sunset with our hobo bags over our shoulders." The episode remains contentious, even among the staff. "To this day, I still think we made the wrong choice on that one," Gilligan laments.

David Duchovny returned to direct **"William"**, in which a horribly scarred Jeffrey Spender reappears trying to pass himself off as Mulder. Spender wanted to neutralize William's powers as revenge against government conspirators who experimented on him. The episode ends with Scully giving William up for adoption, realizing she can't protect him from alien conspiracy.

Chris Owens remembers getting the call to return to the fold: "I moved to Toronto. And then three years later, I got a call from David, out of the blue, saying, 'We're shooting the finale and the second-to-last episode, and I want to bring you back.' I said, 'But you shot me.' And he said, 'Alien injection—don't worry about it. It'll be fun. Well, it won't be fun for you; you'll be under all that shit,'" referring to the heavy special effects makeup required to transform him into "The Breather." "I thought, 'What is he talking about?' And then I get there, and I realize, 'Oh, my God!'"

"Release" features an FBI cadet with psychic abilities who directs Doggett to his murdered son, Luke's, killer. Doggett's feelings for Reyes are explored in light of Doggett's lingering wounds from the tragedy of his son's death.

ABOVE: Michael McKean returns as Morris Fletcher to harass the Lone Gunmen in the trio's final episode, "JUMP THE SHARK"; Frohike, Langly and Byers. RIGHT: Quite a team: Doggett with the Gunmen.

"'I want to bring you back.' I said, 'But you shot me.' And Chris said, 'Alien injection; don't worry about it.'" —Chris Owens

"We never really got the chance to because we ended the show, but I think Monica would have definitely gone further with their relationship," Gish says.

"Mulder's like a Byron, just kind of dark and brooding and troubled. Doggett was just as complicated a human being, but he just seemed more positive, more can-do," Gilligan observes. "He had this terribly tragic back story in that his son had been abducted and murdered."

"Sunshine Days" was Gilligan's valedictory script, which he also directed, featuring a telekinetic prodigy who immerses himself in a TV sitcom fantasy by psychically recreating the world of *The Brady Bunch* inside his home. "They built that *Brady Bunch* set from scratch, which was so astounding that we had people visiting from all over Los Angeles," Gilligan marvels. "People wanted to get their picture taken on *The Brady Bunch* set because *The Brady Bunch* set no longer exists."

"The last time I really watched television on a regular basis was when I was a teenager watching *Gilligan's Island* and *The Brady Bunch*," Gillian Anderson recounts. "So it was wild."

"That was goodbye to the audience, and goodbye to the characters, because I knew that would be the last time I'd ever be writing for them," Gilligan says sadly.

"The Truth" would usher *The X-Files* off the television screen with a bang. David Duchovny returned for the two-hour series finale in which Mulder breaks into a secret government complex and is accused of murdering Knowle Rohrer. A secret trial ensues in which most of the major supporting characters from the past nine seasons are called in to testify.

After Mulder is found guilty in what is obviously a show trial, Skinner and Doggett break him out, and Mulder and Scully escape to New Mexico. Then Mulder confronts the Cigarette-Smoking Man, who tells Scully that the final colonization is set for December 24, 2012. But the conspirators are hot on their heels, and Knowle Rohrer arrives, only to be destroyed by the mineral deposits that are Super Soldiers' Achilles' heel. The Cigarette-Smoking Man is then killed by a missile attack, which *The X-Files* agents escape in the nick of time. The episode ends

TOP LEFT: Scully is baffled by the disfigured Breather (Chris Owens) in "WILLIAM"; Director Duchovny advises his two stars; Patrick and Duchovny enjoy playback of a shot; Chris Carter drops by to see how his director is making out. **RIGHT:** Kim Manners with Robert Patrick—with Doggett's ex-wife, played by real-life spouse Barbara Patrick—as Doggett prepares to finally send the ashes of his long-dead son into the wind at Leo Carrillo State Beach in "RELEASE"; A light moment between takes for Patrick; The unusual Cadet Rudolph Hayes (Jared Poe); Here's the story of a man named Doggett. . . The agents talk with the Brady-obsessed Oliver Martin (Michael Emerson) in Vince Gilligan's "SUNSHINE DAYS", the final standalone *X-Files* episode. The set was built from plans borrowed from *Brady Bunch* (and *Gilligan's Island*) creator Sherwood Schwartz himself, who gave his blessing to the episode; Gilligan (center, in jersey)—whose uncanny name was not lost on the crew or Schwartz—directs the scene.

with Mulder and Scully spending a rainy night together in a hotel room locked in an embrace.

All the stops were pulled for the finale. "It's the end—you don't get another chance. So you'd better put everything you've ever wanted to put in into the episode," Carter explained in 2004. "There were things to distract from what was really going on," Carter added. "The band was breaking up."

"I just remember watching that footage come in on the series-ender there, and thinking this is never going to happen again because TV is constantly in a state of being downsized," Vince Gilligan laments.

Annabeth Gish was impressed by the production: "It did feel like a big movie set. We were on location, there was an enormous budget, and everyone came back."

Gillian Anderson recalls a bittersweet ending to her time on the show: "David and I wrapped at the same time, and we ended up having a water balloon fight. Someone had brought water balloons, so we had a big water fight between David and I and a couple crew members."

"At that point, I knew I was out of the series," William B. Davis says, "It was great that they brought us all back in the finale, that they found a way to get us all in again."

"I can remember the last day on the set. We shot a scene with Gillian and myself, and that was it. And then I had to say goodbye to another family, another crew," Mitch Pileggi recalls. "I almost teared up, and Gillian was standing there looking at me saying 'Okay, go ahead, big guy; get through this.' It was tough."

"It was pretty euphoric, and sad, and all those emotions you can imagine. A chapter's closing, and we're all moving on to something new and exciting," Patrick says. "And yet we were all going to miss each other."

Kim Manners recalls the final moment: "The last shot in the picture was Gillian handing David the baby in her bedroom. David leaned over and gave her a kiss, and the camera then pulled back out of the doorway and just kept going down the hall. We got the shot, and we cut it and printed it; the nurse came and took the baby away. And David put his arms around Gillian, and she put her arms around him, and they stood there for about 10 minutes, and never said a word to each other. The tears were just rolling down their faces, and the whole crew stood there and watched this in silence. It was truly one of the most emotional experiences I've ever witnessed in my life."

And so ended one chapter of *The X-Files* story.

David Duchovny looks back and explains that *The X-Files* was "something that hadn't really existed before on television, and I don't think has since. And that achievement is really due to a kind of loop between the writers and the actors pushing one another, and the hiring of new writers and the stretching of the same old actors wanting to do different things."

FOLLOWING PAGES: Gillian Anderson and David Duchovny ready themselves for more "coverage" for "THE TRUTH".

A day in the sun: the X-Files crew shoots the desert sequences for "THE TRUTH" in Anza-Borrego Desert.
OPPOSITE TOP LEFT: The end of The Cigarette-Smoking Man: Helicopters blast the Cigarette-Smoking Man's final lair; Kim Manners on an interior set; Manners reviews a model and storyboard sketches for the complicated helicopter sequence; Annabeth is ready for takeoff; Doggett and Reyes on the run; A joyful Annabeth Gish gives her director a pat on the back; The full *X-Files* crew poses for one final shot outside historic Stage 8—the home of the series since its move from Vancouver—at Twentieth Century Fox. **ABOVE:** Manners reviews a shot on the monitors with Robert Patrick and Annabeth Gish; The two agents try to stop Knowle Rohrer, though it is not their bullets which finally puts an end to the Super Soldier; Adam Baldwin's Rohrer begins to experience the effects of the surrounding geology, which puts an end to the creature; Gish, Patrick, Manners and crew hard at work in the springtime heat; Manners, posed with his ever-supportive wife, Marline, whom he in no small way credits with his success on the series.

TOP LEFT (left to right): Mulder has come to hear the final truth from a "wise man" in the desert—little does he know the wise man's identity; Gillian Anderson records her one memories of the day on a video camera; The two stars pose together on their last location day on April 26, 2002, just three weeks away from the air date of the series finale. Another good take: Duchovny and Patrick give a thumbs-up after watching a scene on playback; Keeping it cool: The stars take a rest between takes in Anza Borrego Desert. **RIGHT:** "Wait a minute, Bill, you got something plugging your stoma here. . . Kim Manners makes a minute adjustment to William B. Davis's adornment; "Wise Man" Cigarette-Smoking Man in his startling makeup for the finale; Gillian Anderson and David Duchovny drop in from the adjacent courtroom set to visit with Davis; Manners chats with Davis and the Cigarette-Smoking Man's keeper, played by Julia Vera; The Lone Gunmen, who make a ghostly cameo in the episode, are presented with a special "final issue" of *The Lone Gunmen* newspaper by Chris Carter.

"It was the end. The band was breaking up." —Chris Carter

Gillian Anderson agrees that the broad range of moods made *The X-Files* special. "That's what kept it fun, and that's what kept it worth doing all the time. At least there was enough variance between the episodes and when we had an opportunity to play that it shook it up and made it challenging. We were lucky that way."

After *The X-Files*, people would come to me and they'd say, 'Let's go do something that's more out there, more crazy, more wild than *The X-Files*,' and I would say, 'Guys, that's not the secret of *The X-Files*,'" David Nutter explains. "*The X-Files* was a very realistic setting, the people were real, and what they were going through were things that we could all understand."

"I don't know if there will ever be another *X-Files*. They were like movies every damn week," Mark Snow says, "It was the greatest job any composer could ever have."

"With the passing of *The X-Files*, a certain kind of television went away and will never return in my estimation," Gilligan says, mournfully.

"I don't know that a viewer can watch this series and really understand what it means to invest your life creatively into something this magnificent," Paul Rabwin said in 2005. "But it was a crowning achievement, and I will never, never forget that."

"*The X-Files* changed the way television looked," says Tom Braidwood. "It had a huge effect on TV then and TV since."

"It all got filtered through Chris; I don't care who the original writer was," Kim Manners observes. "Chris always put the polish on it, so the shows always had a unique voice, and that was Chris Carter's voice."

"There were so many incredibly talented people who came to work on that show who deserved all the credit they could get for their contributions, but it's a huge accomplishment to gather those people, and to give them a vision that they can serve, and Chris was so clear," Spotnitz notes. "He really just had an amazing vision for *The X-Files*, and it allowed all these talented people to come and do their best work."

"Everyone liked the show for different reasons. There are some people who liked the comedy episodes better than anything, and some who like the stand-alone episodes. And there are people who like the mythology episodes," Chris rter states. "There was something for everyone."

TOP LEFT: Kim Manners directs "THE TRUTH's" "judges," as Nicholas Lea and Steven Williams observe from behind; The disfigured Jeffrey Spender (Chris Owens) also makes an appearance; Kim Manners directs Duchovny and Owens in the scene; The beautiful Marita Covarrubias (Laurie Holden) also makes a return to come clean; Patrick and Manners confer.

RIGHT: David Duchovny has a last laugh in Mulder's jail cell, as Manners works with Mitch Pileggi, Robert Patrick and Annabeth Gish; Pileggi and Manners talk on an outdoor set—imagine what that director's chair is worth today. . . Mulder ponders his fate as Scully and Skinner look on; The episode's—and the series's—final scene finds Mulder and Scully cozy together in a motel. Shades of things to come . . . ; Annabeth Gish studies up on her lines as Kim Manners goes over the courtroom scene with David Duchovny and Mitch Pileggi; Manners works with Laurie Holden in the same scene; Kersh finally comes around and helps Mulder escape; Nicholas Lea and the judges panel (including James Pickens, Jr.'s Deputy Director Alvin Kersh) listen to Manners's direction for the scene; A somewhat confident Mulder thinks he has a plan for the trial, but the outcome is not in his hands.

PART 5

I WANT TO BELIEVE

DON'T GIVE UP *THE X-FILES RETURNS*

A new *X-Files* movie in 2008—so. . . . what took so long? The answer, as with all things *X-Files*, is complicated. Following the success in 1998 of *The X-Files: Fight the Future*, it was clear to everyone that *The X-Files* theatrical films were a good idea. "There was a sound business reason for doing another movie," says Chris Carter, "and we felt there were enough *X-Files* stories to tell that there might be at least one other movie," if not a whole series of movies.

The television series, at the time *Fight the Future* was released, was in its prime, having just finished airing season five a month before, the last season before the move to Los Angeles. The long-awaited feature film was a huge success and was followed later that year with another powerful season (six), which wrapped up the original mythology thread and paved the way for a new era of *The X-Files*: a new mythology and a significant change in cast and crew.

In October 2001, a month prior to the premiere of season nine's "Nothing Important Happened Today"—and three months before Carter decided the series would end with that season—Twentieth Century Fox executive Steve Asbell contacted Chris Carter and Frank Spotnitz. "He said, 'We'd like to do another movie,'" Spotnitz recalls. "But Chris and I both felt, 'Look, we have our hands full now with season nine of the show, and we've got these new characters of Doggett and Reyes we're dealing with,' so we just tabled it." That January, Carter announced that season nine would end *The X-Files* television series. "We still didn't talk about the movie because we were finishing up the series, and then we were just . . . tired."

The two took a break—but not for long. By the end of 2002 and early 2003, Carter and Spotnitz were already meeting in Frank's Beverly Hills office thinking "movie." The two hammered out their story idea and brought it to Asbell and Fox president Hutch Parker, who immediately gave the project a greenlight.

Then there was some business to attend to. Deals had to be struck with David Duchovny and Gillian Anderson, as well as with Carter, which took the better part of a year. "To my recollection, that was around 2004, and they were just about done," Spotnitz says. "David and Gillian's deals were finished, and Chris's was just about done, and then a legal issue came up from the studio of money from the TV series, and everything stopped." As the lawyers hammered out the details, time marched on. "By 2006, I thought this was never going to happen."

By January of 2007, the dispute was resolved, and, says Spotnitz, "Literally, the next day, the movie was back." From April to August, Carter and Spotnitz wrote the script, and then the pressure was on to produce the film. "Fox came to us and said, 'If you want to do this movie, it's now or never,'" recalls Carter. "'There's a looming writers' strike, and if we don't do it now, it could be two years until your movie is in theaters, depending on the length

"By 2006, I thought this was never going to happen." —Frank Spotnitz

TOP LEFT: Chris Carter watches as David Duchovny performs a scene at Mulder and Scully's home; The bearded hermit still wants to believe, but doesn't want to help, as Scully tries to convince him his services are needed by the FBI; Scully brings some bad news: Father Joe is dead; The audience's first view of their favorite nonbeliever—Scully listens in on a teleconference regarding the young Christian Fearon; Anderson pauses between takes of that very scene; An emotional scene between Mulder and Scully, as Mulder comes to the hospital to once again question Father Joe; Beard out, Mulder in: ASAC Whitney and Agent Drummy have a new lead to track from Father Joe. But where will it lead? FOLLOWING PAGE: Chris Carter gives Gillian Anderson some direction between takes in the teleconference scene early in the film.

"Stand-alone stories are what we did most of, and some people thought we did best." —Chris Carter

of the writers strike.' So we chose now over never."

"There was a period when it felt like it was going to happen, and then all of a sudden it stopped," Gillian recalls. "Then, eventually, I met David and Chris for lunch to talk about it. I had literally heard just two days before that that we might do it, and then, at lunch, they said we might start in July. Then they said 'This October,'" which eventually turned into December. Anderson had another film lined up for shooting at the end of 2007, *The Smell of Apples*, which was pushed into 2008, as well as another, *Helen*, which, coincidentally, was due to be filmed in Vancouver at the same time as *The X-Files* movie. "I ended up having to let go of that film," she says; Ashley Judd would end up taking her place.

Stand-Alone vs. Mythology?

Carter and Spotnitz came up with their original story for the new film in late 2002/early 2003. But before that could happen, a choice needed to be made: would the new movie be, like its predecessor, a further delving into *The X-Files* mythology, or would it be a stand-alone story—a single X-Files case? "It was never a question," says Spotnitz. "The studio wanted a stand-alone, and we wanted a stand-alone. The mythology was so complicated after nine years of the series that the thought of trying to revisit it in a straightforward way that would make sense to both fans and nonfans was daunting, frankly, and not even close to what we wanted to do."

"That was the plan from before we even finished filming the series," says Anderson, "that if we were going to do another film, it was going to be a stand-alone."

Explains Carter, "We have the luxury now of not having a television series on, so we don't have to actually worry about a running story line. And also, stand-alone stories are what we did most of, and some people thought we did best, so it was a chance to do that."

Spotnitz agrees, as does Duchovny: "We're honoring the kind of straight-ahead Morgan and Wong-type Chris Carter thriller, early *X-Files* episodes that weren't involved so much in the soap opera of the relationship between Mulder and Scully or the soap opera of the mythology conspiracy episodes. It's really a straight-ahead horror thriller investigative paranormal story that really harkens back to what made the show popular from the start."

A new film in 2008 also needed to appeal to more than just the fans who watched the series in its initial run on Fox from 1993 to 2002. "We have a whole audience out there that were either casual viewers of *The X-Files*, non-viewers of *The X-Files*, or, most importantly, people who were too young when *The X-Files* was on, who are now in college, who may not know what *The X-Files* is, beyond a possible cultural reference," explains Carter. A confusing mythology episode would alienate a curious new audience and not draw them in.

The story idea for the movie came after Carter had seen a disturbing video on YouTube. "It was a head transplant, kind of a Frankenstein thing. There was video of a Russian scientist who had actually transplanted one dog's head onto another dog's body, creating a two-headed dog," he says. "It's quite horrific," adds Spotnitz. "It's really pretty horrible."

Intrigued though, Carter and Spotnitz went to visit an American physician in Cleveland named Dr. Robert White, who had done similar—and briefly successful—experiments with monkeys. "Chris and I flew out there, and we talked about the issues involved in head transplants, and the reason

why, medically, it's inevitable. We can get there," Spotnitz says. "What prevents it from being terribly appealing right now is that you'd be paralyzed—there's no way to reattach the spinal cord, but it is a way to prolong life. If you've got a body that was diseased, you can preserve your consciousness by attaching the head to a new body."

The character of Father Joe—at that time (and actually up until the movie was filmed) known as Father Joseph Patrick Trowbridge—was also in the original story. "I had read a story about pedophiles all living together under one roof, basically policing one another," Carter explains. "I also, like a lot of people, was intrigued by the problems within the Catholic Church with the allegations against priests who were pedophiles." Carter, in fact, had a friend who represented the Catholic Church in nearby Orange County, California, so he was well aware of the issues the priests faced.

Spotnitz, too, had a connection with the topic. "One of my closest friends for the last nine years was a Catholic priest name Joe Burke—Father Joe," he says. Sadly, Burke died just a few months before Spotnitz and Carter started working on the story again in October 2006. "But he stayed with me."

Burke and Spotnitz would meet for lunch or dinner every month or two to talk about various topics —theology, ethics, philosophy. "Mostly he talked and I listened, because he was a very educated man, a lovely man. He used to joke, when I would say, 'How are you doing, Father Joe?' And he'd say, 'Just happy I'm not in the papers.'"

Carter had also been spending time listening to a series of lectures by a philosopher named Alan Watts. "They're very interesting lectures from the 1960s," Spotnitz says. "He was an Englishman, and he had this sort of raspy cigarette cough"—something that would see its way into the filmed characterization of Father Joe.

The X-Files's Father Joe was neither Watts nor Spotnitz's true-life Father Joe, though both stayed in the writers' minds. "We wanted someone who would be creepy in and of himself, so making him a pedophile seemed appropriate. And also someone who needed redemption," Spotnitz describes. The two also liked the idea that their defrocked, convicted priest was a psychic. "The idea that the psychic connection ends up being to one of the boys he'd abused—one of his abductees—that made sense to us. Because the connection of this abductor with one of his victims can read two ways—it can read the real world criminal conspiracy here is that Father Joe is connected to the kidnapper. Or it can read as Father Joe saying, 'This is God forgiving me, giving me a way to save these women by giving me this psychic connection to one of the boys I abused.' Once we had that, we felt we had a whole that made sense."

As an aside, the name change from Joseph Patrick Trowbridge—a name originally created by Carter—was necessitated once production began and names used in the film had to be cleared for use. "It turns out there was somebody who was convicted of a sex crime in Virginia that had the name of Trowbridge, so we changed it to Crissman," Spotnitz explains.

Mulder and Scully's characters did not end up changing significantly from the way they were initially conceived in the original film sequel story concept in 2003. "Scully is a doctor in a small family clinic and Mulder is in seclusion," says Spotnitz. "We had Scully treating a young boy, as in the final film, but we hadn't yet decided where we were going with that."

The two story lines eventually converge, he explains. "The Father Joe

TOP LEFT: Once a priest, always a priest: Former Vancouver *X-Files* Unit Production Manager J.P. Finn pops in for a cameo as a cleric—as he did in season three's "THE LIST" and season five's "ALL SOULS"; Hoping for a connection, visit Father Joe in the hospital to show him photos of two suspects—there is indeed a very important connection. Chris and Frank take a moment for a snap with their young star, Marco Niccoli, who portrays Christian Fearon, the young patient whose case has so strongly engaged Scully's heart and soul; Look familiar? Duchovny and Anderson take a familiar pose, recreating their original publicity still from 1993; Important words: Carter directs star Billy Connolly in scene where an emotional Scully queries him on those three important words: Don't Give Up; Scully's conversation with the Christian's parents is interrupted by Agent Drummy, who seeks info on Mulder's whereabouts.

story line ends up being about the boy as much as it is about finding the missing woman. What the boy story line also did for us is it allowed us to address the mythology of the series without making this a mythology story. Scully has to wonder, as does Mulder, 'Is my refusal to accept this boy's diagnosis, to accept that there's no treatment, related to my own child, my own unresolved issues about having to give up William? This boy's a substitute for my own son,' and that has great resonance to anyone who is a fan of the series."

It was a good four years between the time Carter and Spotnitz had created the story and when they returned to it to write the final script in 2007. "We decided we wanted to keep *The X-Files* story as part of it, the case, but the rest had completely changed," Spotnitz says. "It had changed because so much time had elapsed that Chris and I were different people, as writers, than we were in 2003. And the characters were different. There was just no escaping that, after that period of time, you would look at things differently."

The two convened at Peet's Coffee in Brentwood, California, for two days—just to talk. "It wasn't really even about the story," he says. "It was about life and where we were in our lives. We felt that revisiting *The X-Files* after all this time was a big moment for us, and a big opportunity for us as writers. So we wanted to really take this opportunity to say something that was meaningful to us."

Thus was born—on that first day at Peet's—the idea of "Don't give up"—the message that Father Joe, the disgraced priest, says to Scully in the snow. "As disgusted as she is by him, she's in the midst of this horrible quandary about what to do about this sick boy. So she acts on his belief, or her belief in what he says." By the end of the movie, it seems there's a case that he is to be believed, but there's an equally strong case that he's not. "In the final scene in the movie, there's a culmination of this idea 'Don't give up.'

Scully doesn't give up." Even without knowing whether the priest was credible or not, Scully continues to have faith that she can help this little boy.

"It's a beautiful ending, to me, because it doesn't say there is a God or there isn't a God, it doesn't say the priest was to be believed or was to be discredited, it simply says that we can't give up. We have to act on beliefs."

Knowing where Carter and Spotnitz themselves stood in life was easy to determine; figuring out where Mulder and Scully were was another story. The two writers had to create a back story for what had transpired for the two characters—both as individuals and as a couple. "We had to develop a back story, and then we had to communicate that back story through the characters to a very familiar audience, but we also wanted to communicate it to an unfamiliar audience. So that was a trick," says Carter.

One thing Carter knew he didn't want to do was simply put Mulder and Scully back at work at the FBI and tell an *X-Files* story as if nothing had happened. "That would have been a cheat and a lie, and an unimaginative way to start," he says.

Scully, it was determined, had fulfilled her dream—and that of her family—and become a doctor. As far as her back story goes, Spotnitz says, "I think there was a whole process she had to go through, probably going through some kind of residency or certification process to practice the kind of medicine she's been practicing. We don't explain any of this in the movie, but presumably she felt it was safe for her to come forward and put herself in the phone book, because she was not under any charges herself."

Mulder, on the other hand—bearded when we first see him—has become a recluse, hiding from the FBI and their trumped up charges against him, though, as Scully says in the film, they apparently were just happy to have him out of their hair. "Mulder has gone into a kind of a hermit mode and has begun, once again, to read, study, catalog and collect information on the supernatural, paranormal, and otherworldly," Carter notes.

> "Mulder had been defeated; he'd been driven away from his life's work—he'd been canceled." —Frank Spotnitz

But he is stuck in a holding pattern. "He'd been defeated, he'd been driven away from his life's work—he'd been canceled," Spotnitz says. "He was living in this room collecting this information, but not really impacting the world outside."

"He's essentially been a recluse for an extended period of time," Anderson notes. "And you get a sense that when she comes home and walks into the room, she comes into an onslaught of what to her must sound like gobbledygook from the remaining person that she cares a great deal about."

Between the two of them, though their life might be good because they have each other, Mulder and Scully have suffered a great deal as individuals. "It's part of the poignancy of these two people that they've lost so much," says Spotnitz. "And you can feel it in their performances. One of the great things about *The X-Files* is that it's very underwritten. On the page, it's very simple." It helps having great actors like Duchovny and Anderson around to bring out the messages that are there. "You don't have to say it, because they bring it. Plus, *The X-Files* people find it smart, because you don't have to spell it out. The actors are good enough to bring it out. David lets you see exactly the right thing to let you see. And that's a lot harder for an actor to do than just letting it all hang out. It's risky, because it can look like you're not playing anything, but that never happens, because David is a really smart actor."

Duchovny was well aware that he was not playing the Mulder last seen in "The Truth." "It was important to me, on the one hand, to honor who the character was, but I also wanted to honor the fact that six years have passed since the last time we saw him," he explains. "I wanted him to be older, whatever that means. It was more of a subtle kind of psychic shift."

Portraying Mulder, particularly in this state, was something keenly important to the actor, according to his acting partner. "I think when he left the show, he realized that he really had had something good," Anderson says. "I think he wanted to revisit that again." And the scenes where Mulder and Scully are together were the most important. "You get to see the best of who they are when they are together. And I've heard David say that that's where he felt the most comfortable—that he arrived back in the character when we were together."

The scenes featuring Mulder and Scully together are, interestingly, rare in the film. "That was a choice we made, to withhold," Spotnitz explains. "Because that's what the audience is waiting to see, so we make them hungry for it. Don't give it all to them right up front—make them want it." The two finally do have a real onscreen romantic kiss at the end of the film. "If you're a fan, it's the reward you get. But you have to wait through the whole movie for it."

Indeed, waiting to see how Mulder and Scully would be as a couple in 2008, six years after they were last seen cuddling in a motel room at the end of "The Truth", was one of the most intriguing parts of *I Want to Believe*. "Since they basically rode off into the sunset together," says Carter, "we imagined them together. But we had to imagine them how they would be together, and wanted to use that as both a surprise, but also as a foundation for telling this new story. And we didn't want to come back in a way that might serve 'a good story,' but not serve the relationship the fans had with Mulder and Scully."

"We felt Mulder and Scully had come to a place of great intimacy and love at the end of those nine years on the show, and we weren't going to throw that away," adds Spotnitz. "But we weren't going to try and reset

things as if nothing had happened. We couldn't just go, 'Okay, we're going to trot out the unfulfilled romantic tensions one more time.' We'd done that too many times to do it again."

As a couple, after living together for six years, Mulder and Scully's relationship has changed in some ways—the same ways that most couples' do. "We resist showing their domesticity," says Carter, "but, obviously, they're living together as partners, so the relationship has changed because of all that goes with that."

That brought an interesting challenge—and change—to the actors. "What's interesting is that now this is a couple solving problems, rather than partners," says Duchovny. "There's a different tenor to their disagreements, and that's an interesting change. It's not *The Bickersons*, but there's a little of that in it."

Anderson agrees. "You essentially see them in a marriage, which you've never seen before," she says. "And what that comes with, the kinds of arguments that married couples have, the kind of bickering and things that are said to each other that you've never heard them really say to each other. Mulder says a couple of things to Scully that are pretty harsh. So it was interesting to play, because it's different—it was bizarre."

A Chilling Experience

I Want to Believe was, for the most part, shot back on home turf, in the Vancouver, B.C., area. As one would guess, a new *X-Files* movie drew considerable attention, something the paparazzi couldn't resist. "We had problems with them all through it," says Spotnitz. On the very first night of filming in December, on Homer Street, he says, outside the organ transplant office, "One of them actually rented a hotel room across the street and spent the night taking photos and shooting video." The photographers also managed to get pictures taken in the deep freeze of Pemberton, three hours to the north of Vancouver, where the snow scenes were filmed over a three-week period during the last two weeks of January and first week of February.

Working in snow is an incredible challenge for any director and production team, from a number of perspectives. "You've got to plan out how you're going to shoot things, because you can't trample fresh snow without spending a great amount of effort and expense to untrample it," Carter says. Equipment can't be brought in via truck because wheels can't move well in

PREVIOUS PAGES TOP LEFT: Director of Photography Bill Roe's high-powered lighting pays off, as the nighttime snowscape is lit as the FBI returns to the snow field once again at Father Joe's to find Monica Bannan; Good reception: Director Carter fields a call at the same location, this time during the FBI's initial manhunt. **RIGHT:** Dirty glass: An unbelieving Scully watches as Mulder and Father dig in the snow, finding a severed head in the ice, the "dirty glass" Father Joe had described.

ABOVE: Filming a key nighttime scene—Never forgotten: Scully cuts to the chase with the obsessed Mulder—his concern for finding the missing women is not about their welfare but about something more basic: his abducted sister, Samantha. Note the camera on a camera crane, wrapped in plastic to protect it from the elements; A line of extras prepare to search for the missing agent early in the film; A frozen Frank Spotnitz attempts to keep warm during filming of the manhunt sequence; In a scene deleted from the theatrical release, the 2nd Abductor looks for a good place to dispose of a spare body part; Happy, but cold: Chris Carter pauses for the camera during the Mulder/Scully scene depicted above/left; ASAC Whitney (Amanda Peet) looks to Father Joe: it was supposed to be our missing agent—so whose arm has been found? Scully to the rescue: Scully stops the 2nd Abductor from cutting Mulder to pieces; "It's okay, I have insurance": Gillian Anderson is all smiles with Chris Carter during sequence in which Scully and Skinner find her abandoned, destroyed car while searching for Mulder. **RIGHT:** Camera operator Marty McInally, who performed similar duties during the series' production in Vancouver in the 90s, prepares to grab a shot from the opening manhunt sequence; Xzibit, David Duchovny and Chris Carter chat during sequence when Father Joe cries tears of blood; Leading the charge: Chris Carter prepares to drive his extras on the manhunt; Mulder ponders whether to follow Father Joe as Scully pleads with him not to in what has become one of the most widely-used publicity images from the film; It's in the mail: 25:2—An address, which coincides with Father Joe's clue, referencing Proverbs 25:2, catches the eyes of Scully and Skinner; Drummy, Mulder and Whitney return to the scene of Monica Bannan's abduction, having been led by Father Joe; Not a good sign: Whitney finds the severed head in the ice.

snow, so most was brought in on skids and sleds.

Sound is also an issue. "People are wearing Gortex, and if they're wearing radio microphones to pick up the dialogue, it also picks up the rustling of their jackets. And there's also the sound of crunching snow under people's boots."

But the biggest issue, of course, was the cold itself. "You must stay warm," he says. "If you start getting cold, it actually affects your ability to think." To prepare himself, Carter, in fact, spent his Christmas vacation in Wyoming, doing nothing but getting ready for the cold, trying out different outerwear and six different pairs of boots. "I was in a ski resort, and I only skied once."

The cold also affected the actors, heated trailers notwithstanding. "It was really cold," says Gillian Anderson. "Everybody who worked on the film who has been doing this for 30 years said it was the hardest film they'd ever worked on in their careers. Every single person."

She and Duchovny had long dialogue scenes, what Carter calls "driving, hard-sell" scenes, one in particular that reminded both he and Anderson of the earliest days on *The X-Files*. "There was one scene where Gillian got so cold that it was actually hard for her to speak," Carters says. "She and I looked at each other, because it reminded us both of an experience on *The X-Files* pilot from 16 years earlier," the scene noted in chapter one, regarding shooting the pilot episode in the driving rain. "It was rain we were making then, but it had gotten so cold that her lips froze."

"It's tough for everyone," adds Spotnitz. "It's tough for the crew, but particularly the actors, who are not dressed as warmly as a lot of other people. I can still hear it in many of the scenes—I can hear that their lips are stiff and they're having a hard time articulating, it was so cold."

Returning to Vancouver, thankfully, meant working with some old friends. While *The X-Files* cinematography master Bill Roe came up from L.A. along with Carter, Spotnitz and the cast, second unit photography at Pemberton was handled by none other than original *The X-Files* director of photography John Bartley, under direction of E. J. Foerster and with a little help from his former First Assistant Director Tom Braidwood. Foerster performed similar duties for the glacier scenes in the first *X-Files* movie and in this film shot sequences such as Mulder's car flipping over in the snow. Other old colleagues joined the fray, including casting director Coreen Mayrs, physical-effects specialist David Gauthier and music editor Jeff Charbonneau, among others.

"I'd be on the set, and I'd see a face and go, 'Oh, my gosh!'" Gillian Anderson recalls. "It was really cool in all different departments to see old faces and catch up with people. It was great."

Among the familiar faces was actor Mitch Pileggi, who reprised his role as A.D. Walter Skinner. Carter and Spotnitz, though, were wary of using nostalgia for nostalgia's sake, only bringing back old characters where they served the story. "I'd love to bring back many, many characters from the past, but Chris and I both felt, for this movie, we wanted to be as simple as we possibly could," Spotnitz explains. "The more characters you bring back, the more you have to explain and deal with previous relationships." Though it was briefly discussed bringing back Doggett and Reyes (and The Lone Gunmen—by allowing their van to be seen briefly), it was decided to keep things as simple as possible. "It was only when the perfect opportunity to involve Skinner came up that we wrote him in, which I was very happy to do."

Other cast members returned as well, though from the "guest cast" category. Actor Callum Rennie, who portrays the Russian Second Abductor, appeared twice previously on the series. "He was actually considered for the role of Krycek, and was considered for big roles in all the series we did," Carter notes. Alex Diakun, who portrays the Russian doctor so skilled at headswapping, appeared three times in the series—all Darin Morgan episodes—most notably as the creepy, deformed curio museum curator in "Humbug."

Of the main cast, of course, Billy Connolly is a true standout as Father Joe. Known in England mostly for his work as a comedian, Carter considered him immediately, even while the character was being developed. "I said to Frank, 'I've got an idea who should play this.' He's actually a terrific, undervalued dramatic actor." Carter and Spotnitz, fans of Connolly's work in such films as *Mrs. Brown* with Judi Dench, had actually written a script for Paramount that contained a part for the actor. "That script didn't get made, and maybe never will be made, so when we were thinking about Father Joe, we thought about Billy very early on, and he was the one."

A lifelong Beatles fan, Carter also had heard Connolly's performance

"The part of the two-headed dog was played by a Rottweiler named Okie. So we called the other head Dokey." —Chris Carter

TOP LEFT: The creepy operating set is prepared by the crew. The 2nd Victim's ice bath is seen on the left, and a skillfully-created severed body of Monica Bannan—made by Special Makeup Effects designer Bill Terezakis—is seen on the right. A severed head is seen in a basket in between; The Mulder and Scully of 2008; Parts aside: Mulder assures Whitney that finding body parts in the ice is a good thing—this is The X-Files, after all; X-Files and Millennium veteran (most notably as the deformed curator in Humbug) Vancouver character actor Alex Diakun returns as the Russian-speaking doctor with a thing for swapping heads; An underwater camera tracks the 2nd Abductor (Rennie) as he stalks his next victim (Nicki Aycox) at the Natatorium; Drummy listens intently as Father Joe details the abduction of the 2nd Victim; Not everyone believes Father Joe's story; Just trying to get a head: The 1st Abductor lies awaiting. . . who knows what—on the operating table. Whitney, Mulder and Drummy visit the Natatorium, where they suspect the 2nd Victim was abducted, though the Elderly Gent (Roger Horchow) employee isn't much help. ABOVE: Mulder listens as Drummy doubts during a chat in the FBI conference room.

LOOKING FOR A FAMILIAR NAME?

No die-hard X-Files fan could watch *I Want to Believe* without keeping an eye out for any hidden in-jokes and tributes of the variety typically found throughout the TV series. Just in case you missed them, here are a few:

—Looking for an animal tranquilizer, Mulder drops into "Nutter's Feed Store," named for early trendsetting X-Files director David Nutter.

—When Scully and Skinner go searching for Mulder at the Russians' compound, they pass a group of mailboxes containing the names of the series' most prominent writers: V. Gilligan, G. Morgan, D. Morgan, J. Wong, H. Gordon, and J. Shiban.

—The first time legend in the film is 11:21 P.M. —November 21 is the birthdate of Carter's wife, Dori.

—A hospital is seen called Manners Colonial Hospital, named for the series' incredible 53-episode director, Kim Manners.

—After Mulder crashes in Scully's car, he attempts to dial Scully from his cell phone. Other names programmed into his speed dial are Bowman, Gilligan, and Shiban.

—Seasons seven through nine co-executive producer Michelle MacLaren is honored by having the swimming pool facility where the abductors find their victims named for her—The MacLaren Natatorium.

—Toward the end of the film, Scully pulls a piece of mail from a mailbox sent from Fain Rotter Medical Supplies, named for Chris Carter's and Frank Spotnitz's assistants, respectively, Gabe Rotter and Jana Fain.

—There are a number of FBI offices bearing the names of various X-Files alum: Season nine character former assistant to Chris Carter and Hollywood writer Brad Follmer, First Assistant Director Barry K. Thomas, Spotnitz Assistant Sandra Tripicchio, and another former assistant—now a successfuly writer (and co-creator of **Reaper**)— Michele Fazekas.

—And what X-Files film would be complete without at least one sighting of 10/13? When Mulder calls Scully from the FBI forensics lab, it's 10:13 A.M. —October 13th, of course, being Chris Carter's birthday.

TOP LEFT: The final scene: Chris looks off set for a moment during a break; Chris chillin' with Xzibit for a moment between takes; **RIGHT:** Duchovny, prior to getting into costume, chats with Chris and Gillian.

"The film has a beautiful ending, to me, because it doesn't say there is a God or there isn't a God...it simply says that we can't give up." —Chris Carter

on Beatles record producer Sir George Martin's 1998 release, *In My Life*, in which celebrities performed Fab Four classics, Connolly covering John Lennon's "Being for the Benefit of Mr. Kite." "I heard him, and I thought, 'Billy Connolly can do anything,' and, lo and behold, I was right."

Connolly had a tough task. "He created a sympathetic character out of an unsympathetic character," Carter says—even in the face of constant verbal pounding from our own favorite sympathetic characters, Dana Scully. "He stands up to her with a rational discussion about the quality of faith and the quality of existence."

Adds Spotnitz, "That's the thing that Billy has, which is that you can't help but like him no matter how monstrous he is, because he's got that twinkle in his eye. He's got this impishness about him, because he's a comedian. Even though it's a straight dramatic role, there's something about him that is enormously likeable. But he can also be creepy, which worked very well for this film."

Carter was a fan of Amanda Peet's work in *Studio 60 on the Sunset Strip* before casting her as ASAC Dakota Whitney. "She could deliver a lot of dialogue credibly, which is an important thing on *The X-Files*. And she was believable as an FBI agent, I felt, and pretty enough to be a foil for Scully," he says.

Rapper and host of MTV's *Pimp My Ride*, Xzibit, plays an FBI agent on Whitney's team on the trail of his two fellow missing women. "We read many people for this part," Carter says, "and we read a lot of white guys in the beginning, and then we started reading some comedians, which was an interesting way to go." Fox had suggested Xzibit, whom Carter knew from *Pimp My Ride*. "He walked in the door, without cornrows, and proceeded to simply nail the reading. I told him when he read it, 'You're right for this part.'"

Mulder and Scully came up against one other co-star, one with a particu-

larly memorable face—or faces, rather. "The part of the two-headed dog was played by a Rottweiler named Okie. So we called the other head Dokey," notes Carter.

Okie performed his job to perfection, bearing the Velcro-attached appliance well and growling ferociously on cue from his handler, Paul Jasper. "It was funny because even though he looked like a ferocious dog, he would probably be more likely to lick you death," says Carter. "He's a very sweet dog."

So the big question, of course, is . . . will there be another *X-Files* movie? "That's all dependent upon this one," Carter says. And what would it be about? "That depends on how many movies we do," says Frank Spotnitz. "If we only do one more movie, then I would vote to deal with 2012 and the end of the world in an alien invasion," as detailed in "The Truth." Spotnitz continues, "But if we're going to do more than one, then I would say I would like to keep mixing it up. If there's enough movies, you can do both stand-alones and mythology."

And what of Mulder and Scully—what's in their future? "A fan asked me once on a website, 'Do you think Mulder and Scully are fated to have a tragic life, or an unhappy life?' Spotnitz recalls. "No, I don't, actually. I think what's heroic about both of them is that, ultimately, neither of them gives up. Ultimately they do have hope, and they don't allow circumstances to defeat them. They keep going, and I think that's what makes them heroic and why we love them as characters, because they're indomitable."

To Carter, the new film continues what we've always known about Mulder and Scully. "It's about Mulder's struggle with faith and the supernatural and unexplained phenomena, and it's about Scully's struggle with her faith in science and her personal faith in God. It's about faith. That's why it's called *I Want to Believe*."

Don't give up.

SEASON ONE

1x79
Pilot (M)
9/10/93
Chris Carter*
Robert Mandel*

1x01
Deep Throat (M)
9/17/93t
Chris Carter
Daniel Sackheim*

1x02
Squeeze
9/24/93
Glen Morgan* and
James Wong*
Harry Longstreet*

1x03
Conduit
10/1/93
Howard Gordon* and
Alex Gansa
Daniel Sackheim

1x04
The Jersey Devil
10/8/93
Chris Carter
Joe Napolitano*

1x05
Shadows
10/22/93
Glen Morgan and
James Wong
Michael Katleman*

1x06
Ghost in the Machine
10/29/93
Alex Gansa and
Howard Gordon
Jerrold Freedman*

1x07
Ice
11/5/93
Glen Morgan and
James Wong
David Nutter*

1x08
Space
11/12/93
Chris Carter
William A. Graham*

1x09
Fallen Angel (M)
11/19/93
Alex Gansa and
Howard Gordon
Larry Shaw*

1x10
Eve
12/10/93
Kenneth Biller* and
Chris Brancato*
Fred Gerber*

1x11
Fire
12/17/93
Chris Carter
Larry Shaw

1x12
Beyond the Sea
1/7/94
Glen Morgan and
James Wong
David Nutter

1x13
Gender Bender
1/21/94
Paul and Larry Barber
Rob Bowman*

1x14
Lazarus
2/4/94
Alex Gansa and
Howard Gordon
David Nutter

1x15
Young at Heart
2/11/94
Scott Kaufer* and
Chris Carter
Michael Lange*

1x16
E.B.E. (M)
2/18/94
Glen Morgan and
James Wong
William Graham

1x17
Miracle Man
3/18/94
Chris Carter and
Howard Gordon
Michael Lange

1x18
Shapes
4/1/94
Marilyn Osborn
David Nutter

1x19
Darkness Falls
4/15/94
Chris Carter
Joe Napolitano

1x20
Tooms
4/22/94
Glen Morgan and
James Wong
David Nutter

1x21
Born Again
4/29/94
Howard Gordon and
Alex Gansa
Jerrold Freedman

1x22
Roland
5/6/94
Chris Ruppenthal*
David Nutter

1x23
The Erlenmeyer Flask (M)
5/13/94
Chris Carter
R.W. Goodwin*

SEASON TWO

2x01
Little Green Men (M)
9/16/94
Glen Morgan and
James Wong
David Nutter

2x02
The Host
9/23/94
Chris Carter
Daniel Sackheim

2x03
Blood
9/30/94
Glen Morgan and
James Wong
(story: Darin Morgan*)
David Nutter

2x04
Sleepless
10/7/94
Howard Gordon
Rob Bowman

2x05
Duane Barry (M)
10/14/94
Chris Carter
Chris Carter*

2x06
Ascension (M)
10/21/94
Paul Brown*
Michael Lange

2x07
3
11/4/94
Glen Morgan, James Wong
and Chris Ruppenthal
David Nutter

2x08
One Breath
11/11/94
Glen Morgan and
James Wong
R.W. Goodwin

2x09
Firewalker
11/18/94
Howard Gordon
David Nutter

2x10
Red Museum (M)
12/9/94
Chris Carter
Win Phelps*

2x11
Excelsius Dei
12/16/94
Paul Brown
Stephen Surjik*

2x12
Aubrey
1/6/95
Sara B. Charno*
Rob Bowman

2x13
Irresistible
1/13/95
Chris Carter
David Nutter

2x14
Die Hand Die Verletzt
1/27/95
Glen Morgan and
James Wong
Kim Manners*

2x15
Fresh Bones
2/3/95
Howard Gordon
Rob Bowman

2x16
Colony (M)
2/10/95
Chris Carter
(story: Chris Carter and
David Duchovny*)
Nick Marck*

2x17
End Game (M)
2/17/95
Frank Spotnitz*
Rob Bowman

2x18
Fearful Symmetry
2/24/95
Steve deJarnatt*
James Whitmore, Jr.*

2x19
Dod Kalm
3/10/95
Howard Gordon and
Alex Gansa
Rob Bowman

2x20
Humbug
3/31/95
Darin Morgan*
Kim Manners

2x21
The Calusari
4/14/95
Sara B. Charno
Michael Vejar*

2x22
F. Emasculata
4/28/95
Chris Carter and
Howard Gordon
Rob Bowman

2x23
Soft Light
5/5/95
Vince Gilligan*
James Contner*

2x24
Our Town
5/12/95
Frank Spotnitz
Rob Bowman

2x25
Anasazi (M)
5/19/95
Chris Carter
(story: Chris Carter and
David Duchovny)
R.W. Goodwin

SEASON THREE

3x01
The Blessing Way (M)
9/22/95
Chris Carter
R.W. Goodwin

3x02
Paper Clip (M)
9/29/95
Chris Carter
Rob Bowman

3x03
D.P.O.
10/6/95
Howard Gordon
Kim Manners

3x04
Clyde Bruckman's
Final Repose
10/13/95
Darin Morgan
David Nutter

3x05
The List
10/20/95
Chris CarterWong
Michael Katelman*

3x06
2SHY
11/3/95
Jeffrey Vlaming*
David Nutter

3x07
The Walk
11/10/95
John Shiban*
Rob Bowman

3x08
Oubliette
11/17/95
Charles Grant Craig*
Kim Manners

3x09
Nisei (M)11/24/95
Chris Carter,
Frank Spotnitz and
Howard Gordon
David Nutter

3x10
731 (M)
12/1/95
Frank Spotnitz
Rob Bowman

3x11
Revelations
12/15/95
Kim Newton*
David Nutter

3x12
War of the Coprophages
1/5/96
Darin Morgan
Kim Manners

3x13
Syzygy
1/26/96
Chris Carter
Rob Bowman

3x14
Grotesque
2/2/96
Howard Gordon
Kim Manners

3x15
Piper Maru (M)
2/9/96
Chris Carter and Frank
SpotnitzRob Bowman

3x16
Apocrypha (M)
2/16/96
Frank Spotnitz and Chris
CarterKim Manners

3x17
Pusher
2/23/96
Vince Gilligan
Rob Bowman

3x18
Teso dos Bichos
3/8/96
John Shiban
Kim Manners

3x19
Hell Money
3/29/96
Jeffrey Vlaming
Tucker Gates*

3x20
Jose Chung's "From Outer
Space"
4/12/96
Darin Morgan
Rob Bowman

3x21
Avatar
4/26/96
Howard Gordon
(story: Howard Gordon
and David Duchovny)
James Charleston*

3x22
Quagmire
5/3/96
Kim Newton
Kim Manners

3x23
Wetwired
5/10/96
Mat Beck*
Rob Bowman

3x24
Talitha Cumi (M)
5/17/96
Chris Carter (story: David
Duchovny and Chris
Carter) R.W. Goodwin

SEASON FOUR

4x01
Herrenvolk (M)
10/4/96
Chris Carter
R.W. Goodwin

4x02
Unruhe
10/27/96
Vince Gilligan
Rob Bowman

4x03
Home
10/11/96
Glen Morgan and James
WongKim Manners

4x04
Teliko
10/18/96
Howard Gordon
James Charleston

4x05
The Field Where I Died
11/3/96
Glen Morgan and
James Wong
Rob Bowman

4x06
Sanguinarium
11/10/96
Valerie and Vivien
Mayhew*
Kim Manners

4x07
Musings of a Cigarette
Smoking Man
11/17/96
Glen Morgan
James Wong*

4x08
Paper Hearts
12/15/96
Vince Gilligan
Rob Bowman

4x09
Tunguska (M)
11/24/96
Frank Spotnitz and
Chris Carter
Kim Manners

4x10
Terma (M)
12/1/96
Chris Carter and
Frank Spotnitz
Rob Bowman

4x11
El Mundo Gira
1/12/97
John Shiban
Tucker Gates

4x12
Kaddish
2/16/97
Howard Gordon
Kim Manners

4x13
Never Again
2/2/97
Glen Morgan and
James Wong
Rob Bowman

4x14
Leonard Betts
1/26/97
Vince Gilligan, John
Shiban and Frank Spotnitz
Kim Manners

4x15
Memento Mori (M)
2/9/97
Chris Carter, Vince
Gilligan, John Shiban and
Frank Spotnitz
Rob Bowman

4x16
Unrequited
2/23/97
Howard Gordon and
Chris Carter
(story: Howard Gordon)
Michael Lange

4x17
Tempus Fugit (M)
3/16/97
Chris Carter and
Frank Spotnitz
Rob Bowman

4x18
Max (M)
3/23/9
Chris Carter and
Frank Spotnitz
Kim Manners

4x19
Synchrony
4/13/97
Howard Gordon and
David Greenwalt*
James Charleston

4x20
Small Potatoes
4/20/97
Vince Gilligan
Cliff Bole*

4x21
Zero Sum (M)
4/27/97
Howard Gordon and
Frank Spotnitz
Kim Manners

4x22
Elegy
5/4/97
John Shiban
James Charleston

4x23
Demons (M)
5/11/97
R.W. Goodwin*
Kim Manners

4x24
Gethsemane (M)
5/18/97
Chris Carter
R.W. Goodwin

SEASON FIVE

5x01
Unusual Suspects
11/16/97
Vince Gilligan
Kim Manners

5x02
Redux (M)
11/2/97
Chris Carter
R.W. Goodwin

5x03
Redux II (M)
11/9/97
Chris Carter
Kim Manners

5x04
Detour
11/23/97
Frank Spotnitz
Brett Dowler*

5x05
Christmas Carol (M)
12/7/97
Vince Gilligan, John
Shiban and Frank Spotnitz
Peter Markle*

5x06
The Post-Modern
Prometheus
11/30/97
Chris Carter
Chris Carter

5x07
Emily (M)
2/14/97
Vince Gilligan, John
Shiban and Frank Spotnitz
Kim Manners

5x08
Kitsunegari
1/4/98
Vince Gilligan and
Tim Minear*
Daniel Sackheim

5x09
Schizogeny
1/11/98
Jessica Scott* and
Michael Wolaeger*
Ralph Hemecker*

5x10
Chinga
2/8/98
Stephen King* and
Chris Carter
Kim Manners

5x11
Kill Switch
2/15/98
William Gibson* and
Tom Maddux*
Rob Bowman

5x12
Bad Blood
2/22/98
Vince Gilligan
Cliff Bole

5x13
Patient X (M)
3/1/98
Chris Carter and
Frank Spotnitz
Kim Manners

5x14
The Red and The Black (M)
3/8/98
Chris Carter and
Frank Spotnitz
Chris Carter

5x15
Travelers
3/29/98
John Shiban and
Frank Spotnitz
William A. Graham

5x16
Mind's Eye
4/19/98
Tim Minear
Kim Manners

5x17
All Souls
4/26/98
Frank Spotnitz and
John Shiban (story: Billy
Brown* and Dan Angel*)
Allen Coulter*

5x18
The Pine Bluff Variant
5/3/98
John Shiban
Rob Bowman

5x19
folie a Deux
5/10/98
Vince Gilligan
Kim Manners

5x20
The End (M)
5/17/98
Chris Carter
R.W. Goodwin

SEASON SIX

6x01
The Beginning (M)
11/8/98
Chris Carter
Kim Manners

6x02
Drive
11/15/98
Vince Gilligan
Rob Bowman

6x03
Triangle
11/22/98
Chris Carter
Chris Carter

6x04
Dreamland
11/29/98
Vince Gilligan, John
Shiban and Frank Spotnitz
Kim Manners

6x05
Dreamland II
12/6/98
Vince Gilligan, John
Shiban and Frank Spotnitz
Michael Watkins*

6x06
Terms of Endearment
1/3/99
David Amann*
Rob Bowman

6x07
The Rain King
1/10/99
Jeffrey Bell*
Kim Manners

6x08
How the Ghosts Stole
Christmas
12/13/98
Chris Carter
Chris Carter

6x09
Tithonus
1/24/99
Vince Gilligan
Michael Watkins

6x10
S.R. 819 (M)
1/17/99
John Shiban
Daniel Sackheim

6x11
Two Fathers (M)
2/7/99
Chris Carter and
Frank Spotnitz
Kim Manners

6x12
One Son (M)
2/14/99
Chris Carter and
Frank Spotnitz
Rob Bowman

6x13
Arcadia
3/7/99
Daniel Arkin*
Michael Watkins

6x14
Agua Mala
2/21/99
David Amann
Rob Bowman

6x15
Monday
2/28/99
Vince Gilligan and
John Shiban
Kim Manners

6x16
Alpha
3/28/99
Jeffrey Bell
Peter Markle

6x17
Trevor
4/11/99
Jim Guttridge* and
Ken Hawryliw*
Rob Bowman

6x18
Milagro
4/18/99
Chris Carter
(story: Frank Spotnitz and
John Shiban)
Kim Manners

6x19
Three of a Kind
5/2/99
Vince Gilligan and
John Shiban
Bryan Spicer*

6x20
The Unnatural
4/25/99
David Duchovny*
David Duchovny*

6x21
Field Trip
5/9/99
Vince Gilligan and
John Shiban
(story: Frank Spotnitz)
Kim Manners

6x22
Biogenesis (M)
5/16/99
Chris Carter and
Frank Spotnitz
Rob Bowman

7x01
Hungry
11/21/99
Vince Gilligan
Kim Manners

7x02
The Goldberg Variation
12/12/99
Jeffrey Bell
Thomas J. Wright

7x03
The Sixth Extinction (M)
11/7/99
Chris Carter
Kim Manners

7x04
*The Sixth Extinction II:
Amor Fati (M)*
11/14/99
David Duchovny and
Chris Carter
Michael Watkins

7x05
Millennium
11/28/99
Vince Gilligan and
Frank Spotnitz
Thomas Wright*

7x06
Rush
12/5/99
David Amann
Rob Lieberman*

7x07
Orison
1/9/00
Chip Johannessen*
Rob Bowman

7x08
The Amazing Maleeni
1/16/00
Vince Gilligan, John
Shiban and Frank Spotnitz
Thomas J. Wright

7x09
Signs and Wonders
1/23/00
Jeffrey Bell
Kim Manners

7x10
Sein Und Zeit (M)
2/6/00
Chris Carter and
Frank Spotnitz
Michael Watkins

7x11
Closure
2/13/00
Chris Carter and
Frank Spotnitz
Kim Manners

7x12
X-Cops
2/20/00
Vince Gilligan
Michael Watkins

7x13
FPS
2/27/00
William Gibson and
Tom Maddox
Chris Carter

7x14
Theef
3/12/00
Vince Gilligan, John
Shiban and Frank Spotnitz
Kim Manners

7x15
En Ami (M)
3/19/00
William B. Davis*
Rob Bowman

7x16
Chimera
4/2/00
David Amann
Cliff Bole

7x17
all things
4/9/00
Gillian Anderson*
Gillian Anderson*

7x18
Hollywood A.D.
4/30/00
David Duchovny
David Duchovny

7x19
Brand X
4/16/00
Steven Maeda* and
Greg Walker*
Kim Manners

7x20
Fight Club
5/7/00
Chris Carter
Paul Shapiro*

7x21
Je Souhaite
5/14/00
Vince Gilligan
Vince Gilligan*

7x22
Requiem
5/21/00
Chris Carter
Kim Manners

8x01
Within (M)
11/5/00
Chris Carter
Kim Manners

8x02
Without (M)
11/12/00
Chris Carter
Kim Manners

8x03
Redrum
2/10/00
Steven Maeda
(story: David Amann and
Steven Maeda)
Peter Markle

8x04
Patience
11/19/00
Chris Carter
Chris Carter

8x05
Roadrunners
11/26/00
Vince Gilligan
Rod Hardy

8x06
Invocation
12/3/00
David Amann
Richard Compton

8x07
Via Negativa
12/17/00
Frank Spotnitz
Tony Wharmby*

8x08
Per Anum (M)
2/18/01
Chris Carter and
Frank Spotnitz
Kim Manners

8x09
Surekill
1/7/01
Greg Walker*
Terence Ohare*

8x10
Salvage
1/14/01
Jeffrey Bell
Rod Hardy

8x11
The Gift (M)
2/4/01
Frank Spotnitz
Kim Manners

8x12
Badlaa
1/21/01
John Shiban
Tony Wharmby

8x13
Medusa
2/11/01
Frank Spotnitz
Richard Compton*

8x14
This Is Not Happening (M)
2/25/01
Chris Carter and
Kim Manners*
Kim Manners

8x15
Deadalive (M)
4/1/01
Chris Carter and
Frank Spotnitz
Tony Wharmby

8x16
Vienen (M)
4/29/01
Steven Maeda
Rod Hardy

8x17
Empedocles
4/22/01
Greg Walker
Barry K. Thomas*

8x18
Three Words (M)
4/8/01
Chris Carter and
Frank Spotnitz
Tony Wharmby

8x19
Alone
5/6/01
Frank Spotnitz
Frank Spotnitz*

8x20
Essence (M)
5/13/01
Chris Carter
Kim Manners

8x21
Existence (M)
5/20/01
Chris Carter
Kim Manners

SEASON NINE

9x01
Nothing Important
Happened Today (M)
11/11/01
Chris Carter and
Frank Spotnitz
Kim Manners

9x02
Nothing Important
Happened Today II (M)
11/18/01
Chris Carter and
Frank Spotnitz
Tony Wharmby

9x03
Dæmonicus
12/2/01
Frank Spotnitz
Frank Spotnitz

9x04
Hellbound
1/27/02
David Amann
Kim Manners

9x05
4D
12/9/01
Steven Maeda
Tony Wharmby

9x06
Lord of the Flies
12/16/01
Thomas Schnauz*
Kim Manners

9x07
John Doe
1/13/02
Vince Gilligan
Michelle MacLaren*

9x08
Trust No 1 (M)
1/6/02
Chris Carter and
Frank Spotnitz
Tony Wharmby

9x09
Underneath
3/31/02
John Shiban*

9x10
Provenance (M)
3/3/02
Chris Carter and
Frank Spotnitz
Kim Manners

9x11
Providence
3/10/02
Chris Carter and
Frank Spotnitz
Chris Carter

9x12
Scary Monsters
4/14/02
Thomas Schnauz
Dwight Little*

9x13
Audrey Pauley
3/17/02
Steven Maeda
Kim Manners

9x14
Improbable
4/7/02
Chris Carter
Chris Carter

9x15
Jump the Shark (M)
4/21/02
Vince Gilligan, John
Shiban and Frank Spotnitz
Cliff Bole

9x16
Release
5/5/02
David Amann
(story: John Shiban)
Kim Manners

9x17
William (M)
4/28/02
Chris Carter
(story: Chris Carter,
David Duchovny and
Frank Spotnitz)
David Duchovny

9x18
Sunshine Days
5/12/02
Vince Gilligan
Vince Gilligan

9x19
The Truth (M)
5/19/02
Chris Carter
Kim Manners

9x20
The Truth (M)
5/19/02
Chris Carter
Kim Manners

KEY
* – First episode
appearance
M – Mythology episode

ORDER
Episode
Title
Air Date
Writers (s)
Director

AWARDS

This long running Fox drama lasted nine seasons and focused on the exploits of FBI Agents Fox Mulder, Dana Scully, John Doggett and Monica Reyes and their investigations into the paranormal. From genetic mutants and killer insects to a global conspiracy concerning the colonization of Earth by an alien species, this mind-boggling, humorous and occasionally frightening series created by Chris Carter has been one of the world's most popular sci-fi/drama shows since its humble beginnings in 1993.

Emmy Awards

Outstanding Makeup for a Series for episode *DeadAlive* (2001)

Outstanding Makeup for a Series for episode *Theef* (2000)

Outstanding Sound Mixing for a Drama Series for episode *First Person Shooter* (2000)

Outstanding Special Visual Effects for a Series for episode *First Person Shooter* (2000)

Outstanding Makeup for a series for episodes *Two Fathers/One Son* (1999)

Outstanding Art Direction for a Series for episode *The Post-Modern Prometheus* (1998)

Outstanding Single Camera Picture Editing for a Series for episode *Kill Switch* (1998)

Outstanding Lead Actress in a Drama Series for Gillian Anderson (1997)

Outstanding Art Direction for a Series for episode Memento Mori (1997)

Outstanding Sound Editing for a Series for episode Tempus Fugit (1997)

Outstanding Guest Actor in a Drama Series to Peter Boyle for episode *Clyde Bruckman's Final Repose* (1996)

Outstanding Individual Achievement in Writing for a Drama Series to Darin Morgan for episode *Clyde Bruckman's Final Repose* (1996)

Outstanding Individual Achievement in Cinematography for a series for episode *Grotesque* (1996)

Outstanding Individual Achievement in Sound Editing for a Series for episode *Nisei* (1996)

Outstanding individual Achievement in Sound Mixing for a Drama Series for episode *Nisei* (1996)

Outstanding Individual Achievement in Graphic Design and Title Sequences for *The X-Files* (1994)

Golden Globe Awards

Best TV Series (Drama, 1998)

Best Performance by an Actor in a TV Series (Drama) to David Duchovny (1997)

Best Performance by an Actress in a TV-Series (Drama) to Gillian Anderson (1997)

Best TV Series (Drama) (1997)

The X-Files Today: Series alumni gathered at a tribute at The Paley Center for Media on March 26, 2008. Left to right: Glen Morgan, Dean Haglund, Nicholas Lea, Paul Rabwin, Howard Gordon, Bill Roe, Chris Carter, Frank Spotnitz, David Amann, Steven Maeda, Darin Morgan, David Nutter, Rob Bowman and Mitch Pileggi.

INDEX

PICTURE CREDITS

All photos supplied courtesy of Fox pictures unless

otherwise mentioned below.

Video stills supplied by OmniGraphic Solutions

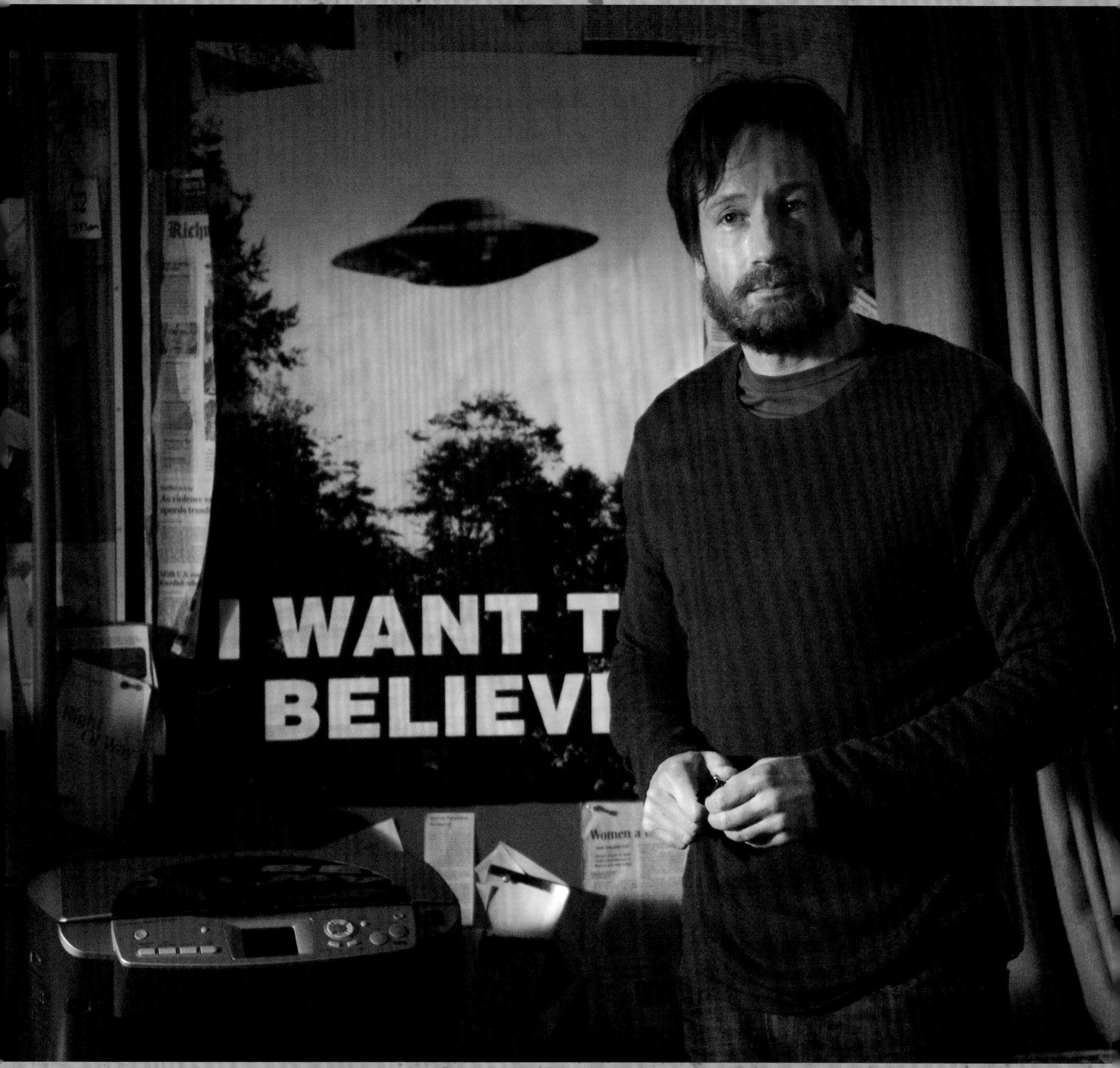
I WANT T
BELIEV

COLOPHON

Publisher and Creative Director: Raoul Goff

Art Director: Iain R. Morris

Acquisitions and Development Editor: Lisa Fitzpatrick

Designer: Jennifer Durrant

Editorial Director: Jake Gerli

Proofreaders: Lisa Angelo and Ashley Nicolaus

Design Assistants: Christopher Maas and Hans Hunt

Production Managers: Leslie Cohen
and Lina S. Palma-Temeña

Production Assistant: Donna Lee

Insight Editions would particularly like to thank Debbie Olshan (Director, Worldwide Publishing) for making this project a reality, as well as many other wonderfully supportive FOX staff: Gianna Babando from the props archive, Anne Lawliss, Dani Fields and Jeffrey Thompson from photo department and Steve Asbell (production executive). Additional thanks go to Gabe Rotter, Jana Fain, David Baranoff, Gabe Ely, Mary Teruel, and Grace Kono-Wells for their support.

FROM THE AUTHORS...

First of all, I would like to thank Brenda Knight, for making my dreams come true, Lisa Fitzpatrick, for being an absolute joy to work with, and Matt Hurwitz, for his incredible ability to pick brains. I would also like to thank Chris Carter for creating this incredible cultural phenomenon, and thank Chris and Frank Spotnitz for inspiring their scary-smart cast, crew and writing staff to push the envelope for so many years. We're all the richer for their vision, inspiration, and Olympian work ethic. (Chris Knowles)

Matthew Hurwitz wishes to thank: Chris Carter, Frank Spotnitz, Gillian Anderson, David Duchovny, Kim Manners, Rob Bowman, R.W. Goodwin, Paul Rabwin, Michelle MacLaren, Mitch Pileggi, Glen Morgan, Darin Morgan, David Nutter, Vince Gilligan, Howard Gordon, William B. Davis, Robert Patrick, Annabeth Gish, Nicholas Lea, Jerry Hardin, Chris Owens, Dean Haglund, Tom Braidwood, Bruce Harwood, Steven Williams, John S. Bartley, Bill Roe, Rick Millikan, Mark Snow, Toby Lindala, Glenn Hetrick, Matthew Mungle, Gabe Rotter, Jana Fain, Steve Asbell, Connie Frieburg, Flo Grace, Rita Runyan, Tom Lavagnino, Terry Lynn Bright/Paley Center, Debbie Olshan, Anne Lawliss, Dani Fields, Mark Kaminky, Steven Tice, Chris Knowles (for saving the day!), Rosie Vidaurri (for listening to Mark Snow's theme music 202 times with me), and Mark Hurwitz.

I'd also like to thank all at Palace Press, particularly editor Lisa Fitzpatrick for her tireless support and enthusiasm, for maintaining the high quality of this project, and for putting X-Philes first.

Chris Carter, Age 10

I MADE THIS

Back in 1993, as *The X-Files* was finally beginning to develop its identity, Chris Carter, as many production company executives were beginning to do, created a logo to play at the end of the show's closing titles. The image displayed the name of his company, Ten Thirteen Productions (named for Carter's birthday, October 13th), but it needed a special look.

"It was one of those nights where I had to come up with something, and I went to the special effects room with Mat Beck," Carter recalls. "We started monkeying around with something, and I came up with the idea of going to a static old movie reel and a sort of old movie effect with the jittering 'Ten Thirteen Productions.'

It is, of course, not the image itself that *The X-Files* fans remember, but the sound that accompanies it—a child's voice declaring, "I made this!" "That's the voice of the son of our supervising sound editor, Thierry Couturier," a lad of 10 years of age at the time named Nathan.

"I don't know where I came up with that. But it's like when you're a kid. You're so proud of your mud patties, that 'you made this,' it's your product. I think that, basically, we're all just big kids making bigger mud patties."

TEN THIRTEEN
PRODUCTIONS

PREVIOUS PAGES (LEFT): Forest creature from season fives "DETOUR"
(RIGHT): Leonard Vance makes his point in "MIRACLE MAN" from season one

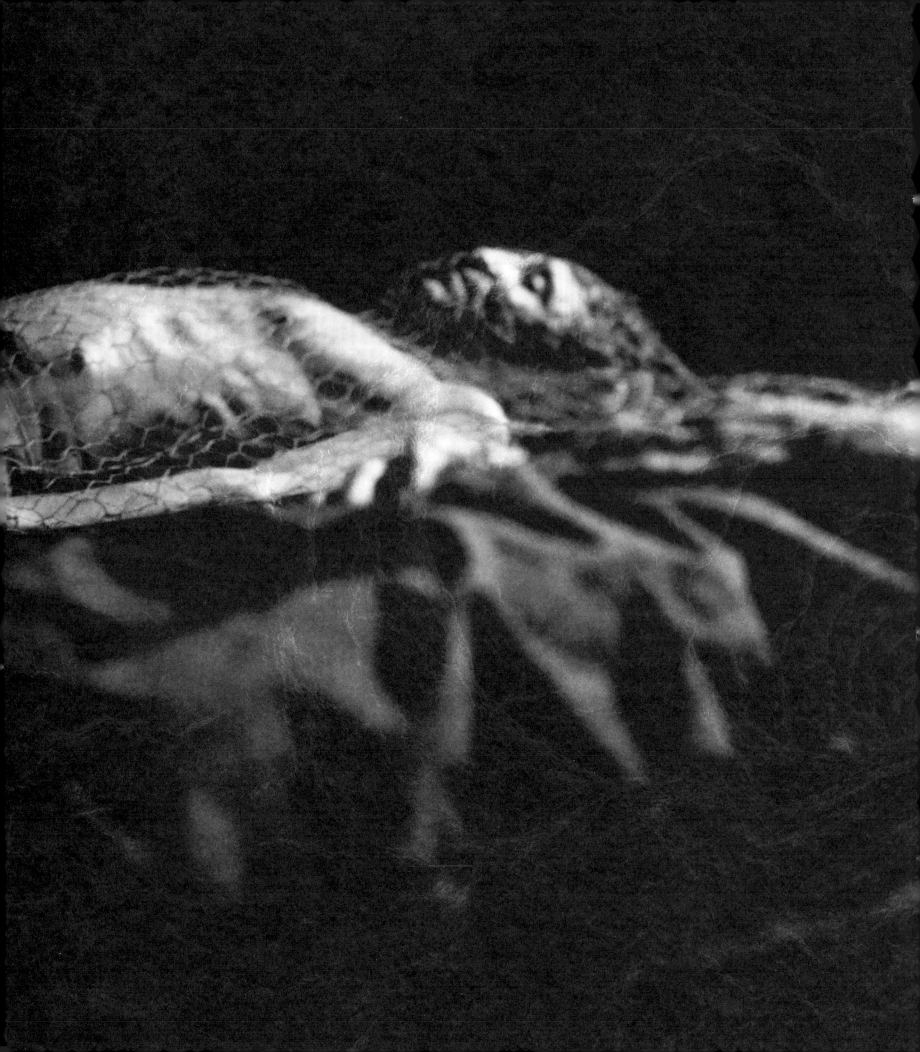